necessary & eternal coexistence
of God & nature. = Pantheism
A theist A deist
Believes in God Believes in God but not
& also in revelation. in a revelation.

M. Lämmel sc.

The Madonna di San Sisto.

THE SCIENCE OF

ÆSTHETICS;

OR

THE NATURE, KINDS, LAWS, AND USES

OF

BEAUTY.

BY

HENRY N. DAY,

AUTHOR OF LOGIC, ART OF DISCOURSE, ENGLISH LITERATURE, &c.

NEW HAVEN, CONN:

CHARLES C. CHATFIELD & CO.

1872.

Electrotyped by E. B. Sheldon, New Haven.

PREFACE.

However abstract and speculative the present treatise may appear to any, the preparation of it was in fact prompted and carried on to a great extent in the closest practical connection with the study and teaching of rhetoric. This art simply proposes as its aim to teach the construction of Discourse; to train to the expression of thought in language,—to the embodiment of idea in suitable form of articulate sound. There were obviously three different things to be regarded in this work,—the thought to be expressed, the word-form in which it was to be embodied, and the act itself of embodying the thought in the word. Most abundant and most unhappy experience had shown how futile the attempt to acquire the power to speak or to write well by the mere study of the rules of grammar or of rhetorical style. However necessary to the highest skill in speaking and writing the knowledge of those principles may be, the demonstration has been most complete that the exclusive or preponderating study of them can never bring skill in discourse. Nor on the other hand was the art of discourse to be acquired by mere study of thought—of its nature, its laws, its legitimate forms. Logic is as really necessary to the writer or speaker as grammar and the laws of style. But more than these, above either or both of them, it was found necessary to know how to put logical thought into grammatical word-form. Here indeed lies the great art of the writer and speaker; here his peculiar characteristic power and skill. To the study of this element accordingly the mind of the pupil was to be predominantly turned; and logic and grammar while they were to be thoroughly mastered, were yet to be held subordinate to it. What this is—to put thought fitly into words—to embody idea in perfect form which is but perfect beauty; the nature, the laws, the forms of this perfect beauty, accordingly demanded his earnest study. To guide and help this study—the philosophy of form—unhappily, however, our literature affords to him nothing of much practical value, and even where the subject was treated at all, in our literature or in that of continental Europe, the treatment was from a point of view too remote and too speculative to be turned to account. Questions were ever arising in determining the processes in the art of constructing discourse which could find no satisfactory solution in these metaphysical or critical discussions. For more than a quarter of a century thus the studies and instructions in rhetoric and the composition of discourse continued to put upon explorations into this field of *form*—of beauty.

It became apparent, moreover, that other arts were groping and stumbling in the same way as that of discourse. Every where was discovered the silly and ever futile attempt to arrive, by a blind leap and jump in the dark, at a perfect form of art

—at a beautiful landscape, a fine poem, an excellent painting or statue, a sweet melody or harmony—at a perfect form of beauty, with no intelligence of what a perfect form is, what form is, and how it is to be created. Indeed the grand defect and bane of modern art in all departments is its utter ignorance of what art proposes to do. Mr. Fergusson, in his History of Architecture, remarks that while in every nation the art was successful, wherever practiced up to the sixteenth century, since then "not one building has been produced that is admitted to be entirely satisfactory or which permanently retains a hold on general admiration." The reason is that ancient architecture built suitably to the purposes of the building;—or as we may express it, grasping first the idea of the building, it then with the best material at hand proceeded intelligently to embody the idea in it; modern architecture, knowing vastly more of materials and of architectural details and having more constructive skill, has overlooked the vital element of old art—the actual incorporation of the idea into the material at its control. It has leaped blindly in hope to realize a perfect form, forgetting that no perfect form can be reached but in the rational way of expressing some idea in its appropriate matter, and that this expressing, this embodying, is the governing element in all art procedure and can never be realized but intelligently and aimingly, that is rationally, and in accordance with the laws of the rational nature.

The fruit of this long labor, occasioned and

directed as stated in these rhetorical studies, appears in this volume. The special preparation of this treatise on the general subject of beauty as perfect form, has been prompted by the observation that English literature is marvelously poor in æsthetic treatises, while a very general and earnest demand exists for suitable text books in this department of study. The importance of the study indeed can hardly be overrated, whether regarded in its relations to the culture of art generally and the right interpretation and enjoyment of art-creations of whatever kind, or to the mere personal ends of personal culture, since most vitally connected with all intellectual and moral culture is the familiar knowledge of the nature of the beautiful as related to the true and the good.

Especial care has been taken to observe the strictest method in the whole development of the study, and to ground the teachings on the firmest foundations of philosophical truth and to exhibit each part of the system in its exact relations to the whole and to every other part. When it is used as a class book for instruction, the judicious teacher will accordingly be careful to omit, at least in the first studies, such portions as are too abstract or foreign to the customary range of thought in the pupil. The plan of the work, so far as respects the mingling of philosophical explanations and argumentations with the statements of the principles, to which summary statements a mere rudimental text-book should perhaps be confined, was imposed as a necessity in the circumstances of the case, which required that sufficient support in reason and fact should be furnished for the teachings so far as novel in form or substance.

The following works have with others been more or less consulted in the preparation of this volume :

Characteristics of Men, Manners, Opinions, Times. In three volumes. By the Right Honorable Anthony, Earl of Shaftesbury. The third edition. 1723.

An Inquiry into the Original of our Ideas of Beauty and Virtue. The third edition. By Francis Hutcheson. 1729.

Elements of Moral Science. By James Beattie, LL.D. 1790.

Elements of Criticism. By Henry Home, Lord Kames. Am. edition. 1838.

A Philosophical Inquiry into the Origin of our Ideas of the Sublime and Beautiful: with an introductory discourse concerning Taste. By the Right Hon. Edward Burke. Am. ed. 1834.

Essays on the Nature and Principles of Taste. By the Rev. Archibald Alison, LL.B., F.R.S. Dublin, 1790.

An Analytical Inquiry into the Principles of Taste. By Richard Payne Knight. London, 1805.

Lectures on Art. By Washington Allston. New York, 1850.

An Introduction to the Study of Æsthetics. By James C. Moffat, Professor of Greek in the College of New Jersey, Princeton. Cincinnati, 1856.

Æsthetics; or, The Science of Beauty. By John Bascom, Professor in Williams College.

Elements of Art Criticism. By G. W. Samson, D.D., President of Columbia College, Washington, D. C. Philadelphia, 1867.

Art Thoughts. By James Jackson Jarves. New York, 1869.

A General View of the Fine Arts. Fourth edition. New York, 1851.

The Literary Works of Sir Joshua Reynolds. London, 1846.

Modern Painters, Seven Lamps of Architecture, Lectures on Art, &c., &c. By John Ruskin.

Imitative Art. By Frank Howard. London.

Joseph Guilt. Encyclopædia of Architecture, Historical, Theoretical, and Practical. London, 1842.

John Billington. The Architectural Director. London, 1848.

James Fergusson. History of Architecture in all Countries, from the earliest times to the present day. London, 1865.

John Henry Parker. Introduction to the study of Gothic Architecture. Oxford and London, 1867.

——— ———. Concise Glossary of Terms used in Grecian, Roman, Italian, and Gothic Architecture. Oxford and London, 1866.

History and Rudiments of Architecture. New York, 1853.

Wonders of Architecture. New York, 1870.

The Architecture of Country Houses. By C. J. Downing. New York, 1850.

Rural Homes. By Gervase Wheeler. New York, 1852.

Homes for the People. By Gervase Wheeler. New York, 1855.

The Landscape Gardening and Landscape Architecture of the late Humphrey Repton, Esq. By J. C. Loudon, F. L. S. London, 1840.

Practical Landscape Gardening. By G. W. Kern. Cincinnati, 1855.

Allan Cunningham's Lives of the most eminent British Painters and Sculptors. Am. ed. 1831.

Richter's Manual of Harmony. Translated by John P. Morgan. New York, 1867.

L. Cherubini. A Course of Counterpoint and Fugue. Translated by J. A. Hamilton. London, 1841.

Logier's System of the Science of Music, Harmony, and Practical Composition.

Adolph Bernard Marx. Theory and Practice of Musical Composition. New York, 1852.

L. H. Southard. Course of Harmony. Boston, 1855.

William Gardiner. Music of Nature. Boston, 1838.

Turner's Vocal Guide. Boston, 1836.

Mendelssohn's Letters.

Life of Mozart.

Cousin's Histories of Philosophy. Lectures on the True, the Beautiful, and the Good, &c.

Cours d'Esthetique par Jouffroy. Paris, 1845.

An Essay on the Nature, the End, and the Means of Imitation in the Fine Arts. Translated from the French of M. Quatremère de Quincy. London, 1837.

The Fine Arts—their Nature and Relations. By M. Guizot. Translated, with the assistance of the author, by George Grove. Second edition. London, 1855.

Du Fresnoy, de Arte Graphica. With Notes by Sir J. Reynolds.

Vasari. Vite de' piu Eccelenti Pittori, Scultori, e Architetti.

F. T. Vischer. Æsthetik, oder Wissenschaft des Schönes. 1846—1858.

Robert Zimmerman. Geschichte der Æsthetik als Philosophische Wissenschaft, 1858.

Hermann Lotze. Geschichte der Æsthetik in Deutschland, 1868.

Wilhelm Hebenstreit. Wissenschaftliche-literarische Encyclopädie der Æsthetik, 1848.

Joh. Winckelmann's Werke. Stuttgart, 1847.

Goethe's Werke.

Schiller's Werke.

Herder's Werke.

Lessing, Laokoon.

Kant's, Kritik der Urtheilungen und Beobachtungen über das Gefühl des Schönen und Erhabenen.

Solger's Vorlesungen über die Æsthetik. 1829.

Hegel's Æsthetik.

Hinkel's Allgemeine Æsthetik. 1847.

Oeser's Briefe an eine Jungfrau, über die Hauptgegenstände der Æsthetik. Leipzig, 1870.

Wilhelm Lubke. History of Art. Translated by F. E. Bunnell. Second edition. London, 1869.

CONTENTS.

BOOK II.

KINDS OF BEAUTY.

BOOK III.

LAWS OF BEAUTY.

BOOK IV.

RELATIONS OF BEAUTY.

INTRODUCTION.

METHOD OF STUDY.

Stages of method. § 1. METHOD in the study of any fact of experience requires of us that we proceed in order by the following stages, viz:—

1. Observation. First, that we ascertain precisely the fact which we are to study in its essential nature and properties:—

2. Generalization. Secondly, that out of the world of facts of our experience we then select those that possess this nature with these properties in order that we may group and classify them:—

3. Laws. Thirdly, that we then interpret the laws which are revealed in these facts thus generalized; and

4. Application. Fourthly, that we apply the science thus attained to the ends proper to all scientific investigation, either theoretically to the advancement of truth in other departments of knowledge, or practically to the improvement of our own personal well-being.

Our method, accordingly, in investigating the phenomenon of Beauty, will be to consider—

I. The Essential Elements or Properties of Beauty;
II. The Classification of Objects of Beauty;
III. The Laws which govern in Beauty;
IV. The Relations and Uses of Beauty.

Or more briefly still:

I. The Nature of Beauty;
II. The Kinds of Beauty;
III. The Laws of Beauty;
IV. The Uses of Beauty.

BOOK I.

NATURE OF BEAUTY.

CHAPTER I.

BEAUTY IN THE CONCRETE—THE RAINBOW.

§ 2. Our first step is to find an instance of beauty;—an instance in which we undeniably feel the effects of what we call beauty;—an instance, to speak more scientifically, in which the beautiful comes into our experience. We are to take first some familiar occasion on which the common fact in question is experienced; and then our next step will be to separate, by a careful analysis of the complicated elements of the phenomenon, such as are essential from those which are merely associated with it whether necessarily or accidentally.

Experience of Beauty instanced in the Rainbow.

We have then, all of us, had our attention arrested by the appearance, near the close of some summer day, of a bow of light, exceedingly brilliant, and of various hues, and in form, undeviatingly circular, without a break in its light or an imperfection in its regular outline, arching the entire circuit of the visible heavens before us, and seemingly resting on a dark, chaotic mass of cloud, with which it appears to be connected in close relationship. The outward sense is riveted to it by a most pleasurable sensation and the inner spirit by a most loving admiration.

This is the familiar phenomenon of the Rainbow; —the outer occasion and the inner experience. It will be unhesitatingly accepted as an instance in which the Beautiful enters into our experience. It has been so in all ages. "Look," says the Son of Sirach, "Look upon the Rainbow, and praise him that made it; very beautiful it is in its brightness; it encompasses the heavens with a glorious circle; and the hands of the Most High have bended it."

It is a complex phenomenon. Let us seek carefully to ascertain its constituting elements and essential properties.

Sensation and Perception in relation to Beauty.

§ 3. There is, in the first place, an affection of the outward sense;—there is sensation. The eye takes in an object of wonderful brightness, of enchanting hue; of vast extension and of most perfect outline. The sense is vividly impressed.

There is, also, together with this lively impression on the sense, an intellectual activity awakened equally decided;—there is perception. The mind perceives a portion of its sensitive organism impressed from without itself, and thus recognizes an object external to itself, distinct from itself. This sensation in which we are passively impressed by the object and this perception attending it in which we actively recognize the object, are each attended by a peculiar pleasure. The eye of the child, whose intelligenee and reason have been developed only to the lowest degree, fastens upon it with obvious delight. This pleasure, however, is the mere pleasure of sense. It is not the feeling of beauty. Both may be experienced together. One may predominate at one time or in one mind; the other, at another time or in another mind. The child feels more the pleàsure of seeing; the mature mind is more absorbed by an entirely different emotion. The sight is necessary to the latter. It is, however, only indispensable condition of it; not the emotion itself. We must go farther in our study to find the elements of this emotion.

Intuition of Power.

§ 4. There is, further, in every full contemplation of the bow, the recognition of a power at work in its production. It is, indeed, a power of surpassing energy—a power bringing a dazzling light and splendor out of darkness and gloom, sudden order out of unmixed chaos; stretching its arm over a vast reach of the heavens, and holding forth its glorious work over a space we are unable to measure; moving its hand, too, in its work with a marvelous skill and dexterity, evincing a shaping as well as a producing energy as it blends with matchless taste and inimitable delicacy of touch the purest of hues and traces its arch with mathematical precision and exactness. This element of a recognized present power of marvelous energy and skill, enters into our mental experience, and necessarily enters, on a full contemplation. The recognition of this present power is a fact in our experience for which it is idle to attempt to account on any other supposition than that the power is there, to be recognized by every beholding spirit as truly as the outward form or outward brightness.

This element—power—it may be remarked, is not, in the sense in which the term is now technically used, *perceived.* It is not a proper object of perception. It is an object of intuition;—the mind intuits it.

Of Intelligence. § 5. Besides this active producing power, a full and true contemplation of this phenomenon universally and necessarily discovers another element—that of intelligence appearing everywhere in the order, in the interior design, in the relation of the parts to one another constituting a perfect intellectual whole. Every part stands in an orderly relation to every other;—the bow to the portion of the heavens in which it is placed and to the cloud on which it rests, as well as to the eye that contemplates it; the parts of the bow itself to one another, in the outline all arranged in the exactest mathematical order and precision, and in the color, each hue in its own place and mathematically definable relation to every other in position and in shading. So precise is this order, that, given any portion of the bow, however small, the mathematical mind can reproduce every other part and reconstruct in idea the whole.

This order is as objectively real as the power that brought the bow into being and shaped the outline and blended the various hues, or the cloud and mass of raindrops from out of which this marvelous creation is produced. Like the power, it is not perceived, but intuited. It lies beyond the mere matter, and is revealed through it, and these intuitions of power and of order are accompanied by the proper pleasure which attend all exercises of the intuitive faculty, varying in degree with the character of the idea or object and the varying character and condition of the intuiting spirit, but, as a distinct kind of pleasurable exertion, of a higher rank than the pleasures of sensation or of perception.

Of Freedom.

§ 6. Still further, a full contemplation of the bow reveals the elements of freedom. The power which we have intuited, and which we have found to move in intelligence, we find to work, also, in perfect freedom. The hand that has laid that bow so gently on the bosom of the storm-cloud, that has so delicately rounded its outline and blended its hues, has moved without checks or hindrances from within or from without. The perfect gracefulness that marks its forming work reveals a freedom unimpaired and without defect and unobstructed by any other outer force. This element, too, is necessarily given in a true and full contemplation, and is accompanied by its own peculiar pleasure.

Of Love.

§ 7. Once more, a full contemplation of the bow reveals to us the element of love. The heavenly Iris is sent on a mission, bearing a purpose. There is good-will, love, expressed. The pleasure which attends each step of the contemplation, is the purposed fruit and result of the revelation, and demonstrates the love that is behind and within. Hence its attractive power upon our souls, and the loving sympathy which it awakens in grateful response in our bosoms. We recognize accordingly and by necessity, a spirit's presence with the same attributes as essentially characterize our own spirits; and this recognition is attended by the peculiar pleasure of sympathy.

Of Spirit.

§ 8. Now as, when the form and the color are given to us in the first stage of our contemplation—first not in time but in logical order—as objects of sensation and perception, we at once and necessarily suppose a material substance in which these properties inhere; as these qualities are the signs, the expressions, the revelations of the matter to which they belong; so precisely when, in the second stage of our contemplation, the elements of power, of intelligence, of freedom, and of love are given to us, we as necessarily and immediately suppose an immaterial, a spiritual substance in which these properties inhere. Power, intelligence, freedom, love, are the signs, the expressions, the revelations of a spiritual being, directly or indirectly concerned wherever they appear.

CHAPTER II.

ELEMENTS OF BEAUTY.

Three constituents in all experience of the beautiful.

§ 9. We have found an object which the world have agreed to call beautiful: an occasion on which the beautiful undeniably enters into our experience. In that experience we have found, first, that which the world have agreed to call matter, producing in us as passively affected by it sensation, and as actively determined by it perception. We have found, secondly, certain attributes just as certainly and as necessarily given to us: those of power, intelligence, freedom, love,—belonging to what the world have agreed to call immaterial and spiritual. In other words, we have found matter and spirit—matter revealing to us spirit, or spirit revealing itself to us through matter. Whatever else may be true of this experience, whatever else may enter into our experience, these three things are undeniably present: first, something which we call matter through which something is revealed to us; secondly, something revealing itself which we may call spirit; and thirdly, the actual revelation of this revealing element or spirit in and through this matter. These three constituents are not only present in the scene, but they are indispensable to whatever we call an experience of the beautiful in contemplating it.

Matter in beauty.

§ 10. That which we immediately recognize through our outward senses in the object is called *matter*. What this is in its essential nature we have no knowledge; we only know that it is not mind, spirit; it is entirely foreign to our rational natures, to our intelligence, to our love. When we seek to define it, we can only say of it, that it has not the properties of an intelligent nature; it is inert, it has no power to move itself; it is formless, is incapable in itself of coming into our intelligence until it has been shaped or formed by some mind; it is chaos, emptiness, being devoid of all intelligible elements or properties and only capable of being filled and so characterized by some acting mind. Matter is best defined, although even then but very defectively, as that which may receive and retain mind.

In its primary and more familiar use, the term *matter* is applied to that which we can see or feel. This is gross, sensible matter. In a derived meaning it is applied to whatever may receive and retain any act or state of mind, although not visible or tangible, so that one state of mind may be the matter in which another may embody itself. Thus a feeling of joy may be embodied in a train of thought, which then becomes the matter in which the joy expresses itself. This derivative use of the term will be made more clear in the sequel. From these uses of the term should be carefully distinguished another use which is very common, in which it is employed to denote the thought or feeling as shaped or determined or embodied, including both that which is revealed and that through which it is revealed. Thus we speak of the matter of a poem, meaning by the expression the thought or sentiment, the object or scene which is shaped and embodied in the poem.

Spirit in beauty —Idea.

§ 11. The second element mentioned, that which is revealed through the matter or is shaped in it, is called *idea*. By this term is denoted any manifested act or state of mind; any expressed thought, or feeling, or purpose, or disposition. We found in the contemplation of the bow ideas of power, intelligence, freedom, love. These are manifestations of spirit or mind. Wherever we recognize either one of them, we recognize there a sure and certain work of mind. None of them belongs to what we call matter, for matter in itself has no power, being absolutely inert; has no intelligence, no freedom, no affection. As we have seen, it is characteristic of matter that it is utterly destitute of these attributes. The most and best that we can attribute to matter is that it may receive these ideas, may be impressed by them, and being inert in itself, may or must permanently retain them, until they are displaced by some cause out of itself. It is heavy; it attracts or resists; it gives out heat or light, simply because it has received these ideas of attractive, repulsive, heating, illuminating force and retains them passively till some occasion or condition comes to it, when it gives up what it had received. As we know of but two kinds of being — matter and spirit — so these ideas of power, intelligence, and the like, which are entirely foreign to matter, we attribute to spirit. These are modes, or acts, or states of spirit, and the term *idea* is employed to denote any such mode or act or state when manifested or expressed in matter of whatever kind.

Revelation of idea in matter—Form.

§ 12. The third element mentioned is the revelation of the idea in the matter. It is not idea by itself without relation to the matter, nor matter by itself, nor both together, viewed otherwise than in this relation—that one is revealed or expressed in the other — that necessarily enters in any proper experience of the beautiful. The word that best expresses this element is *form.* It is a word that etymologically comes from a root denoting *to see,* and hence *to know, to apprehend.* Its proper meaning, accordingly, is an object of sight, knowledge, apprehension, or what may be seen, known, or apprehended. It is the correlative of *idea,* and comes from the same grammatical root. Idea is subjective ; form is objective.

Three elements of beauty: matter, idea, form.

§ 12. The three constituent elements of beauty are, accordingly: matter, idea. form. Matter is that element in which idea is revealed. Idea is that which is revealed in matter. Form is the revelation itself of idea in matter. The matter of the bow is color and outline. The ideas revealed in it are power, intelligence, freedom, love. The form is the revelation or expression itself of these ideas, shaping the outline and attempering the light so that the ideas shall be expressed in it, and thus may be recognized and felt by the mind to which the revelation is made.

CHAPTER III.

BEAUTY OBJECTIVE.

§ 14. We have used language thus far which seems to imply that beauty is without us; that it exists distinct and independent of us; that it comes into our experience from without and is not originated within us. It is of importance to investigate this point directly and closely and to ascertain whether such expressions as import such an objective reality in the beautiful are to be understood literally and exactly. We speak of the sun rising, while science teaches us that this is not so: that it is the earth really that moves. May it not be so with expressions which attribute a reality to beauty external to the mind that feels it. In fact, the prevalent theory in Great Britain and in English æsthetic literature has denied to beauty any such outer existence, and has resolved all our experience of it into mere association. This theory, first propounded by Mr. Alison, was fully carried out and perfected by Lord Jeffrey in the early part of this century. According to this theory, "the emotions which we experience from the contemplation of sublimity or beauty are not produced by any physical or intrinsic quality in the objects which we contemplate; but by the recollection or conception of other objects which are associated in our imaginations with those before us and consequently suggested by their appearance." "Things are not beautiful in themselves, but only as they serve to suggest interesting conceptions to the mind." Consequently, to use the very language of Lord Jeffrey, a friend's "poetry or his slippers, his acts of bounty or his saddle-horse" are equally beautiful, inasmuch as they all alike "may lead to the same chain of interesting remembrances."

Its origin.

§ 15. This theory originated in an opposition to certain other views that had gained currency on the nature of beauty. Like most theories that originate in this way, particularly in the early stages of a science, while effective in demolishing the false or imperfect, it is yet to be characterized as partial and unsound. Mr. Alison's able work overthrew those theories which founded all emotions of beauty in some one principle, as of relation, utility, order and design. It as effectually overthrew the doctrine that matter is beautiful in itself, as Mr. Burke, in his Theory of the Sublime and Beautiful, seems to teach. Mr. Alison rather ranked himself with the Platonic school of philosophers, embracing Lord Shaftesbury and Dr. Hutcheson, who have found all beauty to consist in the idea which is represented, and distinctly maintains in his conclusion that matter "derives its beauty from the expression of mind." His exposition, however, led directly to the bold skepticism which characterizes Lord Jeffrey's speculations. Hume had already maintained that "beauty is no quality in things themselves." Lord Jeffrey accepts this teaching, but attempts to account for the rise of emotions of beauty by the principle of association.

Opposed by the common sense of men.

§ 16. This doctrine that there is nothing in the object itself which awakens the emotions of beauty except some accidental association of it with our past experience is rejected by the common sense of men. No unsophisticated mind hesitates for a moment to ascribe the admiration and delight which the sight of the rainbow occasions directly to something in the object itself, independent of all association and all experience. It is difficult, if not entirely impossible, to conjecture what association common to all men it is which is excited by the sight of the bow producing these emotions alike in all; what experience common to all it connects itself with so as to produce this universal effect. It would be difficult to persuade a candid and unbiased beholder that it is not something in the object itself which affects him, but only a train of sentiment in his own mind to which his admiration and delight attach themselves; that it is all a delusion and mistake to attribute the beauty he feels to the object; and that he unconsciously and illusively transfers the effect from the train of associations which is really the center and source of his admiration to the bow which is simply the occasion of that train of associations. It would be as difficult to convince him of this as to convince him that the bell which awakens him in the morning and becomes thus the occasion of his rising and beholding the beauties of the dawn is the real object of his admiration, or at least as truly so as the gold and purple of a morning sky. There is, then, this strong presumption against the doctrine, that the common sense of men recognizes something out of themselves, something really existing which of itself produces the emotions universally ascribed to beauty.

By language.

§ 17. The universal speech of men is opposed to this theory. Even Lord Jeffrey himself everywhere uses language that is utterly irreconcilable with his theory. He speaks unqualifiedly of the "contemplation of beauty" as if beauty was something that is truly an object of contemplation. He speaks of the "perception of sublimity or beauty" of the "objects which have the power of exciting these emotions." His language sometimes amounts to flat contradiction of his theory, as when in laying down his proposition he affirms of "the emotions we receive from the contemplation of sublimity or beauty" that they "are not original emotions nor produced directly by any qualities in the objects which excite them, but are reflections or 'images' of other emotions which we have already experienced." Here he speaks of beauty as something that can be contemplated, and, of course, an object distinct from the contemplating mind. He speaks also of certain objects which excite the emotions received from this contemplation of them or perhaps from the contemplation of the beauty in them; and then in strange confusion he speaks of the emotions received from the contemplation of beauty as only reflections or images of emotions already experienced. The speech of men has so fully recognized the objective reality of beauty that the very utterance of a theory that controverts this common doctrine involves absurdity and contradiction.

Not warranted by their argument.

§ 18. Further, the argumentation by which Lord Jeffrey sustains his theory shows that his statement is far broader than his arguments warrant or than he himself really believed. His aim was to overthrow the erroneous doctrine that beauty is to be resolved into some one specific principle, as of utility, order, or the like, and the opposite doctrine of Burke that beauty consists in mere qualities of matter. In correcting these errors he has fallen himself into the error of resolving all beauty into accidental association. Yet his arguments which he seems to regard as convincing in the case prove something far different from this ;—they prove that while all beauty is neither utility, nor order, nor mere relation, on the one hand, nor mere physical qualities of matter on the other hand, it is yet real, while expressive of whatever the spirit of man can feel or do. His argument thus shows that "the beauty of a living and sentient creature depends upon qualities peculiar to such a creature rather than upon the mere physical attributes." The beauty of an English landscape, also, consists, he shows, "not in the mere mixture of colors and forms," "but in the picture of human happiness that is presented to our imaginations and affections." What the argument really aimed at seems then not to show that all beauty is merely subjective with nothing objective to determine our sense of it, but that it is human feeling, not dead matter, which forms the object of our emotions. He mistakes in supposing that the human sympathy, which is but the condition of our enjoying the beauties of a landscape, is the proper object that is beautiful in our contemplation of it. The beauty is not in the sympathy; although it may be true that a being destitute of all human sympathy would be incapable of discerning the comfort and enjoyment which are presented to our contemplation in the quiet, the order, the neatness, the prolific richness of cultivated grounds that characterize the supposed landscape. The landscape is beautiful not because of the sympathy, but because of these ideas so well revealed in it.

Does not account for all beauty.

§ 19. But a fatal objection to the theory that the emotions we ascribe to beauty are produced by the accidental association in whatever way of the object with our past experience, is found in the fact that many objects which are thus associated with past feelings of pleasure are not as such recognized by us as beautiful. If the theory be correct, whatever is thus associated or can by virtue of such association awaken a train of feelings and imaginations is beautiful. Then must, in fact, as Lord Jeffrey puts it, "the saddle horse" of his friend be equally deserving of the appellation of beautiful as his "poem"; for either may equally awaken the train of agreeable associations; the one as well as the other may recall the absent friend and bring back the precious memories associated with him.

Hutcheson's theory that Beauty is dependent on contemplating minds.

§ 20. There is another mode of explaining the experience of beauty adopted by some writers which leads directly to the same skepticism. Thus Hutcheson, who not only maintains that beauty is in the object, but also undertakes to show what quality precisely it is which makes an object beautiful—which he finds to be "uniformity amidst variety," — nevertheless suffers himself to admit that "were there no mind with a sense of beauty to contemplate objects" he could not see how they could be called beautiful.

Solger.

In the same way Solger, a German writer on æsthetics, teaches that "beauty being bare form is solely for the percipient." Such teachings involve the very opposite of the real views of the writers. If beauty ceases where there is no mind to experience it, then clearly it can have no independent existence. But the bright round sun would not cease to be bright and round if the sense of sight were to be everywhere destroyed.

Beauty not identical with pleasure.

§ 21. Still another very common mode of representation is in the same way liable to lead to skepticism in regard to the objective reality of beauty. It is that which in testing beauty identifies it with the pleasure which it occasions. "Beautiful" and "pleasing" are often interchanged; and an object is assumed to be beautiful which pleases. But while it is true that the experience of the beautiful like the apprehension of truth naturally gives pleasure, yet these are sources of pleasure other than the sense of beauty. The acquisition of truth, as just intimated, is pleasing; sensation is in itself a pleasure. As we look upon the rainbow there is both the pleasure from the sight of its form and of its brightness and blended hues, and also the pleasure from perceiving the relations of the bow to the cloud on which it rests and to each drop of water which refracts and reflects its own light and to the parts of the bow itself in its perfectly circular figures, as well as also to the arrangement of the hues. The child may be delighted simply through the sensation which the visible form and brightness produces in him, and the philosopher through the perception of scientific laws which he reads in the outer and inner relations of the bow, while neither of them shall have the slightest emotion of pleasure from the object regarded as beautiful. There are besides sources of moral pleasure in the object which are entirely distinguishable from the proper æsthetic pleasure. The bow brought hope and peace to those that had been saved from the general deluge; and the pleasure in grateful hope and peace which came to them as they looked upon it may very probably have absorbed all æsthetic pleasure. While it is true, accordingly, that an object which cannot please cannot be beautiful, it is true besides that it is not necessarily beautiful because it pleases. There is a physical pleasure, the pleasure of sensation; there is an intellectual pleasure; there is a moral pleasure; and besides these there is also an æsthetic pleasure. This last species of pleasure comes from the æsthetic properties of the object and cannot be resolved into any one or all of the other species of pleasure which an object may awaken in us.

The immediate end of Beauty not pleasure.

§ 22. On the other hand we must guard ourselves against the error of those who, like Quatremère de Quincy, teach that the characteristic end of form, of beauty, and the proper aim of art, is pleasure. It is no more so than the end of truth is pleasure. Form gives pleasure, as does truth, when apprehended. But the proper end of form is to effect communion between different spirits—it is the condition and the medium of such communion.

Proofs of Objective reality of Beauty;—1. from common sense.

§ 23. The proofs of the objective reality of beauty are first, that the common sense of men uniformly recognizes some thing inherent in the object which awakens the emotions of beauty. It never questions this reality. It never imagines that these emotions come from a train of associations, and that the object is only the remote occasion of the emotions. It laughs at the notion of Lord Jeffrey, that a man's slippers are just as really and intrinsically beautiful as a poem. The rainbow it recognizes to be beautiful alike at the first observation when there can be little or no possibility of any associations and at the second and any subsequent observations. If the pleasure which is occasioned comes only from its being associated with the memory of some friend in whose society it had been contemplated before, the common sense of men pronounces that this pleasure is not proper æsthetic pleasure.

2. From language.

§ 24. Secondly, the common speech of men recognizes the objective reality of beauty. In all languages of cultivated nations, in all ages alike, this reality is implied in the most common and familiar forms of expression. Even Lord Jeffrey, as already indicated, cannot but use language which disproves his theory.

3. From its own manifestations.

§ 25. Thirdly, this objective reality comes attested to us by all the signs and proofs which attend the presentation to us of any immaterial object. We accept the presentation to our sight of a living man moving before us and producing effects upon our feelings and our thoughts as well as upon our organs of sight as proof of a real object external to ourselves. We may question the reality of this object as reasonably as the reality of beauty.

4. From universal consciousness.

§ 26. Fourthly, universal consciousness attests the reality of beauty. We are conscious of an effect upon us, not of our own producing. We are conscious of an effect which is not that of bodily sensation, nor of mere perception nor of mere pleasure of any kind. The analysis of our experience gives us unmistakably a peculiarity which does not belong to these other effects, physical, intellectual, or moral. The effect is immediate from the object. It is not intermediate through a train of associations, and therefore is not to be ascribed to them, but to the original object itself which produces tne effect while awakening, it may be, divers associations in connection with the proper effect. We are immediately conscious, it is true, only of the effect; but we are conscious of it as an effect not of our own producing; as not arising from our own memories or associations with past experiences. The effect comes, we are conscious, from without ourselves, from a power external and so foreign to us. This effect in us, which we call the experience of beauty, could not be but for the object that is offered to our view. It must be therefore from that; and in that object must be some property which can thus affect us—something real.

Most correctly does Menzel in his review of German æsthetic literature declare in the light of its history: "the science of æsthetics itself is nothing but the theory of objective beauty; that is, of the beautiful as it appears in external objects."

CHAPTER IV.

THE UNIVERSALITY OF BEAUTY.

Universality of Beauty denied in theory of association.

§ 27. If, as we have seen in the last chapter, there is some reality which is external to our contemplation and the proper object of that contemplation in the experience of beauty, the question at once arises: is that objective beauty for all? Is it object for universal experience?

If beauty consists only in a train of associations, it is evident that whatever may be the character of the object presented to the mind, however beautiful to most observers, it cannot be beautiful to him who has not a train of associations to be awakened by it; to him with whose past experience it is not in some way so connected as to awaken pleasant memories. Beauty, according to this theory, cannot be for mind as mind; but only for such minds as have had a special history related to the object.

And of Pleasure.

§ 28. So, too, on the theory that the beautiful is the same as the pleasing, that whatever is pleasing is by very virtue of its being pleasing, beautiful, beauty cannot be universal. For objects that are pleasing to some are displeasing to others. We ourselves are at one time pleased with objects that at another are positively displeasing. The child is pleased with toys; the man puts away childish things, finding no longer satisfaction in them.

And of Utility.

§ 29. Still further on the theory that beauty consists in utility, or other specific relation, beauty cannot be universal; for where this relation is not recognized there can be no beauty; and our sense of beauty is dependent not on the object itself but on that something else to which it is related. Whether any individual mind has been brought to know that related object is a matter of accident. If a weed, otherwise lacking in all beauty, becomes beautiful simply by virtue of its being useful for food or in healing, it cannot be beautiful to us, till we have learned this utility.

Doctrine of universality involved in the analysis given.

§ 30. But if beauty consists, as we have seen, in form as a revelation of some mode or act of mind through some medium, then it must be alike for every mind that can receive such revelation through such a medium. The sense of beauty must be independent of any such accidents as associations founded in past experience, of any casual changes in the condition of our feelings that capriciously are now pleased, then displeased with the same object, and of any recognition of utility or other relation in the object. Beauty must be for all minds alike that are capable of apprehending it. Its proper effect it must produce alike everywhere and by necessity wherever the conditions are supplied.

Not contradicted by facts.

§ 31. This doctrine of the universality of beauty implying a necessary uniformity of effect whenever the conditions are supplied, although it would seem to be well nigh self-evidencing, may yet, at first sight, seem to be in contradiction to our common experience and observation. We find, thus, that the same object is beautiful to one, while to another it is, perhaps, positively hateful. So, too, some persons seem wholly insensible to beauty. Yet these facts are entirely reconcilable with our proposition. They give, indeed, no more difficulty here than we encounter in other kinds of experience. We assert, thus, that sound is universal—is for all. Yet all do not hear. Some are absolutely deaf. Others who have the organ of hearing in its full perfection and who are, moreover, in the proper relation to the origin of the sound so far as external circumstances are concerned, yet often fail to hear. The clock strikes its hours : but the student engrossed in absorbing study, the youth in the excitements of pleasure, the anxious mother striving by her care and love to hold back the spirit of a child that seems struggling to depart,—men absorbed deeply in thought, in enjoyment, in care, heed it not. Sound is not to them. If it strike upon the outward ear, it reaches not the apprehending spirit. But the truth remains that sound is for all men endowed with the organ of hearing, when the outer conditions are supplied.

Analogy of sound.

Of truth.

So we assert that truth is universal—necessarily apprehended by every mind placed in proper relations to it. But the truth of the equality of the angles of an equilateral triangle so readily apprehended by the geometrician when especially the figure of such a triangle is before his eyes, the mass of men fail to apprehend. Is truth, therefore, not universal? Do we conclude from this that it is not necessarily apprehended by the mind in suitable relationship to it? Certainly not. Truth present to mind as mind is apprehended by it necessarily and with the peculiar pleasure that attends the apprehension of truth.

Apprehension of truth and beauty relative to culture.

§ 32. Nor do we feel the necessity of modifying the proposition that truth is for all minds—alike to be apprehended with the proper pleasure of such apprehension, in order to meet the fact that there is a difference in truths as it respects their capability of being apprehended. The trained mind at once apprehends the equi-angularity of an equilateral triangle exhibited in diagram before it, or even without such diagram; the infant mind apprehends no such truth in a diagram ever so perfectly constructed and distinctly observed by the outward eye. So with beauty. To apprehend some forms of beauty, a developed capacity of apprehension may be requisite. Still, beauty, like truth, is for the mind as mind. The more mind, the greater mental capacity there is, the fuller will be the apprehension as well of truth as of beauty. The germ of the capacity in each of these departments of exertion is in every mind. At least, the human mind wants an essential property, if it lack either capacity; it is but a monstrosity of mind. That ever such a monstrosity existed is without proof. Truth and beauty, we conclude then, are alike for mind as mind ; possible to be apprehended by every mind, necessarily apprehended by every mind when present to it, and ever apprehended by a legitimate necessary satisfaction or pleasure.

Necessary principles of Taste.

§ 33. If this doctrine of the universality of beauty be correct, then there must be universal or necessary principles of taste. There must be a criterion of beauty. In other words it must always be possible to determine whether any given object, a rainbow or a landscape, a painting or a poem, any product of nature or any work of art is beautiful or not ; as it must be possible to indicate whether there be in it that which produces the effect of beauty on mind as mind. It must be possible always to indicate in what respects it must be regarded as beautiful and in what, not ; as that element in it which makes it beautiful can if present be shown by its like effect on every mind. There is possible, consequently, a science of taste, that shall unfold the principles which preside over the creation of form, that is over the revelation of idea, and over its interpretation ; that shall show on universal grounds how idea is to be revealed and how it is to be apprehended by the mind to which it is revealed. There is such a thing as sound taste, as valid criticism ; and these are grounded on the universality of beauty.

Reconcilable with a diversity of tastes.

§ 34. The popular notion of a diversity in tastes which has passed into a familiar adage, need not occasion any serious difficulty in accepting this doctrine. In the first place, it will be necessary to determine precisely in what sense the term *taste* is used, for it has a diversity of meanings. Among these meanings two are to be particularly noted here—one denoting a sensibility to impression or the awakening of that sensibility ; the other, the judgment which acts on that impression. When it is said that a man has a taste for the beautiful, it is meant that he has a lively susceptibility for it, and the term is used in the first of these two meanings. When it is said that he has a good taste in objects of beauty, it is meant that he judges readily and accurately upon objects that awaken that susceptibility—that he refers the impression to that element in the object which actually produces it. It is evident that one mind may be very susceptible to impression from a landscape or a painting without being able to point out at once what are the particular elements in it which impress his susceptibility, and may be a very poor judge ; while another mind, less susceptible may be a very accurate judge ; inasmuch as he may be able to point out in the complex object precisely what it is that makes it beautiful.

In the next place, in the application of the adage the same confusion of the beautiful with the pleasing that has been before indicated, is often to be remarked. Thus Lord Jeffrey in maintaining "that it is not only quite true that there is no room for disputing about tastes, but that all tastes are equally just and correct, in so far as each individual speaks only of his own emotions," grounds his opinion on the fact that inasmuch as an object gives him pleasure, it is beautiful. In the sense that all things do not please alike, the adage holds true.

Still further, it should be borne in mind that the same complex object may reveal in many different ways or through many different elements. One mind may by effect of peculiar disposition or habit more readily recognize one of these ways or elements; another mind more readily fastens upon another. One mind may not find in an object that which another may at once discern. Thus it is said of a celebrated mathematician that he could never find any thing sublime in the Paradise Lost; but "he could never read the queries at the end of Newton's Optics without feeling his hair stand on end and his blood run cold." There is no object presented to us which we may not view in one or another of manifold aspects. In contemplating the rainbow, the regularity of the curve may absorb the mind of the mathematician, while its relation to the cloud and to the sun may engage that of the philosopher, to the exclusion from the consciousness in both observers of the sentiment of beauty, which sentiment on the contrary may wholly fill the mind of a third beholder.

That there should be diversity of tastes and that even in the contemplation of the same object different beholders may see different elements of beauty, and some have no sense of beauty whatever awakened by it, can thus be satisfactorily accounted for in entire consistency with the doctrine that beauty as such is for all human minds as such; and consequently that there are fixed determinable principles of taste and grounds for a true science of criticism. It is correctly observed by Jouffroy that every object and every event is the sign of an idea. Every object is consequently in some respect beautiful, and may be recognized as such if regarded in that respect; while if that respect be disregarded it may be ugly. An object may have manifold elements of expression, some of which may be in beauty, and others not. According as the contemplation fastens upon one or the other class, the object as a whole will be held to be beautiful or not.

CHAPTER V.

THE RELATIVENESS OF BEAUTY.

Kinds of relativeness.

§ 35. It is remarkable how universally the relativeness there is in beauty has been recognized and how vitally it has seemed to shape the various theories that have been given of its nature. From Plato down we find everywhere the influence of this recognized attribute in shaping theory. We find it, indeed, in widely diversified ways, as relativeness may exist in various modes. We may distinguish thus a relativeness in degree and a relativeness in kind.

Of degree.

The relativeness in degree, Plato, in his dialogue entitled the Hippias Major, seems to have desired to exhibit in beauty, when he represents the face of a beautiful maiden regarded by itself as undeniably a true object of beauty; but as becoming absolutely ugly when coming into the presence of angelic or divine beauty. So, as he proceeds to instance, the maiden-face, a horse, a harp, a kitchen-pot, may be unquestionably beautiful in themselves, but become ugly in presence of a higher beauty.

This kind of relativeness consisting only in degree, we are prepared by what has been already seen, to recognize as belonging to beauty. Beauty is of a higher or lower degree, according as the idea is more or less perfect or more or less noble, the matter more or less suitable, the embodiment more or less exact and complete. In this sense, as it respects degree, an object of lower beauty may be said to be relatively ugly in comparison with one of a higher degree. Beauty in this sense is relative. But this kind of relativeness is to be carefully discriminated from that which lies in the intrinsic nature of beauty.

Of kind.

§ 36. Relativeness in kind may be external or internal. It may exist externally between the object and the contemplating mind, or internally between the several elements that constitute it as a complex whole.

External.

We are prepared by what has been considered to recognize a kind of relativeness of the first kind. It is true that beauty can be apprehended only by an energy that can grasp ideas revealed in matter. To the contemplating mind beauty is not, so far as it is not or cannot be apprehended; just as an object of sight is to the blind as if it were not; as music of the richest melody is as if it were not to the deaf. Still farther, as before intimated, the higher beauty demands a higher, riper mental energy; so that, it may be, a real beauty shall be hid from the less cultivated that is manifest to the maturer and more vigorous capacity. If we add to this the further consideration that by its power of abstraction the mind may confine its view to any one or more of the several elements of a complex object to the exclusion of the others, we shall be ready to admit that this attribute of relativeness between the viewing subject and the contemplated object of beauty may have a large place in the actual experience of beauty.

From the observation of the extent of this attribute of external relativeness and, as it would seem, without a careful determination of its true nature, the Scotch theories of beauty have run off into utter skepticism as to the objective reality of beauty. There can be little doubt that the whole skeptical theory in regard to the objective reality of beauty has no other foundation than the mistaken apprehension of the nature of the relativeness which there is in the contemplation of beauty.

Internal.

§ 37. There is still another kind of relativeness to be recognized in beauty —an internal relativeness existing between the several elements in its complex nature. Of the reality, the character, and the extent of this kind of relativeness, we have taken already a sufficiently distinct view in the exposition of the nature of beauty as idea revealed in form. It is only needful here to expose a remarkable error into which philosophers have fallen in misconceiving its true nature. Recognizing an internal relativeness in the elements of beauty, they have admitted only a mere discursive relationship between the idea and the outer form, shutting out from their view entirely that vital union which is implied in a revelation and embodiment. Thus Zimmerman, in commenting on Plato's expositions of the experience of beauty as composite in its nature, leaps at once to the conclusion that, as composite, beauty must be object of the faculty of comparison, the judging intelligence alone. The discursive faculty compares the idea and the matter, and in this comparison lies the true essence and characteristic of the experience of beauty. So he concludes, "the pleasure in the beautiful rests on a comparison of different things with one another, accordingly on a judgment."

In the same way Kant, and in this he is followed by the German philosophers generally,* as well as by Sir William Hamilton, makes beauty mere object of the understanding, or of that faculty whose function is to think the particular under the universal. Only, therefore, in the mere discursive relation, as that in which a plurality of objects may be thought as one, does this theory recognize the elements of beauty; a mere relation of logical dependence. But this is by no means the true internal relation in which the elements that constitute the beauty there is in an object stand to each other. To admit this would be to admit that the experience of the beautiful is indistinguishable from the experience of the true or the real. The unity in an object of the discursive faculty is a unity of the part with its whole; the unity in an object of beauty is a revelation, not a mere attribution, uniting subject with attribute.

---

* "The reference," says Zimmerman, "of the beautiful to a harmonious activity of the understanding and the imagination, the exposition of the beautiful from its subjective origin, not from its objective laws, is the fundamental principle of all æsthetics after Kant, with exception of Herbart."

There are other relations besides that of parts to their respective wholes ; and it is only this last that the understanding regards. Altogether too loosely and too ambitiously is the Comparative Faculty styled the Faculty of Relations, if simply because the revelation of soul in body, of idea in form, is a relation, we must infer that beauty is alone apprehensible by it. On the other hand, when its function and its sphere are accurately determined, its sole prerogative is found to be to identify—to detect and apprehend the sameness, total or partial, the total or partial unity of a plurality of objects or attributes ; and its domain is only over what can be thought as one among many. Revelation of soul in body, of idea in matter, is not mere identification of soul and body, of idea and matter as one. More than this, the contemplatingm ind recognizes here a vitalizing element altogether foreign to mere soul or to mere body ; to mere idea or to mere matter, and more than any mere aggregation of them. The union is not logical, but organic.

CHAPTER VI.

THE IMAGINATION.

Imagination correlative of Form.

§ 38. The fact that Beauty is objectively real implies that there is something in the human mind which answers to it as such object. This department of mind may, in best accordance with the use of language in our most recent literature, be denominated the *Imagination*. Form as object and Imagination as subject, are correlatives. The one is for the other and each implies the other.

Passive and Active.

But Imagination may be viewed in a double aspect ; as *passive* or recipient of form ; or as *active*, creative of form. Activity and passivity, as Sir William Hamilton has well observed, are always conjoined. "In every mental modification active and passive are the two necessary elements or factors of which it is composed." By our power of abstraction we may attend to the one side or to the other side of any mental modification, to the partial or entire exclusion of the other from our view ; and in this way we may characterize the same modification as either passive or active. It is so with knowledge or intelligence. In all perception of physical objects there is necessarily sensation. Perception is the active side, sensation the passive side of the same mental modification.

Defined. The Imagination is accordingly to be viewed both as active and as passive. It may be defined *the faculty of form*, or *the capacity of form;* according as, for the purposes of the definition, it is viewed as active or creative, or as passive or receptive.

Commensurate with Beauty. § 39. The sphere of the Imagination is thus precisely the sphere of the Beautiful, taken in its largest sense The Beautiful is the proper object for the Imagination. It is ever produced by the Imagination as the Faculty of Form; it is ever apprehended by the Imagination as the Capacity of Form. The observation of the elder Mendelssohn is as just as it is profound, that beauty—that is, objective beauty—or perfect form is ever the companion of sensibility.

Other names. § 40. There are other designations of this department of mind in current use, suggested by its different aspects or modifications. Such are the Contemplative Faculty, the Æsthetic Faculty, and the Theoretic Faculty, which regard Beauty or Form as object presented to the mind, and the mind as active in the contemplation; Internal Sense, Æsthetic Sense, Artistic Sense, likewise Æsthetic Taste, suggested by the passivity of the mind in this experience of Beauty; Phantasy and in the abbreviated form of the word Fancy, etymologically pointing to the essential nature of Beauty, as form or appearance, but in use rather applied somewhat capriciously to special modifications of the Imagination; the Creative Faculty, the Poetic Faculty, looking to the production of form as beauty; and the Artistic Sense and Artistic Faculty, limiting to a specific use and meaning.

Place among mental faculties.

§ 41. It will be of service to fix the precise place and relation of the Imagination as thus defined among the faculties and capacities of the mind. In doing this the defects or errors in certain theories of Beauty will come under our consideration.

Imagination, then, and Form being correlatives, related to each other as subject and object, and occupying precisely the same sphere, it is plain that as the Imagination is not the same as physical sensation, so the beautiful is not object merely for the bodily sense. This is the theory of Sir Edmund Burke in his classic essay on the Sublime and the Beautiful. Beauty, he maintains, "is no creature of our reason," but "is for the greater part some quality in bodies acting mechanically upon the human mind by the intervention of the senses;" "the qualities of beauty are merely sensible qualities;" and so he concludes that "beauty acts by relaxing the solids of the whole system." The Sublime, in like manner, he finds to have its source in whatever produces an extraordinary "tension of the nerves." According to this theory the sublime and the beautiful reach the mind only so far as they contract or relax the nerves, and are consequently sole objects for the Sense, precisely as are perfumes and flavors of

Theory of Burke.

bodies, objects only for the senses of smell and taste. The fatal defect in the whole theory is that it exalts a mere accidental concomitant in the experience of beauty to an essential element; indeed, makes this accident the essential element. That in the experience of the Sublime the animal nerves are sometimes tensely stretched, and that in the experience of beauty they are sometimes relaxed, is doubtless true. That it is not universally and necessarily so, hardly demands formal argumentation. Besides, in many cases, certainly the tension or the relaxation is the effect of the mental experience or contemplation, not the cause or object of it.

Imagination and Perception.

§ 42. Again, the æsthetic Imagination is not a proper faculty of the Intelligence; it is not a cognitive power. Accordingly, Beauty is not the immediate object of the Intelligence; the proper experience of the beautiful is not a mode of knowledge, is not a cognition.

It is not a proper perception; for this is but the active side of that mental state of which Sensation is the passive side. As the passive imagination is not Sensation, so the active imagination is not perception.

Nor Intuition.

§ 43. Nor yet is the Imagination a kind of intuition. Intuitions, as distinguished from perceptions in the literature of English psychology, have for their object ideas not presented to the mind through the bodily senses; although some authors also exclude the phenomenon of self-consciousness, and limit the application of the term *intuitions* to such ideas as identity, quantity, substance, cause, and the like. But intuitions like perceptions are cognitions, forms of the intelligence. Imagination is not an intuition. Its object, form, is not as form, as the beautiful, for the intelligence. The intelligence may indeed lay hold of it for itself; may perceive the rainbow as the effect of reflection and refraction, as in perfect circular figure; may study it as a matter of science. But in this exercise of the intelligence there is necessarily no proper experience of the bow simply as a thing of beauty.

Nor judgment.

§ 44. Nor, once more, is the imagination a form of the understanding or faculty of comparison; nor its exercise a proper thought. And the beautiful is not proper object of the understanding. Such, as already stated, is the theory of Kant and of Sir William Hamilton, as also of more recent German writers on æsthetics. "A thing beautiful," says Hamilton, "is one whose form occupies the imagination and understanding in a free and full, and consequently in an agreeable activity." But with Hamilton the imagination is only the representative or reproductive power of the mind by which it calls up past experiences and recombines them; and the function of the understanding is to bring the manifold given to it into a unity. When it can perform this function easily and perfectly, "the object," he says, "is judged beautiful or pleasing." But if this theory were correct, then wherever the greatest variety is combined in the most perfect unity, there should be the highest beauty. A perfect generalization ought to rank thus in the highest sphere of beauty; and to gratify our love of the beautiful in the most exalted degree, we must leave the domains of nature and art and range in the fields of abstract science.

Moreover, this theory mistakes the order and relationship in the complex experience of a beautiful object. The understanding acts only upon what is given to it; only upon what is already in the consciousness. Although it is true that it perhaps always attends upon the apprehension of the beautiful;—although in contemplating the bow, besides judging of the order of the blending hues and of the circular figure, we also may judge that it is beautiful and so exercise a proper taste-judgment in respect to it, yet this taste-judgment follows in order of nature upon the imagination. The proper sense of the beautiful is thus prior to the exercise of the understanding and so different from it and independent of it; for clearly we cannot judge an object to be beautiful until we have felt its beauty, as we cannot pronounce an orange to be sweet until we have tasted its sweetness. This theory overlooks the very fundamental law of the judgment, that it acts only upon what is already in the consciousness; that the subject and the attribute which it is its function to unite must be already in the mind before there can be any exercise of this its sole function. It must ever have as the prime condition of its action a *datum* consisting of an object and some attribute. In the case of a taste-judgment, his *datum* is the object and its attribute—beautiful.

Instead, therefore, of resolving the imagination into a judgment, into a comparison, into any mental act uniting the manifold into a unity, every judgment in matters of beauty presupposes the imagination as the faculty or capacity of form. The taste-judgment then proceeds to affirm respecting this form, in respect to all the manifold attributes which it may recognize in it, as well those which respect its interior as its elements, and the divers relations of these elements to one another, and its perfectness and also its exterior relations to time, place, contemplating mind, and the like.

In all the gradations of the consciousness in the contemplation, the judgment ever waits on the consciousness and acts ever only in immediate reference to that. When in the perception the idea that is revealed in it is apprehended, the judgment affirms the reality of the apprehension, and so the reality of the idea revealed ; and in the same way affirms the revelation. If the perfectness of the revelation passes into distinct consciousness, it affirms in reference to that—it affirms that the revelation is perfect. The whole complex process of æsthetic criticism is but a series of judgments on the several parts of the whole revelation of the idea in its form,—first, the conformity to an ideal of the idea revealed ; secondly, the form in which it is revealed ; and thirdly, the revelation itself : or on more particular points comprehended severally in these, as those parts are already presented in the consciousness.

The judgment, thus, is not the ground of the experience of beauty,—we do not first compare and judge, and then apprehend the beautiful. Beauty is not reasoned out by a process of the discursive or comparative faculty. The order is : we first apprehend beauty ; and then, in that act of consciousness, we judge in relation to it ; the judgment being grounded on the consciousness and pertaining immediately to that.

If the question be put : Do we not then judge immediately of beautiful objects ? it may be replied that, in the first place, we judge certainly in regard to such objects only as we apprehend them. Our fallible natures may err in their apprehension and so far may involve us in erroneous judgments. No judgment of ours can be absolute in regard to the nature of objects external to us. We judge them only as we apprehend them ; so that our judgment really rests upon that ; has that—the apprehension—for its object, not the real qualities of the objects concerning which we judge.

The imagination, consequently, is not properly a form of the intelligence. Psychologists have, indeed, treated it as belonging within that department as they have also Sensation ; but they have probably so treated both only because they are conditions of intelligence, sensation being the condition of a perception, the affection of the imagination being the condition of a taste-judgment.

Relation to Form. § 45. The place of the imagination among the phenomena of mind and its proper character may best be represented perhaps in its relation to form. It is, as we have seen, the capacity and also the faculty of form. It apprehends form and it creates form. As the mind is always really active even when more prominently viewed as passive, as its activity and its passivity both are engaged in every mental state or act, it follows, that even when it apprehends form passively, its active nature responds to this passive affection and re-creates for itself the form which it receives in more or less prominent extent. The musician thus reconstructs the forms of sound, its melodies and its harmonies, while he hears them; the painter in the same way pictures in his own consciousness the figures, the groups, the colorings of the paintings which he studies. So too in creating, in producing music, in designing paintings, the artist holds up the forms he constructs before his own contemplation and is passively affected by them. A great part of the enthusiasm with which his work is inspired comes from this passive affection from the forms his active genius creates. The imagination then is precisely defined as that department of the human mind whose object is form, and form as that attribute through which mind communicates with mind. It is the line or surface of contact between the mind expressing and the mind apprehending.

As will be more fully shown in a subsequent chapter which treats of the matter in form, the medium through which form reaches the mind may be the bodily sense—sensation—or the sensibility of the mind which receives only supersensible ideas. As form includes both idea revealed and matter in which it is revealed, we have diversities of form characterized by the specific kind of matter as also by the specific character of the idea.

CHAPTER VII.

ÆSTHETIC SCIENCE.

Æsthetics coördinate with Logic and Ethics.

§ 46. From the exposition given in the preceding chapters of the essential nature of beauty it will readily be presumed that it may properly be made the subject-matter of a special science. Indeed it would be easy to show that the science of beauty is coördinate with the sciences of the True and the Good,—with Logic and Ethics; and, Psychology being regarded as introductory, with them makes up the three departments of the science of the human mind. As coördinate with them and complementary of the general philosophy of the mind, it reciprocally sheds light upon them and receives light from them; shapes and colors them and is shaped and colored by them.

Has Scientific matter.

§ 47. Beauty has been shown to be objective and real; to be an attribute of objects existing externally to us. This attribute we have found to embrace several constituents or elements; as those of matter, idea, and idea in form, precisely as we find that the conception of the human involves the three elements of body, soul, and soul in body. As man is not mere body, nor mere soul, but a vital union of soul and body which vital union constitutes the essence of what is properly human, so beauty is not mere matter, as Burke's doctrine logically implies, nor mere idea, as Shaftesbury's writings seem to suppose, but idea embodied in matter;—idea in vital relation to matter, having its more essential and characteristic nature seated in this union. It is the same with truth, a truth is not mere subject, nor mere predicate; but the agreement of the predicate with the subject in the vital form of the proposition which unites the two. There can be no truth without a subject; none without a predicate or attribute: yet the most essential and characteristic nature of truth is seated in the vital union between the two, which union constitutes the proposition as such.

Science can make this analysis of the beautiful; can recognize these three elements in their several relations to one another; can in reference to them distribute the different kinds of beauty presented to the human mind; can also from the properties or relations that are given by these elements, severally determine the laws of beauty and its relations whether to science or to use.

Founded on Experience.

§ 48. Like every true science, æsthetic science starts from a *datum*,—from something given to it,—starts in other words from experience. The beautiful must be given as a reality in experience at the start. Science then detects the essential characteristic or attribute of the beauty given in this experience. This being ascertained, we are prepared to go forth into the world of experience and wherever we find this essential attribute which makes beauty what it is we know we find true beauty, however modified in degree or in relation to other things. Farther, we may now with the sure guide of science gather up all these modifications and distribute them into classes, we can scientifically enumerate the various leading kinds of beauty that exist in nature and art. Proceeding a step farther we may interpret out all the laws of these several kinds of beauty with scientific accuracy and thoroughness, inasmuch as these laws will be but essential attributes of beauty as modified by the nature of the objects which it characterizes as beautiful, or so far as beautiful. And, finally, we can reach with the same assurance of scientific method the various uses of beauty whether in nature or in art, whether to science, or to personal culture.

The whole procedure may be thus marked with a strict scientific character, and the result which we may thus attain will be a true science.

Its object the Beautiful, in the fullest sense.

§ 46. The term *beauty*, like its related terms *truth* and *duty*, in its strictest import points only to a single department of the whole science. The Science of the true treats not only of what is true in the more restricted and proper sense of the word but also of the false, the fallacious, the partially true, the mixed of truth and error. The science of duty treats not only of the right and the good, but also of the wrong and the evil, of the action that partakes of the two, that is wrong in intent and yet in a sense good in effect, and of the right in intent followed through the imperfection of the agent or the distortions of a corrupted world, by positive evil. All these three grand sciences thus treat not only of the perfect in their several fields; but of the imperfect also as well. The science of beauty thus treats of the ugly as well as of the positively beautiful; of the sublime and the ludicrous as well as of the properly beautiful. The science of beauty is commensurate with the entire sphere of form as the embodiment of idea in matter. The beautiful is indeed the perfect in form; but science must regard equally the negative and the positive; must regard also the practically perfect and the mixed in respect of its complex constituents as well as the absolutely perfect and the purely beautiful.

Here precisely appears one of the uses of a true science of beauty that by exhibiting the possibility of the combination of divers elements in every beautiful object, either one of which may be more or less perfect irrespectively of the others, it accounts for the proverbial diversity of tastes and at the same time points out the grounds of agreement, thus laying the foundation of a legitimate and trustworthy science of æsthetic criticism.

We have found beauty to be a proper object for the imagination; and the sphere of the imagination accordingly to be exactly commensurate with the sphere of beauty or form. As science of the one is, with the slight modifications which the diversity in the points of view occasions, the science of the other, it is a matter of little or no importance from which the sphere common to both observations is contemplated; much less is it of importance whether the science be called the science of Beauty or the science of Æsthetic Form, or the science of the Imagination.

History of Science in literature.

§ 50 The name *Æsthetics* was first given to the science by Alexander Baumgarten in a work the two parts of which were published at Frankfort on the Oder respectively in 1750 and 1758. The name was derived from the passive side of the imagination, Baumgarten's theory being that the beautiful consisted in addresses to the sense. His work was a very imperfect and partial one; but it immortalized itself by its occasioning a name to be fastened on the science. The criticisms upon the name as pointing to an erroneous theory of beauty are hardly just; since no name could well be selected which should not be associated with one element more closely than with another; and all words denoting spiritual objects were originally applied to material things.

The science has been cultivated with far more assiduity and success in Germany than elsewhere. The catalogue of German writers on æsthetics is long, and the works devoted to the science voluminous. Even the histories of the science, as those of Vischer, Zimmermann, and Lötze are more bulky than the aggregate of treatises on the subject in English literature. The leading writers after Baumgarten, or contemporary with him, are Winckelmann, Lessing, Kant, Schiller, Herder, Schelling, Solger, Schleiermacher, Herbart, Hegel, Weisse, Hinkel.

The French literature is meager in æsthetical works. The most important are the contributions of the Abbe Batteux, Cousin, Quatremère De Quincy, Jouffroy, and Taine.

The British authors of most importance in this field are Shaftesbury, Home, Hogarth, Hutcheson, Burke, Alison, Jeffrey, Coleridge, and Ruskin. In the metaphysical works of Reid, Stewart, Brown, Hamilton, as well as more recent writers, the subject of beauty receives a more or less thorough consideration. In the periodical literature the subject has been touched from divers points in manifold forms; and numerous treatises on special departments, such as Knight on Taste, Price on the Picturesque, Repton on Landscape Gardening, are to be found scattered along the path of British literary history.

In America besides the more formal treatises of Moffatt, Sampson, and Bascom, and the special works on Architecture, Landscape, and Painting, there is no work of commanding interest.

Histories of theories of beauty.

§ 51. The History of the theorizing on the nature of beauty, as it appears in literature, both before and since the formal inauguration of Æsthetic science by Baumgarten, demands a brief notice. It is remarkable how speculation here has turned upon the several elements which we have found to unite in all beauty—idea, matter, and the union of the two in all form. One theorist has emphasized one of these elements, another, another. The schools of speculation in different ages have repeated the same story. The review will furnish strong corroboration of the view we have attained of the true notion of beauty.

Grecian theories.

Beginning with Greece, the cradle of art as of science, we find Plato strongly inclined everywhere to identify beauty with idea. He holds back from any articulate determination of the essential notion of beauty; but it is evident that the idea was in his undetermined apprehension of its nature the ruling element, the characterizing, the essential element. In Aristotle, on the contrary, while he too abstains from any precise determination of its nature, we discover as strong a tendency to recognize the essential characteristic of beauty as lying in the matter. In Plotinus, who united the Platonic with the Aristotelian philosophy, or rather modified the former by the latter, we find the distinct recognition of both elements, idea and matter; but the uniting element he puts in the contemplating mind; there is with him no objective reality in beauty further than this, that the two terms of beauty are objective; the copula, the link, is in the viewing mind; so it is the soul only that is truly beautiful. As he says " never could eye that had not been made sunlike, ἡλιοειδής, have seen the sun, neither can soul that has not become beautiful see beauty."

§ 52. In modern times the philosophy of beauty has run nearly the same race. It has reached greater definiteness of statement with fuller development of meaning; but its movements have been in the directions indicated by the Greeks.

British.

In Great Britain we have Shaftesbury emphasizing the idea, and following hard in the track of the Plotinus philosophy. His conclusion in the long discussion, called "The Moralists," is "that there is no principle of Beauty in body." Mind alone is the principle of all beauty. "The beautiful" he says,* "the fair, the comely are never in the matter, but in the art and design; never in body itself, but in the form or forming power. Does not the beautiful form confess this, and speak the beauty of the design whenever it strikes you? What is it but the design which strikes? What is it you admire but mind, or the effect of mind? 'Tis mind alone which forms. All which is void of mind is horrid; and matter formless is deformity itself."

Burke, as we have already seen, went in the opposite direction and emphasized the matter. Beauty with him is wholly for the sense.

Alison in his zeal to correct the errors of both these opposite views, laid the foundation for the rejection of all objective reality in beauty; and ac-

---

Characteristics, Edition of 1738, vol ii, p. 405.

cordingly in Lord Jeffrey the skeptical theory of beauty appears in the place of the pantheistic or absolutist theory in Germany, and the Plotinus view among the ancients.

French. § 53. In France, the matter-side of the nature of beauty, the Aristotelian view, has been the prominent one. In the Eclecticism of Cousin we find the first intimations of a change; and with him it is the Platonic view that prevails. "The inward alone is beautiful." Beauty lies back of the revelation. "It makes itself known" is his language, "by sensible traits, whose entire beauty is merely the reflection of spiritual beauty." And again, "the three conditions of beauty are the moral idea, unity, and variety." "The most important element in the beautiful is the moral idea; unity and variety should be impressed with it, and serve only to exhibit it; consequently, the most important element in taste and in genius is the sentiment of moral beauty. That which is internal in man can alone perceive the internal in nature. It is my soul that feels the soul of the universe." Thus he slides quickly into the new-platonic philosophy as expounded by Plotinus, and expressly adopts its doctrine that "the beautiful is enveloped in forms without being constituted by them; we must disengage it; the beautiful is simply moral beauty, an idea, a sentiment," and the end of all is absolutism, pantheism. "God is the foundation of truth, beauty, and goodness; the absolute, who is reflected wholly in all his manifestations, or in ordinary language, in all his creation. The Deity is both in nature and in man; and here is found the explanation of man's sympathy with nature."

Jouffroy maintains the twofold element in every æsthetic object; the visible which is the sign, and the invisible which is the thing signified, or what we have called idea; "but of these two elements that which acts upon us æsthetically is the invisible." He immediately adds what indicates an unsettled judgment in the matter. "Perhaps, however, the invisible would not act upon us æsthetically if we could see it face to face and stripped of forms; at least in the present state the invisible which alone moves us must, to move us, manifest itself by forms or material signs."

German theories.

§ 54. In Germany, Baumgarten, following the lead of the speculation of his times, puts all beauty in the matter and allows it being only for and by the sense, holding in logical consistency with this 'that beauty cannot exist without desire for its possession, and that the true aim of beauty consists in awakening desire; the highest beauty is where the sense-known perfection is greatest, that is in nature. Hence the highest art is to imitate nature. All fiction is hateful.' In these views he is mainly followed by Eschenburg and Eberhard.

The Aristotelian or matter side of beauty thus took the lead in time in Germany. The Platonic or idea side was a subsequent development of æsthetic science there. It was the logical result of the idealistic philosophy. The idea was in this view everything. "The idea comes out of the object to meet the mind." But this partial view could not remain. Matter and idea came to be both recognized as indispensable in all beauty, and it was their union in some way which constituted the beauty. Kant placed this union, the uniting act, in the judgment as the faculty by which all multiplicity is gathered into a unity. And since Kant, the prevalent theory has been that beauty essentially consists not in the idea merely, or in the matter only; but in a union of the two effected by the faculty of the judgment. The unity is essential; but it is a mere subjective unity, which of course, as we have seen, denies all objective reality in beauty, and a subjective unity effected specifically by the judgment.

It is apparent that if we but drop the subjective coloring of the German speculations and adopt the doctrine that beauty has a true objective reality, we must pass directly to the theory presented in the preceding chapters;—that while both idea and matter are recognized as essential in all beauty, the union between these elements is objective like them. This theory is thus the legitimate result of all speculations on the nature of beauty to the present time and must be accepted as the teaching of the history of æsthetic philosophy when exploded errors are rejected and generally admitted truths are received.

BOOK II.

KINDS OF BEAUTY.

CHAPTER I.

PRINCIPLES OF DIVISION.

Division founded on the essential attributes of Beauty.

§ 55. In classifying, as there may be ever as many classes as there are attributes to be recognized, it is indispensable for any thorough, scientific study, that the ground of the division or classification be clearly indicated. It is the essential attributes of course which give the strictest scientific division. If these attributes be correctly taken, if they be the comprehensive attributes so far as the essential nature of the subject is regarded, and if they be properly coördinated, the resulting classification will be scientifically correct.

But it is to be remarked that while the essential attributes must give the proper scientific division, these attributes are never found in actual objects of beauty single or pure and unmodified. We find no object thus that is beautiful solely either in respect to its matter, or to its idea, or to its revelation. Material beauty, Ideal beauty, and Formal beauty ever unite in varying degrees, so that no object is wholly destitute of either. It is consequently the predominance of one or the other of these attributes which characterize the object as of one or the other kind. A poem, thus, that is characterized as rhythmical, must have some degree, although, it may be, a very low degree, of ideal beauty. In the same manner we speak of a *senseless book*, when we by no means intend that there is no sense at all, no idea in it. In the same way we characterize a man as intellectual, because intelligence predominates over sensibility and will, although no act of intelligence is possible in a soul utterly destitute of these other capacities.

In determining the kinds of beauty, we should thus found our classifications for scientific study on the essential properties of beauty. These we have found to be three:—1. the idea; 2. the matter; 3. the embodiment of the idea in the matter. All beauty may be correctly and completely characterized, accordingly, in reference to the idea, the matter, and the embodiment of the idea in the matter, so far as its essential nature is concerned. It would be differently characterized and differently classified if it were to be considered in reference to its laws or its uses and other relations.

Distinctions of Kind and Degree.

§ 56. But each of these prime constituents of beauty may appear in any object in different degrees, both absolutely and relatively. The idea may be of a higher or lower grade; or the matter more or less meet; or the embodiment itself more or less perfect. It becomes necessary to recognize this principle in the study of form; especially as the very term itself, beauty, suggests at once the expectation of something more or less perfect.

On these two principles accordingly, of degree and of essential nature, we proceed to mark out the different kinds of beauty.

1. Gradations. The one of the two principles named, that of degree, will guide us to those kinds of beauty which are characterized as more or less perfect in respect to all or either of the several constituents of beauty. It will give *the gradations* of beauty.

2. Kinds of beauty. The other principle, that founded in the essential nature or constituent elements of beauty, will guide us to the kinds of beauty characterized in reference to the prominence of the particular elements in the object. It will give us the *kinds of beauty* in the narrower sense.

This last named classification of beauty, founded on the several essential elements of beauty—idea, matter, form—will contain the more important divisions, to each of which it will be necessary to devote a separate chapter. The subdivisions here will be:

1. Beauty distinguished in respect to the idea revealed;

2. Beauty distinguished in respect to the revealing matter; and

3. Beauty distinguished in respect to the revelation itself of idea in matter, or proper form.

1. Ideal.
2. Material.
3. Formal.

We may, without dissenting from authorized usage in language, denominate these higher classes of beauty respectively: 1. Ideal Beauty; 2. Material Beauty; and 3. Formal Beauty.

Cautions:—1. As to use of terms.

§ 57. It will be necessary in the use of these denominations of beauty to guard against the ambiguity arising from the different meanings which have been attached to them. This diversity of meaning is an unavoidable necessity until the science becomes fixed and mature. In the use of language by some, particularly by those who found all beauty in idea alone, the denomination *ideal beauty* would include all kinds of beauty, and the expression would be tautological, meaning only beautiful beauty. So the denomination *material beauty* is not unfrequently used to distinguish that which is expressed in physical matter from other kinds of beauty; and to one who accepts the theory of Burke all beauty is material. In the same way the expression *formal beauty* is sometimes applied to that kind of beauty which appears in visible figure or outline as opposed to other kinds of beauty, such as those given in painting or in discourse. But if the three elements named are recognized to be distinct constituents of beauty, then it is clear we may distinguish beauty in reference to the attributes which belong respectively to each of these elements; and the higher class, which comprises the several groups of attributes found in each element, may properly be named from the element itself.

It will of course be understood that when a particular kind of beauty is denominated *ideal*, it is only because that element predominates or characterizes those objects; or because perhaps that it is one of the characteristics which belong to it. It will not be supposed that the other elements, those of matter and of form, do not appear at all in the object; but only that they do not appear as those which are to be regarded at the time. There is, for illustration, as we shall see, a species of beauty called *propriety*. It is founded in the idea revealed. Wherever it appears in an object, the object may be characterized as having that attribute of ideal beauty,—as being *proper*, *fit*, *decorous*, or the like; that is, as having a certain attribute of beauty attaching to the idea revealed in it, not to the matter as of marble or color or language, nor yet to the form itself or mode of embodiment as sublime or comic.

This danger of ambiguity, until the nomenclature is fixed by use, is encountered everywhere in abstract science. The terms at first borrowed from common speech are used metaphorically and hence loosely, sometimes with a wider, sometimes with a narrower import, occasioning danger of error or even of contradiction. Thus in moral science we have an exact analogy. In every moral act there must be motive, end, and action from the motive to that end; there must be love as the starting point, good as the goal or end, and the actual movement of love to the end or result. Yet the term *love* properly pointing to the motive, is often applied to the whole moral character of the act. So also *goodness*, which properly looks only to the end or result, and *rectitude* which regards the movement itself from the starting point or motive to the goal, are each in the same way often applied to the whole concrete act. They are correctly so used because each implies the other. There can be no moral act except as involving a motive, an end, and a movement from the motive to the end ; hence no love without good or without right ; no right without love and good ; no good without love and right, in the proper moral sense. And precisely as in ethical science we have antagonistic systems of morals, one founding all morality in the motive, love—another in the end, good,—sometimes good narrowed to mere utility,—and a third in rectitude, so we have in æsthetic science, analogous theories founding beauty, one in the idea, another in the matter, a third in the mere union of the two. The literature of æsthetics as of ethics accordingly abounds with diversities of usage in the terms employed. Hence the importance of guarding against the ambiguities to which such use of language gives rise. And particularly here it may be remarked that the terms *ideal, material,* and *formal* are used to denote the several kinds of beauty which may be distinguished when we regard the different attributes belonging severally to the three great elements of all beauty ; when we regard the attributes that respectively belong to the idea, to the matter, and to the form itself in an object of beauty.

2. As to Classifying. § 58. It is, moreover, ever to be borne in mind, in all classifications of objects, in whatever department of study, that there may be fault or imperfection of result by reason of either of two errors in the procedure. If we proceed exclusively in reference to the attributes which we have by our methods of abstraction and selection been enabled to recognize and enumerate, we shall be liable from the imperfection incident to all human effort to overlook some kinds of beauty, or to misplace others. Our very enumeration of attributes may be partial or inaccurate. If on the other hand we proceed from observation, and enumerate the different kinds of beauty as they happen to offer themselves to our view, we shall be liable to fail in completeness and also in scientific order. The only safe way for us will be to begin with the ascertained elements of beauty and with the analysis which our study of them may give us, and then go out into the outer world of beauty and seek after the objects which may be characterized respectively by the several attributes we have distinguished. It will be only by the careful combination of both methods of procedure that we can hope to guard ourselves from error. If we find that our *a priori* classification is fully sustained by our observation as it sweeps over the entire field of beauty, we may feel a legitimate confidence not only in the validity of our classification, but also in the correctness of our enumeration of the essential attributes of beauty.

CHAPTER II.

GRADATIONS OF BEAUTY.

Gradations of Beauty as Perfect or Imperfect.

§ 59. The first grand distinction of beauty, founded on degree, gives us at once the characters of *Perfect* and *Imperfect* beauty. All beauty must, in some respect, either in itself or relatively to the mind that contemplates it, be characterized by us in our imperfection, as imperfect. To the infinite eye the creation all appeared good, perfect,—a faultless *cosmos;* while to the finite mind that can take in but a part and cannot see everything in its full relationship, it must of course seem imperfect or faulty. Perfectness, accordingly, is with us only relative; it never is discovered by us as absolute. It is so with truth; it is so with duty. We speak of a perfect truth,—perfect in itself, and perfect in its expression; while we do not mean absolutely that in none of its elements it were not possible even for the Infinite one to add to its perfectness. So we denominate an action as perfectly right; while yet we do not mean at all that it was utterly insusceptible of improvement in any respect. It may be that we are unable to see how there may be change or addition in respect of any element or any relation; yet we would be far from maintaining that an all-seeing eye might not discern a spot or a defect. We may accordingly with propriety and in accordance with the established usages of language, speak of gradations of what we even call perfect beauty.

Gradations of Perfect Beauty.

§ 60. Perfectness in beauty may regard the aggregate of the elements which enter into our complex idea of it, or these several elements individually. We may speak of an object as being perfectly beautiful in itself as a whole, or in respect of one or more of its parts or of its relations.

Perfect beauty, in the former of these two applications of the term, exists where the idea revealed, the revealing matter, and the embodiment of the idea in the matter, are each perfect in their relations to one another.

Lower gradations of perfectness in beauty are dependent on the degree in which the several elements enter into the object. It may be characterized as perfect in respect of its idea, when that is of the highest, purest, richest order, not indeed absolutely in itself but as an element of form ; as something to be revealed. Then its perfectness must be judged in reference to the matter in which it must be embodied. One idea is fit only for a certain matter; another for another. Ideas of affection, of tenderness, sympathy, kindness, and the like, are more perfectly expressed in color ; those of skill and power, in outline; and, once more, those of motion, of action and event, in music, or poetry. Still further, perfectness of form, even in respect to idea, must have respect to the eye that is to contemplate it.

In like manner in respect to the matter of form, we find gradations of perfectness both in itself and in its relations to the idea and the design of the object. The ideas of majesty and solemnity which appropriately belong to the architecture of a temple find in the massiveness and durability and firmness of stone a more perfect embodiment; the ideas of seclusion, quiet, cheerfulness which should enter in the architecture of settled home-life may be better expressed in brick or wood or concrete; while, further, the ideas of movement, of celerity, and change which characterize the life of a nomadic tribe or of a military host, are pictured best in the light movable tent of canvas.

The third and the more vital element of beauty, also admits of its peculiar gradations of perfectness. We shall find different kinds of beauty characterized in respect of this element. Each of these may be perfect in its kind. For a single illustration the rendering which would be recognized as perfect in the comic would be utterly condemned and reprobated in tragedy. The same variegated subject of human experience in its strange mixture of reason and passion, joy and sorrow, and, in the same matter of color or of word in sound, would be rendered with characteristics of diverse perfectness by Hogarth and by Guido Reni, in a Midsummer Night's Dream and a King Lear.

Of Imperfect Beauty. § 61. Imperfect Beauty is characterized by corresponding gradations. Either of the three constituents may be in a greater or less degree of imperfectness in itself or in relationship. We may distinguish indefinite gradations from those instances in which the faintest, lowest, most imperfect idea, or the most unmeet matter, or the rudest rendering just admits the object within the domain of beauty or of form, up to the very vestibule of its perfect being.

Subjective gradations of Beauty.

§ 62. But inasmuch as Form is for the observer as well as the producer, we must recognize a subjective as well as an objective perfectness in beauty. There may be a perfect man while we fail to discern the perfection. What is perfect in itself may to our imperfect vision appear discolored, distorted. So the perfect man appeared to the distempered vision of his people. To our experience of perfect beauty there is requisite perfect discernment by us.

Not only is undistempered vision required, but a certain degree of power is necessary that will vary with the kind of beauty to be apprehended. The phases of Venus, its approaches and withdrawals to and from the sun, revealing to the astronomer a law of unintermitting force and unvarying regularity, are to him beautiful in a high degree; he contemplates them with a profound admiration and pleasure; but to the uninstructed eye no beauty of this kind appears, for it has no capacity to apprehend it. The beauty is real; but to be experienced there must be a corresponding capacity in the subject to which it is to be revealed.

A certain degree of mental energy is thus necessary in the apprehension of beauty. Certain forms of beauty may be apprehensible to an infant's capacity ; certain forms, it might be, can be apprehended only by an angelic capacity. And between these limits there are innumerable gradations of beauty in respect to the facility with which they may be apprehended, requiring corresponding gradations of mental energy. It is just so with truth. That the world turns round on its axis is a truth beyond the capacities of apprehension to some undeveloped minds who can demonstrate its utter falseness and absurdity most conclusively to themselves by the fact that their bodies do not fall off when the earth in its revolution brings them under.

Especially worthy of notice here is the consideration that this imperfect apprehension arising from mere want of capacity will perhaps more generally show itself in its grasping but a part of a whole revelation of an idea. The sense that can only apprehend the strong coloring of a Titian will condemn and reject paintings in which the effect is designed to be in the outline rather than in the color, which yet the world of cultivated mind have recognized as masterpieces of art.

Not only may particular properties escape the apprehension of an incompetent observer, and so the whole object appear to him mutilated, incomplete, and therefore ugly, but, what is more common still, the relations of the object may fail to be apprehended, and, in this way, real beauty be unnoticed. That famous city of blockheads, Thracian Abdera, it is fabled, rejected a statue of colossal proportions with correspondingly gross features and rough outline, that had been carefully proportioned by the skillful artist to be seen and admired on the top of their lofty citadel by observers on the ground, because it was so gross and rough, as they criticized it close at hand; and they accordingly elevated instead a five foot statue of Venus, which was, indeed, a master-piece of Praxiteles, but on the distant summit appeared to all observers only an unmeaning excrescence and deformity. So the universe of God, the grand fabric of the All-wise may, when apprehended only in a part of its properties and relations seem wanting in beauty; while a full apprehension shall recognize it as a perfect *cosmos*.

These gradations of perfectness in beauty which are determined in reference to the eye of the observer, both relatively to the object as a whole and also to its parts in their relations to the whole are well indicated by the poet.

> Some figures monstrous and mis-shaped appear,
> Considered singly, or beheld too near,
> Which but proportioned to their light or place,
> Due distance reconciles to form and grace.
> * * * * *
> In wit as nature, what affects our hearts
> Is not the exactness of peculiar parts;
> 'Tis not a lip or eye, we beauty call,
> But the joint force and full result of all.
>
> *Pope's Essay on Criticism*, 171–4; 243–6.

CHAPTER III.

IDEAL BEAUTY.

General Divisions.

§ 63. Under that class of attributes of beauty which pertain to the idea revealed we find as many kinds of beauty as we distinguish modifications of the idea. By this term *idea*, we understand any modification of mind; any expressed thought, or feeling, or purpose—§ 11. The familiarly recognized departments of mind guide us at once to the subordinate divisions of ideal beauty. These departments are Intelligence, Sensibility, and Will.

Beauty of Action and Beauty of Repose.

§ 64. But mind in whatever state or modification maintains its essentially active nature. All idea is consequently but a form of activity. But as perception lives on in memory; as a thought that when first excited comes forth fresh and active and then sinks back into seeming unconsciousness, yet lives a hidden life that may be called up again and thus proves its permanence; so, generally, idea, however essentially active, may rest in quiet and then offer no disturbance to the consciousness. We have these two modifications of ideas accordingly;—ideas of activity and ideas of repose. We shall have consequently kinds of beauty which we may characterize respectively as beauty of *action* and beauty of *repose*. This distinction will reveal itself in all the kinds of beauty which are to be noticed.

1. Intellectual Beauty.

§ 65. The first class of attributes, pertaining to the idea in beauty, embraces those founded in the intelligence. Of these we find recognized in familiar literature two leading divisions. They are founded respectively on the two great classes of the forms of the intelligence,—*immediate* and *mediate*. Immediate cognitions embrace perceptions or cognitions of material objects and intuitions or cognitions of immaterial objects, whether as originally given by their respective objects or as retained in memory and reproduced in recollection Mediate cognitions are the operations of thought, or the faculty of comparison, or of judgment.

Beauty of Truthfulness.

§ 66. In order that the intelligence may apprehend its object, whether in perception or intuition, it is necessary that it be taken as a whole, consisting of congruous parts. This is a prime condition of all knowledge, all intelligence, all truth, that its object be a whole made up of harmonizing parts. Truth of reality, whether in object by itself, or in relation, is but a whole—a unity made up of harmonizing parts. Truth of apprehension—that is intelligence, is but such a whole of harmonizing parts and relations brought into our apprehension. Truth of representation is but such a whole made up of original and copy, the corresponding parts of which harmonize with each other. The source and origin of that admirable designation of the universe by the classic minds of Greece and Rome as *Cosmos* and *Mundus*, seems to lie in the fundamental connection between beauty and this harmony of parts and relations, Wherever we recognize this revealed truthfulness,—this internal propriety, this wholeness of all the parts that are proper to an object—that belong to it all in harmony so as to constitute the parts into one whole, we recognize beauty. It is an essential attribute of intelligence that it apprehends its object as one whole. The revelation of an object as one whole, as a harmonized diversity, is a characteristic work of intelligence. This quality of truthfulness is an essential in all beauty. As a characteristic quality, when it reigns paramount over other attributes, it constitutes a class—a kind of beauty. We have, accordingly, what may legitimately be denominated a truthful beauty.

Of Fitness

§ 67. Closely allied to this is the kind of beauty which we apprehend in the revelation of external propriety—of fitness. Instead of the harmony in the parts as making a united whole to our apprehension, it is the harmony of relations between an object and other objects which taken together make up a larger whole. In other words, here, instead of the relation of parts to a whole, it is the relation of parts to parts that is regarded. This attribute, founded on the apprehension of an object in harmonious relations to other objects around, is the *decorum*, *quod decet*, of the Latin tongue, and the Greek τὸ πρέπον, in the more common use of those terms.

There is then a beauty of fitness. It is the kind of beauty which most characterizes refined and pleasing manners—when all the conveniences, proprieties, fitnesses of the place, the time, the occasion, the persons, the attending circumstances generally, are regarded. We take little notice of the personal qualities otherwise,—the power of intellect, the grade of passion, or the characters of energy, the qualities of bodily form or complexion, the dress, except as they appear in these external relations, when we contemplate the beauty there is in manners. So in the orator, it is the observance of these external relations,—to the occasion, to the persons concerned, and the like,—which mainly constitutes the beauty of fitness—the *decorum*, the *quod decet* on which Cicero dwells so much and which he denominates the chief thing in art, and which Milton also speaks of as "the grand master-piece to observe." The general prominence of this element of beauty is recognized by Plato, as he represents Socrates leading Hippias to admit that a stirrer made of figwood is more beautiful than one of gold because more fitting to the use of such a utensil;—it would not break the porridge-pot and so spill the porridge, while it would besides give flavor to the porridge.

Of Unity. § 68. Truthful beauty includes under it several distinct species. First and most important is that of Unity. So universal is this kind of beauty in all perfect form that it is easily accepted more as the condition of beauty than a distinct species or element. It is requisite in all form because perfect form is essentially the expression of perfect idea, the most fundamental characteristic of which is unity.

Of Harmony. § 69. A second variety is the beauty of Harmony. All harmony is grounded on a fundamental unity—on an underlying identity. Harmony is diversified unity; or diversity in unity. It is of all degrees; from that lowest degree in which the diverse is hardly discernible in the predominant oneness, as a cloudless sky which displays only the diversity of a deep zenith blue with the paler blue of the horizon, up to that in which the diversity approximates irreconcilable contradiction or outreaches the capacity to take into our experience. What we denominate a perfect harmony is thus that which affords the largest and richest diversity that our contemplating capacity can without labor apprehend. Thus in music, the lowest grade of harmony is in the union of different voices sounding the same note which are said then to be in unison; a higher grade of the harmony of unison is that where the different voices sound a tonic and its octaves; still a higher degree of harmony occurs when different voices sound the tonic and dominant. The harmony is enriched by the larger diversity of voices or instruments, and of consonant sounds, all finding a ground of union in the sameness of the tonic or key note.

Of Contrast. § 70. This diversity in unity may be viewed either more prominently in respect to the harmonizing unity, giving as we have seen proper harmony, or more prominently in respect to the diversity, giving the form of intelligence called Contrast.

Contrast thus is pleasing because it is a form of the intelligence. It is a defective view which ascribes the pleasure it gives merely to the increased activity which it requires of the contemplating mind in order to apprehend it. Wide and rich contrasts do indeed call forth an active intelligence, and increased pleasure attends upon this enhanced energy. But the revelation of contrast as a legitimate and genuine form of the intelligence itself gives pleasure of a peculiar kind to the mind that apprehends it; and this peculiar pleasure is but intensified and enriched by the rich and wide contrast. A large orange is sweet not because its size prolongs or magnifies the gratification of the palate or more engrosses the taste than a small one; it has independently of its size the quality of sweetness, which increased size only intensifies and augments.

Of Proportion.

§ 71. Comprehended under the beauty of harmony in its wider scope is the beauty of Proportion. This is a harmony of a whole with any of its parts. An edifice has this kind of beauty, is beautiful in its proportions, when for example, the hight is in harmony with the building in respect to the other dimensions, and each member is in harmony with the whole. So extensive does this kind of beauty reign in architecture that some writers have been led to regard it as the one only kind which this art need respect.

Of Symmetry.

§ 72. Akin to this beauty of proportion is the beauty of Symmetry, which is founded more immediately on the relation of the parts to one another, while proportion looks more directly to the relation between the parts and the whole.

Proportion and symmetry are both concerned with quantity. Proportion may be exactly defined as the harmony of quantity as seen in the relations of any part to its whole; and symmetry as the harmony of quantity as seen in the relations of one part to another.

We have, besides, those species of the beauty of harmony which are not included under proportion and symmetry, for which however language has provided no particular names. Thus we have the beauty arising from the harmony of color, of tone, and the like.

Of Æsthetic Number.

§ 73. Still further under this general kind of beauty is that of æsthetic number—called Eurarithmy. It is a species of beauty which is relative to the contemplating mind. The human mind can easily take in but a limited number of parts,—of members, of features, of hues, of sounds. It is offended by excessive multiplicity, by a manifoldness which it finds difficulty in gathering up into a whole, and in comprehending as one. An infinite mind might comprehend an infinity of objects or features; a finite mind, only a few. And as form is *for* mind as well as *of* mind, the number of parts must be limited to the capacity of the contemplating mind, in order that the form may be perfect.

Generic, Catholic, or Typical Beauty.

§ 74. The other form of the intelligence indicated is that of thought or mediate cognition. It is the proper positive function of this faculty to recognize the agreement or identity between substance and its attribute, and under this recognized identity in the objects presented to it to unite them together and so to construct classes, or to generalize. In exact correspondence to this function of the human intelligence the universe around us is made up of objects that resemble one another; that have, in other words, identical attributes. There is in the boundless diversity an ever prevalent sameness—a true type-form after which all things are made. The infinite thought appears thus everywhere; and it is because of this thought shaping all objects that they can be thought by us; that they can be gathered into classes.

On this identifying and unifying form of the intelligence, we have founded certain kinds of beauty which have been recognized in our literature. We find there what is termed *generic* beauty, *specific* beauty, *ideal* beauty—the term *ideal* being used here in the old Platonic sense of *generic.* These terms all point to this one original notion—that there is in the universe of being the ground of distinguishing what is common to many, in other words, of the generic; that there is a common type of things which is but the expression of the creative thought. Just so far as this attribute is recognized, there is idea revealed which gives beauty of a peculiar kind. So the monstrous is but another name for the ugly—the contradictory of beautiful. It is on the foundation of this broad principle that the law of productive art is based, which requires that not the individual, but the specific be preferred. Whatever straggles off in art to the individual, the peculiar, shows the want of controlling thought; indicates imperfection in the idea. Sir Joshua Reynolds thus observes with his characteristic soundness of judgment:—"There is an absolute necessity for the painter to generalize his notions; to paint particulars is not to paint nature; it is only to paint circumstances."

This kind of beauty may appropriately be denominated either *generic* or *catholic* or *typical* beauty. The two first terms point at once to that attribute of universal or generic,—of class,—which characterizes all the movements of a perfect infinite intelligence; the other term points to that oneness of form which the one source of all being has given to all creation. The three terms, it should be remarked, have been used in other relations and with other meanings.

Recognized in erroneous theories of Beauty.

§ 75. The extent and importance of these properties of beauty are sufficiently evinced by the fact that in variously modified forms they have been ranked by some of the writers on beauty as the essential, characteristic properties of beauty, and the kinds of beauty founded upon them as comprehensive of all beauty.

Theory of Utility.

That theory of beauty, thus, which resolves it into the revelation of the useful, limits all beauty to the mere relation of external propriety, or fitness of objects to result in good. It is true that this revelation of idea is proper beauty. The reasoning of Burke in which he seeks to show that beauty does not consist in utility, fails from the fallacy common to most theorists in this field of science ;—of mistaking the part for the whole. Because utility is not the exclusive ground of beauty, therefore, he concludes it is no ground at all. This is the principle of his fallacious reasoning,—appearing openly and in form, and also disguised in his denial that there is any beauty at all in the presence of a higher beauty,—the old form of the fallacy which we detected in Plato who made the beautiful maiden instantly become ugly in the presence of the spirit of heaven.

The relation of utility, of means to end, is a proper idea of beauty ; which when revealed to us in proper form ever introduces us into the proper experience of beauty ; but is far from being the only principle of beauty, as some have maintained.

Of Unity in Variety.

§ 76. There is another class of theorists who make the universal principle of beauty to be but that of unity in variety. If we could be allowed to engraft the admission of an objective beauty upon the theory of Kant and of Hamilton before mentioned, this logically would be the true principle of beauty under that theory. For if beauty subjectively,—beauty in experience, be but the free and vigorous exercise of the understanding, the merely aggregative faculty, its object can be only that of diversified unity. As in the case of the theory of utility, this theory can substantiate its claim only to a partial validity. The revelation of the manifold and diverse in the one is a revelation of intelligence—of an idea; it is, wherever apprehended, beautiful. It is, however, only a single form of beauty.

Of Order and Proportion.

§ 77. Still another class of theorists would resolve all beauty into order and proportion. Substantially the same criticism is to be passed upon this as upon the other theories just noticed. Mind, as essentially intelligent in all its manifestations, must evince more or less prominently this essential attribute. We must at once pronounce that to be a monstrosity of mental revelation, which contradicts the essential principles of intelligence and belies its characteristic nature. All intelligence must be in order and proportion, so far as it is intelligence; for order and proportion are but expressions for those necessary relations in space and time in which all intelligence must apprehend its objects. Order is but the relation in space of the directions of the parts of a single whole relatively to each other, or the relation in time of the succession of those parts. And proportion, in the larger sense as including symmetry, is the relation in space of comparative magnitude of parts and in time of importance of parts. These are the two comprehensive relations in each of those fundamental and universal forms of all intelligence—space and time. If, then, the intelligence must apprehend its objects in these relations, then the objects must in their nature be susceptible of being apprehended in these relations,

The world without must correspond to the mind within, or it cannot come into its apprehension.

We cannot then exclude order and proportion from the domain of objective beauty. They are real principles of beauty; but they are not exclusive principles of beauty, for they are not the only attributes of mind that can be revealed in appropriate matter.

II. Emotive Beauty.

§ 78. The second kind of Beauty given in a division founded on its idea or content is that in which the spirit is revealed prominently and characteristically as feeling. We may term it Emotive Beauty.

While feeling as attribute of the same single spirit must more or less accompany all forms of the intelligence, yet it often rises to a controlling element in the revelations of spirit, and gives character to them. Thus it is in ordinary life. We characterize a man as in a mood of passion; although it may be, we discern the passion only in actions that receive their direction immediately from the intelligence. So too in discourse, we characterize certain discourse as passionate although appearing in words which are in themselves only the forms of thought. Passion reveals itself through the thought and then through the word; but as it rules and becomes the predominant, characteristic element, it determines the discourse as passionate. There is thus in strict propriety and truth, an emotive, in distinction from an intellectual beauty. We cannot steadily and fully contemplate the rainbow in its glowing brightness and the delicate blending of its hues, reposing on the bosom of a dark and angry cloud that rolls its deep thunders within and darts out its wrathful flashes, without recognizing certain feelings as really expressed, as present and revealed. We see wrath assuaged, and passing into love and kindness. So in the revelation of nature everywhere we discern the features of a feeling soul revealed.

Its specific modifications it would be difficult, from the present imperfect state of the science of the Feelings, intelligently to enumerate with scientific precision, and it is unnecessary. We distinguish, it may be sufficient here to observe, an emotive beauty :—

I. In the mere revelation of a feeling-spirit, of mere sensibility and sympathy ;

II. In the revelation of more specific forms of rational sentiment, as in the more personal forms of joy and sorrow exercised in respect to present good or evil, or of hope and fear in respect to future and possible good or evil ; or in the relative forms of kindness, confidence, and reverence.

While intellectual beauty appears more appropriately in the spacial or extensive relations of the matter of beauty ; in the figure,—the outline, and interiorly in the positions and proportions of the constituent parts, emotive beauty, on the other hand, appears more in the intensive relations—the color, the tone of the object. Its distinctive character is recognized in language that speaks of a form of beauty as warm and glowing or the contrary ; as gladsome or sombre ; as tender and loving ; or that characterizes beauty by its tone.

III. Free Beauty or Grace. § 79. The kind of beauty as determined in respect to the idea, is that in which the spirit is revealed characteristically as *will*.

The will, in its normal condition, at least, is characterized as free. Freedom is the peculiar, the exclusive attribute of will. Its proper definition, thus, is the free activity of rational being.

The revelation of this principle constitutes that specific kind of beauty which is familiarly denominated *grace*. The distinction between this and the other kinds of beauty indicated is fully recognized in ordinary language. We never predicate gracefulness except of motion, or of repose the result of motion, for here as elsewhere we find an active and a resulting beauty ; nor of any motion except as in appearance free. But will in expression—will revealed, is free motion.

If in nature, which in its very nature seems to exclude freedom and admits only the stern sway of necessity, we sometimes alight upon what we designate as graceful, we are ever forced to interpret the appearance as a revelation of grace. The poet's nice sense so reads such natural objects. The graceful rivulet, Wordsworth at once apprehends as "winding by his own sweet will." And Thompson in his "Castle of Indolence" exemplifies his characteristic delicacy and accuracy in his interpretation of nature when he tells us of "free nature's grace." Nature is in no sense more a bond-slave of necessity, than she is blind and unfeeling. She is sage, she is loving, she is free, because there is a spirit breathing in her. God reveals himself in all her forms; and speaks in all her utterances. Therefore is the face of nature beautiful; her voices, music; and her various movements decked with grace. It is characteristically when nature appears but matter, inert as inertiá itself, that she is stiff, ungraceful in her motion. When the creating or revealing spirit shapes her features, or sends out an animating glow into her countenance, or freely bends her inert limbs, then is she beautiful.

Recapitulation.

§ 80. The first division of Beauty, then, distributed into its specific kinds in reference to the idea revealed in it, gives us those—

I. Of Intellectual Beauty, with its subordinate forms of Truthfulness, Fitness, and Catholicity;

II. Of Emotive Beauty; and

III. Of Free Beauty or Grace.

CHAPTER IV.

MATERIAL BEAUTY.

Kinds:—I. Inorganic Beauty.

§ 81. Proceeding now to the distribution of Beauty in reference to its second element—the matter in which the idea is revealed,—we shall find the natural principle of division in the closer or remoter affinity of the matter to the idea.

Beginning, on this principle, with the matter most remote in its nature from idea, the most heterogeneous, we place at the first and lowest stage, the polar opposite of spirit, pure inorganic matter. Wherever spirit enters matter, revealing itself through it, beauty appears. Matter, before formess, now is formed, and reveals beauty. There is, thus, a true inorganic beauty rising in specific grades of perfection, from the lowest rank of well-nigh chaotic matter — orderless, colorless, motionless mass, to the highest orders of inorganic beauty in the regular forms of the crystal, the soft brilliancy of the rainbow, the graceful motions of wave, or stream, or curling vapor.

There is beauty in water, earth, and sky, peculiar to each great element; and each of these general forms is specifically characterized by the idea revealed. There is beauty, thus, for a single illustration or two, in ocean—in its limitless expanse, imaging the infinity of the creating spirit, in its purity of hue as it deepens from the bright green of its face where it nears the habitations of men on solid earth to the deep azure of its distant, fathomless depths, reflecting the pure heart and profound affection of the God of heaven above it; in the easy sweep of its billowing waves also, and the gentle roundings of its shores. There is beauty, too, in earth, in the regular strata of its mass beneath, in the majestic piles of its peaked mountains, in the kindly blended hues of its variegated surface, in the mingled wild and gentle of its rock and hill and vale reposing in such grace. And in all the smaller distributions of these various masses of inorganic matter, we find more specific forms of beauty, each expressing in its own peculiar way the several characters of the diversified idea.

II. Organic Beauty.

§ 82. As we pass from this polar opposite of idea,—from gross matter, we come next to the manifold forms of living beauty, and first to its lowest grade of mere vegetable life. At this stage we find matter, in which the idea may incorporate itself, more akin to the pure nature of idea itself. We are now out of the realm of gross matter. Yet this life is found only in matter which still retains its original capability of embodying spirit and admits, accordingly, all the modes of beauty which could before be shaped in it. But as it is pervaded with life, we recognize a new beauty—different altogether in kind and higher in degree. The masses of earth put on a new charm when a free life wreathes its towering hights with coronets of forest-green, or decks its quiet vales with wavy grain or spreads upon them its tapestry of foliage and flower. Earth comes nearer to us, enters deeper into the spirit's sympathies, when she robes herself in forms of life, even in her more massive shapes. And in her minuter parts, how far above the beauty of mere matter, is the regularity and fitness, and ideal or specific harmony, which vegetable life so universally evinces; the expressive depth and brilliancy of its various hues, too, their graceful blending, and delicate gradations, showing everywhere the tracings of a divine pencil?

III. Sentient Beauty.

§ 83. Another step in the gradations of matter for the revelation of idea brings us to sentient being. As we enter here we at once become sensible of an introduction to a world entirely new. As a medium more homogeneous with itself than vegetable life, the idea reveals itself here in altogether new and incomparably richer, more perfect forms, and comes still closer to us and penetrates into deeper sympathies of our spiritual natures. The idea itself, as finding a medium more meet for its uses, puts out higher grades of its own activity. If there be intelligence revealed in the regularity of the snow-flake, soul in its purity and softness, and freedom in its easy, graceful fall; if these same attributes of spirit appear in higher forms in the fitnesses, the sympathetic relationships, and the graceful luxuriance of organic-life;—as, for instance, if in the modest violet we discover a higher intelligence in the harmonious adaptations of its various parts to each other and to all the demands of locality and of season, a higher scale of sensibility in its characteristic humility and love of retirement, as well as a higher freedom in the graceful rounding of its foliage and the delicate blending of its hues than in any of the revelations of inorganic matter ; yet as we enter the region of sentient being, still richer, more essential, more perfect grades of the ideal meet us. In each of its several forms, we find the idea at a higher point of perfection. Thus, for instance, the wisdom of design in the adaptations of organic function in the complicated structure of the lamb, the innocence, gentleness, joyousness of its sportive nature, and the freedom of its graceful gambolings, are of a higher order than the corresponding forms of the idea in the snow-flake or the violet.

It is to be observed, moreover, that all these forms peculiar to sentient being are embodied in those of organic life as these again are enwrapped in the grosser forms of inorganic body.

IV. Spiritual Beauty.

§ 84. One step higher in the gradations of matter introduces us into the world of spiritual being. The spirit has forms. In a true sense, every particular exertion it puts forth goes out in a form determinate and characteristic. There are forms of intelligence,—forms of apprehending, forms of identifying, or of classifying ; there are forms of sensibility,—forms of joy and sorrow, of hope and fear,—forms of relative emotion,—of kindness, trust, and reverence ; there are forms in which free power goes out in

graceful expression—forms of skill, of achievement. These proper spirit-forms may be enwrapped in forms of sentient life, as these in mere organic bodily forms, and these again in those of matter; but they are distinct, peculiar; and are of a still higher type and order. The divine idea reveals itself in these, as in matter more homogeneous to its own nature, in higher perfection and in richer beauty. We obtain a deeper insight into the mind of the Infinite through these forms of spiritual revelation than through the lower. So too, in art, the ideal form of the artist by far outstrips in perfectness and beauty the outward sensible form in which he enshrines it. We possess ourselves, moreover, of his full and exact idea in the revelation, only as we separate this ideal form—this spirit form in which it is embodied—from the grosser, more external forms of matter.

The artist ever, in all departments of art, has what we justly term his ideal which in the consummation of his art he is to embody in forms perhaps of mere physical sense. He necessarily begins with this ideal. It has a distinct, real existence in his imagination, shaped out, determined in form and feature, before he touches pencil, or chisel. This ideal may be improved, may be perfected, as he proceeds to incorporate in those sensible forms of marble, or of the canvas; but it exists first necessarily in his own mind in a true actual form. The melodies and harmonies of a musical composition all form themselves in the composer's mind before he ever gives visible representation to them in his written staff, and in the various signs or symbols of musical notation. The last stage of the full realization of his ideal in actual sound follows as an entirely separate, independent exertion of artistic skill. The composer may be dumb himself, and deaf even; none the less the true spirit of beauty arrayed in perfect dress walks before his internal eye, distinct, impressive, ravishing mind and heart as he moves along over these mute forms of ink and paper. This ideal itself is a form of beauty, as it reveals the mind and spirit of the artist. We admire thus the grandeur of thought and soul which Michael Angelo reveals in all his ideals whether they are to be wrought out in sculpture, or in fresco or in architecture. There is this style of beauty in his mere ideals.

The process in art-interpretation is the exact counterpart of this. The gross matter, through which alone, at least in our present condition of being, we can be introduced to idea, to spirit external to us,—the gross matter is first presented to us. We may discern in this certain forms of the revealed idea. Mere outline and color may reveal such modes of the idea as may be embodied in gross matter. Regularity of contour, warmth of hue, delicate curving and color-blending, reveals the spiritual principles of intelligence, affection, and freedom. The child is captivated with these lowest forms of art. But through these outer forms, in a landscape, the artist may in the character of his trees and his foliage reveal his idea in fuller degree and correspondingly richer beauty. With admirable art have two American painters, Cole and his pupil Church, revealed moral ideas in the forms of mere landscape—of vegetable life. A true interpretation of these products of art must seize in addition to the inorganic the living forms also. The Flemish school of painters, further, has characterized itself by incorporating in these outer forms of organic and of inorganic being, also forms of sentient life. The range of ideas, suited to this medium of representation, are in some respects of a higher order than the other. But what we have here to remark is that they are not material; that they are separable from all the material forms although apprehended through them, being revealed in them. In the schools of Italian art, we meet a higher rank of forms in their master-pieces of historical painting. In the multiform modes of rational life, themselves incorporated in forms of irrational as mere sentient, organic, and inorganic being, we recognize an entirely new medium of revelation. We cannot begin to interpret these magnificent achievements of art except as we seize the spirit-forms in which the artist reveals his idea. How is it possible, thus, to attain the lowest degree of any proper interpretation of Raphael's Madonna della sedia, without a distinct apprehension of the mother's placid fondness, the purity and elevation of her child, and the reverence of the infant John, and the other forms of rational sentiment which glow in this revelation?

True art-interpretation proceeds thus up through the grosser to the last and inmost, the proper spirit-forms.

§ 85. There are to be recognized then these four grades of æsthetic matter in which idea may be revealed: 1. gross inert matter; 2. vegetable life; 3. sentient life; 4. rational life.

The inner grade may be embodied moreover in the outer,—the ideal in the proper animal, this in vegetable life, and all in gross inert matter. Now in order to a division of the kinds of beauty in reference to these different grades of matter, it becomes important in view of this incorporation of the inner in the outer, to determine which of the grades is to be selected as containing the proper embodiment of the idea. This is especially necessary in the distribution of the products of art to their proper classes. It will not do, as has sometimes been done, to distribute such objects in reference always to the outermost matter in which it appears. Literature and architecture both reveal their products in visible outlines. But while visible figure traced in gross matter is the proper embodiment of the latter, and consequently the beauty of the building is to be apprehended in this outline, the beauty of a discourse or a poem is not characteristically in the printed page which reveals it to us. In criticising the one, this visible outline is an essential element to be regarded; in criticising the other, it is wholly excluded from view. The proper matter in which poetry reveals itself is first and chiefly in the ideal; then in language which itself reaches the contemplating mind only through the letters of the printed page. We are led thus to distinguish two leading kinds of beauty according as they are characteristically revealed immediately or mediately, in the matter in which they finally embody themselves. We have forms of beauty revealed immediately in sensible matter, as architecture, and music. We have other forms which do not characteristically reveal their true nature to the mere outer sense.

Senses addressed in beauty.

§ 86. We here encounter another difficulty that of determining the senses immediately addressed by beauty. There is far from agreement in regard to this among our leading writers on taste. Lord Kames expressly limits beauty to the sense of sight.

Errors of Lord Kames.

"The term *beauty*," he says, "in its native signification, is appropriated to objects of sight: objects of the other senses may be agreeable, such as the sounds of musical instruments, the smoothness and softness of some surfaces; but the agreeableness denominated *beauty*, belongs to objects of sight."* In another place, he extends to sounds the power of raising passion or emotion, but declares that "the most pleasing feelings of taste, or touch, or smell, aspire not to that honor."†

The literature of art, however, has more generally admitted the sense of hearing to share with that of seeing in the high honor of receiving the addresses of beauty. It has excluded from this rank the three other senses; and denied to them any susceptibility to the impression of beauty, any ca-

---

* Elements of Criticism: chap. 3.

† Id. chap. 2.

pacity as organs to convey beauty to the contemplating mind.

The question at once confronts us : is this a well grounded distinction between the senses as organs of beauty ? What in the nature of the case forbids the revelation of idea in any of the qualities of matter, to any of the senses which matter as formed can impress ? Certainly, unless there can be indicated some positive ground for rejecting the three lower senses from this relationship to beauty, we are prohibited from doing it by the consideration of their all partaking in the common, essential property of sense—that of being the medium of communication between the mind as subject and external being as object. If beauty, indeed, be essentially revelation of idea in matter, then, no sense through which such revelation can be made, can on any *a priori* ground be excluded from the function proper to sense.

Still less do we find, in fact, reason for this restriction of the admission of objects of beauty to two of the senses. The divine idea is most impressively revealed to us in the forms of fragrance and of savor. How much of the beauty of nature is associated in our minds with the sweetness of its fruits and the perfume of its flowers ? Rob our imaginings of Paradise of these forms, and how large a share of its beauty is taken from them ?

But as incorporated in other forms, we find the objects of these senses entering largely into the revelations of beauty. Our richest poetry abounds in them. It were a work of supererogation to cite instances in proof either of the fact or the extent of this use of the three lower senses in literature.

Strange, indeed, is it that æsthetic science should disown a sense, from which she has derived her maiden name and from whose stores she has taken her most familiar, her every-day attire; in whose livery, indeed, she is chiefly recognized as an acquaintance or treated with favor or respect. How has it come about that, in all languages, beauty has introduced herself ever under the array of *taste;* borrowing from that sense all her terms and means of introduction to the human mind, if taste and beauty be utterly alien from each other; if the domain of taste be entirely foreign to the nature of beauty?

§ 87. Still more unaccountable is it that some philosophers should have made a quality that addresses only the lowest of the three rejected senses —smoothness—an indispensable requisite to beauty, if these senses lie wholly out of the domain of beauty.

Of Burke.

Burke, in his essay on the Sublime and Beautiful* speaks of smoothness as "a quality so essential to beauty, that," he says, "I do not now recollect any thing beautiful that is not smooth. In trees and flowers, smooth leaves are beautiful; smooth slopes of earth in gardens; smooth streams in the landscape; smooth coats of birds and beasts in animal beauties; in fine women, smooth skins; and in several sorts of ornamental furniture, smooth and polished

* Part III. Section xiv

surfaces. A very considerable part of the effect of beauty is owing to this quality; indeed, the most considerable." And in another part of his essay, he accounts for this prevalence of smoothness in the effect of beauty, in the light of his own theory, that smoothness in bodies is a peculiarly relaxing quality.*

In like manner, he calls "sweetness the beautiful of the taste." †

Of German and French writers.

§ 89. Yet in Germany and France, as well as in England, we find this view prevailing, that but two senses have any part in beauty. Vischer, a recent voluminous writer on Æsthetics, discards peremptorily touch, taste, and smell; from them, he says, "beauty is excluded." ‡ And Cousin in his "Lectures on the True, the Beautiful, and the Good," oracularly pronounces: "of the five senses which man is endowed with, smell, taste, and touch are incapable of transmitting the beautiful to us." "Taste, for instance, appreciates the agreeable and not the beautiful; it is the servant of interest, of the stomach; and all those senses which do not judge in a disinterested manner, cannot judge the beautiful. Scent is a little less at the service of the body, but by itself has nothing to do with the idea of beauty; one never thinks of saying that a scent has any beauty in it." "So of touch, also, which judges only of

* 2d. Part IV. Sect. xx.

† 3d. Part IV. Sect. xxii.

‡ See Review of Vischer's Æsthetics, Bib. Sac. for 1859: Vol. xvi, p. 473

hardness and softness; in both of these there is neither beauty nor ugliness." "There remain only two senses which can discern the beautiful,—sight and hearing."

On the other hand, we find Schelling formally admitting tastes and scents into the domain of beauty.

Source of error. § 89. Can we account for this extensive prevalence of the opinion which excludes the lower senses as organs of æsthetic impression? In the first place, very much of this restrictiveness as to the organs of beautiful impressions may be attributed to imperfect and hence erroneous theories of beauty. These theories have failed generally to draw the line definitely between sensation and emotion—between feeling as bodily affection and feeling as pure spiritual affection. That beauty is object for a feeling, higher, purer than sensation, they could not but admit; while yet having but vague notion of the true nature of feeling or accepting the rude and false notion of it, that feeling is but pleasure or pain, they readily resorted to the expedient of severing the senses into two classes, one, as they supposed, giving ideas, the other only sensations, and so excluded the lower senses from all part in beauty, retaining the two higher, as if this resource would extricate them from the difficulty. The whole ground of the exclusion is removed with a correct philosophy of the feelings.

Æsthetic Gradations of Senses. § 90. There is, further, it is to be remarked, a true distinction in the senses in their relation as organs to beauty.

It is, however, a distinction in degree not in kind, and therefore does not justify this separation of the senses into two classes, the one class being organs of beauty, the other not. The true character of this distinction may be clearly indicated in the light of our theory of beauty as a revelation. A revelation implies a revealer and a mind to which the revelation is made. These terms are in a revelation directly opposed,—placed over against each other. The more decided this opposition the more perfect the revelation. Just so far as a revelation becomes mingled with our own spontaneous activity, it loses in power, in effect, in its essential character. In a perfect revelation the idea revealed must stand out in distinct and bold relief, in clear opposition to the contemplating mind. And the more objective the idea appears to us in the revelation, the more perfect the revelation.

Now the five senses stand in a clearly recognizable relation to each other in respect of the degree of objectiveness in which they introduce material bodies to us. The sense of sight reveals to us objects most distant, most remote from us. The impressions on the nerves of sight can hardly ever be confounded with merely subjective experiences. Revelations of idea to this sense are in the highest degree objective, and are consequently the most perfect. Of all the material forms in which beauty is revealed, accordingly, those that address the sight, visible objects of beauty, are of the highest rank and character.

Next in rank is the sense of hearing which gives

us distant objects, but less remote than those which sight may give. There is but little more difficulty, however, here in discriminating the external object that is presented to us from our own self-moved changes of experience, than in the case of sight. The two senses rank nearly together; at least the difference in regard to the degree of objectiveness with which the object is given us is far less than between the sense of hearing and any of the lower senses. It is this wider separation between the two higher and the three lower senses which has probably suggested the thought that the latter are by their own nature insusceptible of beauty. It is obvious however, that the distinction is merely one of degree; and the gradation we can easily trace from the highest to the lowest;—the three lowest ranking in the order, first, the smell, then, the taste, and last of all, the touch; as sight decidedly outranks hearing in this particular.

If we take into consideration, further, the fact that corresponding with this gradation in objectiveness in the senses, is the degree of facility with which they receive idea to be revealed, we shall need to look no further for a solution of the question, how philosophers could have come to make the exclusion unless they had recognized a ground for it in the nature of things; especially as they have nowhere indicated any reason for the exclusion but have given their mere arbitrary declaration that such is the fact, and as, moreover, all *a priori* considerations are against their doctrine, as also the actual facts that the lower senses are largely engaged in the revelations of beauty in nature and in art.

Arts classed in respect to senses addressed;—Architecture.

§ 91. Distributing now objects of artistic beauty in reference to the matter in which they are embodied, under the class of immediate forms, we have first, the products of the great art which is cognizable through the highest in order of the senses—the sight—the art of architecture. Inasmuch as there are two qualities of material bodies with which the organ of vision is conversant—outline or figure and color, corresponding to the extensive or spacial and the intensive relations of bodies, all architecture must recognize primarily and universally these two properties and all principles of the art must ground themselves on these as essential.

To the next class under inorganic forms embracing those which immediately address the ear, belong the arts of Music and of Spoken Discourse.

Music.

Of these Vocal Music or Song in which the idea as formed in words is made a prominent element and also Spoken Discourse, both oratory and recited poetry, so far as it is contemplated in any degree apart from the form of sound as effect on the ear, present this peculiar feature—that they are complete arts furnishing complete revelations irrespectively of the matter of sound—in which they ultimately incorporate the idea. They so far come under the class of Mediate Forms. Merely that Music which is effected through the voice, apart from words, and Elocution or Recitation therefore, strictly speaking, belong here, when they appear predominantly, not as rendering thought, but only as immediate expression of idea through mere modifications of voice.

Perfumery.

The arts which address the other senses either so exclusively regard some end of utility, as the culinary arts and the art of Perfumery or are in such a degree subordinate to other arts that no recognition of them as coördinate with those that have been enumerated as addressing the senses of seeing and hearing, has prevailed or is for any purpose desirable. We should be far, however, from denying them on this ground all admission into the domain of beauty.

Landscape.

Passing to the next higher class of forms, we come to those of organic life, where we find the art of Landscape addressing itself predominantly to the sense of sight, but not with entire exclusion of the others, as it does not confine itself to mere organic forms; but masses of rock, of earth, of water in their degree and subordinately engage its interest. Still Landscape, or as it is familiary known under the more cumbrous designation, Landscape-Gardening, is an art that characteristically and chiefly addresses the sight and in the forms of organic life. It is on these characteristics chiefly that its laws or regulative principles are grounded.

Sculpture and Painting.

The second general division of objects of visual beauty so far as products of art, embraces those which reveal characteristically in mediate forms. It includes the two great arts of Sculpture and Painting. Taking the highest product in each—the human form, we see at once that the character which they undertake to reveal is first conceived as it shows itself in the bodily feature, figure, and attitude. The artist first possesses himself of the character and then of the form as thus embodied ; and it is this bodily form in which his ideal is immediately revealed. A distinct process of art renders this embodiment of his original ideal in marble or in color.

Pantomime, Vocal Music, and Elocution.

Entering now the immediate forms of sentient life we find the various arts of bodily expression, as those of Pantomime and of Gesticulation addressing the eye, and those of Vocal Music and of Elocution addressing the ear, including the proper theatrical or histrionic arts, and of a lower order those which simply exhibit muscular agility and strength without other expression of idea.

In the art of the stage, we find the arts of pantomime and of elocution, as also of discourse, all singularly blended, and concurring in revelation of idea, to eye and ear.

Discourse.

We come, next, to the revelations of idea in proper spirit-forms. The great art which here introduces itself is that of Discourse. That it belongs here appears at once from the fact that, although idea can reach another mind only through the outward sense, and discourse therefore requires the medium of the written or spoken word, it may adopt either, and proves thus its proper essential form to be really supersensible. So in the interpretation of discourse, while it is possible for us to contemplate, also, the worthy incorporation of the idea in the last form of the Pantomime or of the Recitation and admire the art that appears there, we must, in order to interpret the orator or the poet, contemplate, apart from these same outward forms, the proper immediate forms in which he has revealed his idea.

CHAPTER V.

FORMAL BEAUTY.

Formal Beauty comprises the higher kinds of Beauty.

§ 92. The third principle of division applicable to objects of beauty distinguished in respect of their essential nature, is given in the revelation itself of idea in matter. If we have rightly apprehended this as the essential, vital element of beauty, we should find here the higher, more important sets of the various possible divisions of beauty—such as are more distinctive, characteristic, and essential.

Fundamental Analysis, giving the general divisions.

Looking now at this element of beauty —the revelation itself—in order that we may detect what in its very nature can furnish the ground of important, fundamental divisions of beauty, we recognize in it at once the nature of an *activity*. Revelation is of mind, an act, a process, of mental, of rational energy. Further it is a uniting act, uniting idea and matter, incorporating the one in the other. It is obvious, then, that the revelation of idea in matter may be contemplated in three different aspects: 1. The revealing activity may regard more itself—its own procedure in the revelation; or, 2. it may regard more the tendency and resulting effect of its work; or, 3. it may regard more the relation of the two terms which it is its function to unite, that is, the relation of the idea to be revealed to the revealing matter. In other words, in a revelation, we may in our analytic study fix our eye more on the revealing activity and in our interpretation of it emphasize that; or we may look more at the result and the revealing act as completed and emphasize that; or, in the third place, we may turn to the idea to be revealed in its relation to the revealing matter, and emphasize that in our interpretation.

I. Artistic Beauty.

§ 93. Beginning with the first emphasized character in the relationship of a revelation of beauty, that of the revealing activity itself, we are furnished at once with that important distinction of beauty which marks it in its closer relation to the revealing activity itself. When this predominates to our view in the object we recognize what we call *Artistic* beauty. It contrasts itself at once with those two kinds of beauty named, one of which, looking more at the idea, we have called Ideal Beauty, the other, looking more at the matter in which the revelation is effected, we have called Material Beauty.

The reality of this distinction we meet everywhere. It may be illustrated, to some degree at least, in three of our greatest poets. In Spenser, we find proper ideal beauty characteristic. It is in the richness, variety, perfectness of his idea that we find the charm of his poetry. In Milton, on the other hand, it is material beauty which reigns predominant and characteristic. We are ravished with the luxuriance and expressiveness of his vocabulary, the admirable harmony and melody of his verse-forms; the inexhaustible supply of material of every kind at his command, inorganic, and living, vegetable, animal, human, and angelic,—the control of all the stores of expression in nature or in art, in literature and science. The richness of idea is eclipsed by the magnificence and exuberance of its investing matter. In Shakespeare, we admire the proper artistic energy, the marvelous, matchless power of revealing. You may find elsewhere greater profusion and elevation of idea, a fuller, more beautiful vocabulary, and more luxuriant representative imagery; nowhere such power of grasping idea and matter and incorporating the one with the other in such inseparable bonds, in such unalterable relationships. We recognize the same distinctions of beauty in three of the princes in modern German literature. In Schiller it is the ideal, —the thought, the feeling, the character, the spirit, the event,—in short the theme to be revealed, which ever occupies him, which engrosses the reader's mind. In Jean Paul Richter, it is the wonderful richness of his matter—more particularly in his spirit-forms,—his proper imagery—that transports us as we read his works. While in Göethe we have the artistic power which plays with idea and matter as with toys, combining them at will with a most admirable dexterity and skill. In Painting we find the same distinction exemplifying itself. In ideal beauty, in the richness and grandeur of his idea, Michael Angelo reigns conspicuous in art; in material excellence, in his command of outline we admire chiefly Guido Reni and of color, Titian; while in artistic power,—in power to reveal given idea in given matter, Raphael outranks all.

It is in that species of art which reveals in mediate forms that we find this distinction more imposing. Here we often encounter what we discriminate as a *rendering* energy, or as a facility and grace of execution, which is but this artistic virtue that we have distinguished. We recognize it also in those arts which we denominate *mechanical*. Here we often meet with a true beauty that excites our warm admiration which lies merely in the artistic excellence that characterizes the product. We dwell not so much on the idea—the design to be put into the material; not on the material but on the artist's work itself in incorporating the one in the other. We admire the intelligence that has guided his hand in perfect regularity and order, observing every relationship of internal propriety and external adaptation, without stumbling or erring, avoiding all that is monstrous ; or the soul that is poured into the work, the heartiness, the joyousness which gleams everywhere from it, which charms and gladdens us although the intellect can find no characters in which to interpret or by which to denominate the particular features or parts in which the charm is concealed, which speaks to our hearts and to which our listening hearts respond, feeling the wide contrast there is between such a rendering and one that is proper but cold, skillful but heartless ; or still again we admire the wonderful freedom in which the revealing activity has moved throwing around the work the girdle of grace, characterizing the product not for its brightness, not for its warmth and glow, but for its proper gracefulness.

II. Free Beauty, and Dependent Beauty.

§ 94. The second ground of distinction in beauty given in an analysis of the revelation itself, is its relation to the result or effect ; or if we view this result as anticipated and designed, its relation to such designed object or aim. We have here at once presented to us the grand distinction of *Free Beauty* and *Dependent Beauty*, as we conceive of the revelation looking only to itself as its end or aim, or as looking to something ulterior or outside of this. Free beauty we recognize when the revelation of idea is merely for that purpose, for mere expression, mere realization, mere embodiment. Dependent Beauty we recognize in a revelation made for some ulterior object, not for the mere embodiment itself.

The validity of this distinction, as well as of a lower distinction which we shall notice in Dependent Beauty, is too obvious to require prolonged discussion. The nature of these distinctions is equally obvious. Idea is attribute of mind, which is in its essential nature an activity, and in its proper and higher form a moral activity. This activity can readily be regarded as for its own sake, seeking only expression, or as in relation to an outer world, either as seeking simply to communicate itself in its own essential nature to other activity of the same nature, or to impress itself upon such activity. Mind may, in other words, be regarded as simply acting, as acting out in certain form, or as acting out a result on the world about it. Idea may be regarded as mere idea, as idea in meet form, or as idea impressing itself on other natures for good or evil. To this distinction corresponds the distinction in the mind that regards it. Idea, as mere idea, addresses itself to the perceptive or intuitive faculty; idea, as mere revelation or expression, to the contemplative or imaginative faculty; idea, as impression on others, to the approving faculty. Psychology has sometimes marked the distinction in the mind addressed as that of intuition, imagination, conscience, but is at discord with itself in its nomenclature.

All revelation of idea being in the domain of beauty and constituting that domain, the distinction of free beauty and dependent beauty becomes at once a natural one. If the idea be perfectly free in its outgoing, that is, if it consult only itself, its own nature, its own properties in assuming natural form, it is properly denominated *free*. If it reveal itself with a view to an end out of itself, it is so far *dependent*, as it so far modifies its proper embodiment. Its form is one in its free expression; another in its expression for the sake of imparting itself in its own interior nature to foreign apprehension; still another when it seeks in its expression to impress results exterior to itself. We recognize here a common nature, with palpable modifications. In all revelation of idea there is beauty, truth, and good. One revelation we recognize as beautiful, for the idea is revealed for the sake of its own expression and embodiment to be admired; another is true, for the idea is revealed for the sake of what it is in itself to be known; a third is good, for it is revealed to impress a result in blessing. An object of free beauty, as a poem, contains ever a truth to be known; as such it may by virtue of the abstracting power of the mind be regarded simply in that relation, and when so regarded, it is recognized simply as truth. So a form of truth regarded as simple revelation may be contemplated as so far beautiful. We speak of a beautiful demonstration in mathematics. Philosophy not only teaches, it pleases as a beautiful revelation; and also, as it imparts good, it blesses. Proper science is true in its idea, beautiful in its form, blessing in its object. Poetry not only pleases as beautiful, it also teaches: and moreover blesses. Proper art must please in its form, instruct in its idea, bless in its appropriate result.

With this common nature we recognize the several modifications. Revelation for the form's sake is beauty ; for the idea's sake, is truth ; for the end's sake, is goodness. As the one or the other of these features predominates, it gives character to the revelation. The same product as a poem or a painting is characterized as beautiful, as true, or as good, according as it is regarded more in respect to its form, to its own interior relations, or to its effect in blessing.

The distinction furnishes to us at once laws or guiding principles in all the arts—laws and principles most vital to perfection, yet almost of necessity obscured and hidden until the distinction recognized reveals them. Free beauty governs itself by essentially other principles than Dependent Beauty. The only difficulty will be in determining the extent of the applications of the diverse principles which the two classes respectively originate.

Division of the Arts as Free or Independent.

§ 95. Entering now the society of the arts with this principle of distinction we find it exactly shaped and adjusted to the cleavages familiarly recognized, showing their source and direction, and straitening out and harmonizing what is clearly distorted and discordant in them, illuminating all and revealing all in beautiful order.

We find no difficulty now in discriminating the Free Arts, otherwise termed the Liberal Arts, the Fine Arts, the Elegant Arts, from those diversely denominated the Useful Arts, the Mechanical Arts.

Passing to the individual arts, Architecture we readily see belongs under the denomination of

Dependent Beauty ; for it characteristically seeks an end of utility. Yet it has all gradations from the mere sheltering cabin to the free beauty of a temple. It appears sometimes as properly free art. The beautiful temple which a grateful memory has erected by the grave of Robert Burns, on Carlton Hill in Edinburgh, is an instance of Architectural free beauty.

Music is free beauty in its most prevalent form. But in the service of religion or of country, it modifies itself and becomes dependent. In recitative it marks its lowest gradation as dependent beauty ; in wordless voice or instrument, its highest degree as free beauty.

These three characters which revelation when analyzed in its own nature thus unfolds to us, it will be remarked, are all of them essentially relative. They are through and through, characters of relationship. This property of relationship we must never drop from our view as we proceed to trace out the distinctions of beauty which are here to be indicated.

Analogy of an act of judging.

It may, perhaps, be helpful to a recognition of this ground of distinction, of its reality and its nature as well as significance, to revert again for illustration to the analogies of an act of judgment. In every act of judging there are the three elements concurring: there is something of which we judge, something judged of it, and the judging act. The judging act is in the copula, so called. Now we may consider apart and separately that of which we can judge—

all possible subjects. We can distinguish subjects. classify them; characterize judgments by them In the same way we can proceed with the predicate or attribute, and classify judgments in respect to the particular characteristics of the predicate. So, also, we may classify the judgment by the particular qualities of the copula or judging act itself. And in this, still further, we may find still other grounds of distinction. We may, for instance, emphasize the copula in respect to its own essential nature as a mere judging, a mere identifying activity, or we may emphasize the result, the product of the act—the judgment itself in its nature and relations; or, finally, we may emphasize more the mere relationship of subject and attribute to each other. And in this analysis of the judging element itself as the uniting, constituting element of the complex act in a judgment, we may ground distinctions that are relatively to all others, more essential and more significant and important.

Discourse is clearly distinguishable as free characteristically in Poetry; as dependent in Oratory, History, and Scientific Discourse. Yet Poetry modifies its freedom when it enlists in the service of philosophy or morality; and may be but little more free than some of the forms of Prose Discourse. Much Didactic Poetry is as dependent as some prose Oratory.

Landscape is predominantly free. As it bends to the sway of utility it becomes so far dependent, and binds in its proper freedom.

Pantomime in all its forms is perfectly free. In spoken discourse, it likewise becomes dependent.

In the same way, Sculpture and Painting are predominantly free arts. In Portrait Painting, in Statuary from living objects, it serves an end out of itself; it becomes dependent.

III. Distinctions founded on the revelation itself.

§ 96. The third ground of distinction in beauty given in the analysis of the revelation itself—the copula of the two terms, idea revealed and matter revealing—was found in the relationship which the revelation expresses between the two terms. We discover here as before three possible distinctions, under which all others must fall and be subordinate. First, the terms—the revealed idea and the revealing matter—may be in perfect equipoise and harmony; or, Secondly, the revealed idea may overbear or outspan the revealing matter; or, Thirdly, the revealing matter may preponderate over the revealed idea.

Proper Beauty

§ 97. The first kind of beauty indicated as given by this distinction is that in which the terminal co-efficients of beauty, the idea and matter, are revealed as in perfect harmony. This may be denominated *proper beauty*. It is the kind of beauty which, for the most part, we have in view when we attribute this quality to any object and pronounce it beautiful. This circumstance, it may be remarked in passing, has perhaps occasioned in a great degree the vague, indefinite, supposition that this is the only allowable application of the term; that only such objects should be called beautiful as express the idea and matter in this perfect harmony. But we should treat this only as an instance of unwarrantable narrowness of view precisely paralleled in that which we have noticed in our early writers on beauty who limit it to objects of sight, excluding music and poetry as well as all objects that address the other senses, from the sphere of beautiful things.

Its nature.

Proper Beauty, then, is that species of beauty in which the revealed idea and the revealing matter are in perfect equipoise and harmony. That there should be such harmonious relationship, even in appearance, relative to the contemplating mind, implies not only an *a priori* correspondence of idea and matter in all its forms as already indicated, — inorganic, organic, sentient, and ideal,—but an actual commensurateness between the terms in every instance of proper beauty.

We need here, as before, to observe carefully the distinction between beauty in itself, and beauty as apprehended by the contemplating mind. As we have seen, a true revelation, which, as such, in itself, may be strictly an object of beauty, may, by the mind that views the revelation, be regarded only as expressive of the real as idea to be known, and so be no beauty to it; or in relation to the result of the revelation, as morally right or good, and in this case, also, be no longer beautiful to it; so here it is in the power of the contemplating mind to see a revelation as one of either of the three several classes given by the distinction in hand.

Its effect.

The effect of Proper Beauty on the viewing mind is that which we should at once anticipate from this view of its distinctive nature. The experience of proper beauty is ever in undisturbed tranquillity and repose. There may be degrees in intensity of emotion as of vividness of view; but the effect is, ever and characteristically, one of perfect satisfaction and quiet enjoyment. The mind rests in contented contemplation. So the creator, as he contemplated his creative idea filled out in perfect fullness in the realized creation, pronounced it good and rested. Infinite idea in infinite universe of matter, if language sanctioned by use yet literally absurd may be used, is not merely infinite, but perfect beauty. Finite idea exactly filling finite matter is also perfect beauty. When the finite mind so contemplates it, it is in the experience of proper beauty perfect in its kind.

The Sublime;—Its Nature.

§ 98. The second kind of beauty, indicated as given by this distinction, is that in which the revealed idea is in preponderance as it respects the revealing matter. In this species of beauty, the idea asserts its superiority over form,—spirit over matter; the idea overmasters the form, breaks through it as it were, and stands forth in the majesty of its own divine, unparticipating nature. It is that kind which is familiarly recognized as *the sublime*.

Its effect.

Its effect on the contemplating mind exactly corresponds with this view of its peculiar nature. The mind is disturbed, unbalanced, as it were. It is no longer, as in the contemplation of proper beauty, in harmony and repose; it is in unrest and disharmony. It is attracted as in all beauty, but it is awed, not simply satisfied. The proper emotion in the experience of the sublime is awe, not simple admiration.

Authorities. § 99. It is hardly necessary to adduce any corroboration of this view of the nature of the sublime from generally recognized authorities. Reject from these authorities what we must regard as imperfect or erroneous in their theories, and we find a substantial agreement as to the admission of the proper characteristics of the sublime, whether determined from its own objective nature, or its effect in experience.

Schiller. "Reason and Sense" says Schiller,* "harmonize under the sway of beauty, and it possesses attraction for us only on account of this agreement. * * * On the contrary, reason and sense do not harmonize in the sublime, and in this very opposition between both lies the magic whereby it invades our mind."

Richter "So Æsthetic sublimity of action," says Richter evidently speaking under the lead of the same view, and in reference to one variety of the sublime, that of action, as distinguished from that of mere vastness or degree, "stands in an inverse relation to the importance of the sensuous symbol, and only the smallest is the sublimest; in this case, Jupiter's eye-brows moved more sublimely than his arm or himself."

Hamilton. Sir William Hamilton, closely following Kant here as elsewhere, who with Schelling makes the sublime to consist

* Æsthetic Papers; Upon the Sublime.

in a mere relation of quantity—that of the relatively Infinite,—distinguishes, as his theory of feeling as mere pleasure or pain, and of beauty as that which engages the mind in an agreeable activity, compels him to do, proper beauty from sublimity by this, that beauty engaging a free and full activity "affords a feeling of unmingled pleasure," whereas the "feeling of sublimity is a mingled one of pleasure and pain." "The beautiful has reference to the form of an object, and the facility with which it is comprehended. For beauty, magnitude is an impediment. Sublimity, on the contrary, requires magnitude as its condition; and the formless is not unfrequently sublime."* The implication of quantity in the essential nature of the sublime and also of quantity in the idea relatively to the form, in these extracts is obvious. In beauty, this relation of quantity does not appear, for the co-efficients, idea and matter, are commensurate; in sublimity, quantity forces itself necessarily on the contemplation, for it is in the quantitative disproportion between the co-efficients, that its distinctive characteristic resides.

Cousin.

Allowing for specific difference in their theories of feeling and of objective beauty, we find the leading French philosophers agreeing with the authorities already cited. "When intuition," says Cousin,† and by intuition here he means simply sense-perception, "When intuition alone is satisfied, there is only an *agreeable sensation*, stifled by the displeasure of

---

* Metaphysics; Lecture XLVI.

† The Philosophy of the Beautiful.

reason, which is unable to grasp unity; and imagination cannot rise to the conception of beauty. When, on the contrary, we arrive at unity, and intuition cannot comprehend all the variety inclosed in the object, the beauty we perceive, and which occasions a displeasure in our sensible organization, and at the same moment a delight in our mind, has been called the *sublime.* But when the parts of an object are not so various and numerous as not to be comprehended, and when at the same time, the whole can be easily seized, and we feel a perfect accord between the various and unity, between the senses and reason, we stay and regard the spectacle with delicious emotion, and this is *the beautiful* properly so-called. "We determine the nature of beauty and of sublimity *a priori,* or, as it were mathematically." Cousin, like the others, makes the distinction of beauty and sublimity to lie in the relation of quantity.

This view of the essential nature of the sublime as that kind of revelation in which the revealed idea outmeasures and predominates over the revealing form forces upon us the thought that the idea revealed is not necessarily bounded by the revealing form; and compels us to reject all that reasoning, as essentially fallacious, which would strive to prove that the finite spirit cannot know the infinite on the simple ground that knowing implies limitation both in the object known and also in the subject knowing, and therefore cannot transcend the limits —the finiteness implied in form. The object known is not, in the sense which this reasoning implies, limited either to the limits of the knowing mind or to the limits of the revealing object. The child knows a greater spirit than itself in every recognition of a guiding, supporting, cheering parent. The still small voice—a revealing form of the narrowest limits by every measure that can be applied to form —reveals the great Jehovah; yes, better, more impressively, more fully, than the thundering storm or the rending earthquake.

Divisions of the Sublime.

§ 100. The most essential sub-divisions of the sublime will be grounded, of course, on the relation of objects to this attribute of quantity. Kant thus distinguishes the two species, of mathematical, and dynamical; that is, those of extensive magnitude, and of intensive greatness or of power. Hamilton adds to these species, which he denominates the extensive and the intensive, that in the relations of time, viz.: the protensive—"the sublime of Space, the sublime of Time, and the sublime of Power"—which he speaks of as "the three quantities."

But we cannot stop with these. There are more than these three quantities. Indeed, the relation of the last quantity named, that of power, to the second, that of time, should have at once suggested the analogical correlative to space, viz.: substance, that with its attributes fills space as power with its operations fills time.

Nor should we stop here. We are hardly yet in the proper domain of spiritual activity; space, time, substance, power—all of which quantities give us peculiar instances of the sublime—are in mere being, and the forms in which we apprehend being. There are other quantities, as of character and of truth. Not as mere substance, not as mere power, does the idea strike us as sublime in the revelation of Jehovah to Elijah in the still small voice. We speak accordingly of great, sublime characters; of the sublime in action. The more complete and scientific division is founded on the three-fold discrimination of mental experience—the three-fold discrimination of ideas or phases of spiritual being: Power, Thought, and Passion.

The Comic.

§ 101. The third kind of beauty indicated as given by the distinction in hand, is that in which the revealing matter is in preponderating disproportion to the revealed idea. We have here the species of beauty indicated by the names of the diverse varieties, such as the comic, the pretty, the diverting, the entertaining.

Its nature.

Matter seems to gain ascendancy over spirit, form over idea; or at least idea is not prominent. A face is beautiful when character is perfectly and harmoniously revealed in fitly expressive features and complexion. It is pretty when the features and the complexion are faultless, but it is expressionless of idea—character, soul, perfection of spirit is in defect. The great concerns of the human spirit, its great ever-pressing cares and struggles, its mighty achievements, its immortal destinies, constitute the sublime; the lighter affairs, the transient, the entertainments of the hour, and all the un-reason of the life make up the comic.

Language has furnished no fit appellation for designating this species of form ; its failure in this respect is attributable to the fact that its characteristic nature, as distinguished from the other species, has not been accurately ascertained. Dr. Thomas Brown, in his lectures on the Immediate Emotions, drops the remark: "There are similes which are sublime, similes which are beautiful, similes which are ludicrous." He here seems to have in his mind a vague conception of the fundamental distinction of form into these three species ; but the name *ludicrous* which he applies to the third can properly denote only a variety of the species. A like objection might be urged against *comic;* yet this term seems best adapted to this designation. We will accordingly adopt it, and signify under it all that species of form in which the matter predominates over idea.

Divisions of the Comic.

§ 102. We may readily distinguish two gradations of the comic, to use the term in this large generic sense, as we start from its nearest affinities to proper beauty. They are the *pretty* and the *proper comic.*

1. The Pretty.

The *pretty* is that gradation in which the idea is simply depressed and the form fastens the contemplation on the matter rather than on the idea expressed in it. It may be characterized as beauty but deficient in expression. Its effect is more like that of proper beauty ; it charms, while it does not convulse with laughter, as in the grossly ludicrous. Yet, while beauty never tires, and we return to contemplate it with ever fresh delight, the pretty soon satisfies, and we do not care to return to it. It is found in objects in which the outer form is more perfect, while the inner idea is not suitably expressed. Dress is pretty when viewed apart from its relations to the wearer ; when accordingly the mere internal and essential idea of dress does not fitly appear in it. A landscape is pretty when the forces of nature are but feebly revealed, while the outer dress is all in beautiful variety, harmony, and fullness, considered only in reference to that, and the creative idea is suppressed. A poem is pretty whose outward form, its rhythm and flow and harmony, are perfect, but idea is relatively feeble or obscure.

There are many varieties of this gradation. There is the *fantastic*, in which idea forgets its true nature as rational and shows its weakness by running off into the wild and capricious. There is the simply *odd*, that is disconnected from the order of things, and stands off by itself alone. There is the *queer*, which goes athwart the regular course of things ; the *quaint*, which is studied and cultured ; and the *capricious*, that lacks both study and reason.

Under this gradation we recognize also the proper *mirthful*, in which, as so beautifully painted in Milton's L'Allegro, the idea goes forth characteristically as activity, movement, perfect freedom and grace, while it leaves behind the deeper nature of the soul, its great concerns, all care and seriousness, and riots in this freedom. "With wanton heed and giddy cunning," it appears in a form that mocks and yet heeds its essentially rational nature, and plays blindfold with its intelligence while yet it even sees—contradicting while yet following the law of reason.

Proper comic. § 103. 2. A second gradation of the comic is found in the proper comic, where the idea is not merely overshadowed, but appears as positively weak. In contemplating it the attention is turned more upon the idea itself than on the outward form or matter. Here are to be found manifold varieties. A leading division is into the *intentional* and the *unintentional*.

Of the intentional comic is the *facetious* with all the different kinds of witticisms. True wit combines keenness, quickness—mental power which stirs our admiration—with the comic which moves our laughter. The two are congruous and each heightens the effect of the other. The comic element in it is the manifestation of something that is not according to reason.

There is of course in true wit that which surprises; as that which is not according to reason, we do not expect. But the surprise is an incident in the effect of the ludicrous, not an element of it. There is likewise in it, as not according to reason, some incongruousness. The idea, as wanting in reason, may be incongruous in its parts or elements, or in its relations to its source, or to the surroundings, or to its form of expression. Caricature thus delights to represent some feature in incongruous proportions to other features, or brings incongruous elements together.

The play upon words derives its power to amuse

from this incongruity between mind and its expression. Word, as the product of reason, should from its very nature, ever be the embodiment of certain, unambiguous idea. When it is used to signify widely different things or admit widely different applications, the incongruity becomes comic; as when in a tedious legislative debate, a speaker who had wearied out the assembly by a stupid harangue stopped to take a glass of water, was called to order by a waggish member who claimed it was not in order for a windmill to go by water.

The intentional comic has found a large sphere in the amusements of all nations. The love of the ludicrous has nowhere so freely or so largely indulged itself as in the Saturnalia of the ancient Romans, the Carnival jollities of the moderns, and the grotesque festivities of northern Europe. Thus at the annual feasts of asses in France, an ass was invested in sacerdotal robes and a mock service performed before it by the pope of fools with chants that burlesqued in every imaginable way all serious things. So in more recent times festivity is wont to run into the incongruous as the very soul of the comic, which either depresses or actually mocks at the rational.

The Bull.

The unintentional comic is exemplified in the familiar *bull.* Sir Boyle Roche has the reputation of being the father of the proper Irish bull. The comic incongruity in every form,—incongruity between the parts of the idea, in respect to its relations, and in respect to the expression,—characterizes his blunderings.

"Single misfortunes," he uttered in profound wisdom, "never come alone; and the greatest of all misfortunes is generally followed by a much greater." In the Irish House of Commons he had in debate remarked, that he did not see why we should put ourselves out of the way to serve posterity. "What," said he, "has posterity done for us?" A burst of laughter put him on an attempt to explain. "By posterity, Mr. Speaker, I do not mean our ancestors, but those who are to come immediately after them."

These comic blunders often occur in translations when the unfixed significance of words occasions ludicrous mistakes. Thus a French translation renders the last part of the Shakespearian verse:—

So dull, so dead in look, *so wo-begone,*

thus: *Ainsi douleur! va-t'en,* as if he had read, *so, wo! begone.*

BOOK III.

LAWS OF BEAUTY.

CHAPTER I.

NATURE AND DIVISIONS.

Laws are essential attributes.

§ 104. The Laws of beauty are learned from its attributes. Indeed, the characteristic properties of an object of beauty are but its laws seen from another point of view. In the same way we regard heaviness, gravity, as a property of matter, when we are concerned with an analysis of its attributes; but we speak also of the law of gravity, meaning only that matter, in order to be matter, must always gravitate —must be heavy. So soon as we recognize an essential attribute of an object, we recognize a law of its being, or of its acting. The term *law*, however, carries with it the notion of universality, which does not necessarily belong to an attribute as such, but only to an essential attribute, or such an attribute as always belongs to the object in the conditions to which the law applies. For we may have laws that are derived from attributes of relation as well as from essential attributes or properties. It is a law of the solar system that the planets revolve about the sun in elliptic orbits. Yet the essential attributes of the sun would remain the same were there no planets and consequently no relations between sun and planet, upon which a law of revolution could be founded.

In order to determine the laws of beauty we have only to replace before our minds the attributes which we have already found to belong to beauty. We study them, however, from a different point of observation. In the first place, we found the kinds of beauty, as given by its different attributes under the lead of an analysis of beauty into its constituent elements, and proceeded from the general attribute itself of objects—their beauty—to the different modifications of it in objects. Our method was from the attribute to the object. Our course now is the reverse of this. We proceed from the object to the attribute: we take a class of objects of beauty and proceed to determine from their essential nature, as belonging to such a class, what must be their attributes or their laws.

Further, in the study of the attributes of beauty we look at it as an object presented to us for our investigation; in the study of the laws of beauty we regard rather the mind producing or interpreting beauty. In the one case, we inquire what are the different forms of beauty as they are respectively characterized by the relative predominance of this or that element; in the other case we inquire how we are to create beauty or to apprehend beauty.

The laws of beauty will direct and govern us in putting beauty into objects, in forming objects that shall be beautiful, or in interpreting beauty out of them.

Twofold division of laws: 1, of Production; 2, of Interpretation.

§ 105. There are, accordingly, two classes of laws of beauty: The one class pertain to the production of beauty; the other class to the interpretation of beauty. Form, indeed, has two sides, the one looking to the embodying or communicating mind; the other to the contemplating or apprehending mind. It implies a revealing and also a receiving mind. Not that if there were no observing mind in any particular case there would be no beauty. But form is as really for a mind as of and from a mind. It is the line of contact between the two; as the German metaphysicians might say, the indifference point between subject and object; the place of union between inter-communicating minds. The imagination is both active, creative of form, and also passive, receptive of form. Hence the division of the laws of beauty, of form, of the imagination as the faculty or capacity of form, into the two classes of laws of production and laws of interpretation.

Beauty of nature and of art.

§ 106. Still further, beauty exists both in nature and in art. It appears both as of divine and of human origin. It is the same in both, however, in its essential attributes. That cannot be admitted to be beauty in art which is contradictory of what is recognized as beautiful in nature. As the forms of nature are the revelations of the divine idea, so the demand that art follow nature has a plausible ground of validity.

As mind is essentially ever the same—as the human mind is in its characteristics as mind god-like, so ideas and forms, in the workings and expressions of all mind as mind must be alike under the general law of mind. Yet the expression of one mind is quite different in its modifications from that of another. The forms of beauty in nature as the embodiments of the divine idea are specifically different in divers modifications from those of art. There is a beauty characteristic in nature; there is another beauty characteristic in art. Least of all is copy of nature of itself true creative art. It may be purely mechanical; and so far no proper revelation of original idea.

But while beauty in nature and in art is ever subject to the same laws of interpretation, the laws of the production of beauty must of course look chiefly and prominently to art.

After presenting these general laws, which are applicable to all production of beauty in whatever department, and which are derived immediately from the three constituents of beauty, we will consider the more specific laws as applied to the arts. And, in respect to the fine arts, considerations of utility will lead to a selection out of all the possible kinds of art of those only which have evinced their high claim to the regard of every cultivated mind by the extent and the degree of perfection in which they have actually appeared in history. Six stand out in grand preëminence before all others. They are: Architecture; Landscape; Sculpture; Painting; Music; Dis-

Six leading arts.

course. The first four of these address the eye. The first three reveal through outline mainly, although landscape cannot wholly overlook light and shade, or even proper color in the disposition of its vegetable growths; the fourth mainly through color. The last two immediately address the ear; but the last also mediately through the ear reveals a proper ideal form for the super-sensible imagination. Next below these, but at a wide interval, has been ranked the so-called histrionic art, including both elocution and pantomime. Then come the arts which address the lower senses, which have hardly as yet even a place in the Æsthetic circle.

CHAPTER II.

LAW OF IDEA.

Selection.

§ 107. Beauty is perfect form. The first law accordingly in all art production, in all æsthetic creation is that the highest perfection in all the elements of form be aimed at which the nature of the case will allow. There are, as we have seen §§ 59–62, gradations of beauty determined respectively by the relative perfectness of the idea, the matter, and the embodiment. There may be ideal excellence, or material excellence, or rendering excellence. There are gradations of ideas ; one is æsthetically higher than another. If the idea to be rendered be free of selection, this subordination of one idea to another should be regarded. In like manner there may be room for selection in regard to the matter, as also in the modes of embodying ; and when selection is free, there should be rational deliberation and choice in order to the highest success in art. This law of deliberate and careful selection applies to all the three elements of form.

Requires:—
1. Earnest Study.

§ 108. A more specific law relates to the treatment of the idea itself to be revealed. This law of ideals requires several things. First it requires that the idea to be revealed should be perfectly fashioned out into a distinct, fully outlined ideal in the imagination. Just so far as art production is attempted with no distinctly formed ideal, with no distinct imagination of what is to be revealed, the production must fail. Perfectness of material, skill in rendering, will not atone for this fundamental defect. The product will be empty, meager, unsatisfying. Distinctness and richness of idea are indispensable in all art. The first work of an artist is to shape this ideal into the most complete and definite outline, and to fill it with the fullest and richest spiritual content, of intelligence, of feeling, of energy. Here almost universally there is room for long, patient, earnest, and loving labor. The imagination is subject like all human activity to the conditions of time; and can perfect its work only as it is allowed to intensify its power and elaborate its products. The artistic labor required here is too generally overlooked. In all the arts the ideal receives for the most part too little study. Yet nowhere is artistic work more advantageously expended. The ideal in architecture, what precisely is to be brought out in the design of a building; the ideal in a landscape, what precisely is to be expressed in the disposition of the grounds and of tree and flower; the ideal in discourse, to exemplify no farther,—what precisely is the theme to be presented and the object for which it is treated;—each demands a care, a study, that can hardly be excessive, before any embodiment of it is attempted. This ideal may be expected to grow in richness and in perfectness even in the very work of embodying; but this growth can only be assured by this previous study and will also be greatly aided by it.

II. Conformity to laws of mind;—

§ 109. Secondly, this law of the idea requires that it be carefully conformed to the nature and laws of the mind or spirit. The mind is simple and although for convenience in the study of its operations we distinguish different faculties as of knowing, feeling, and willing, yet the mind is ever the same one power, never ceasing to feel or to will when it acts as intelligence, and never dropping its intelligence when its states are predominantly those of sensibility or of will. It is ever intelligent, ever feeling, ever acting as will. Every ideal of perfect art must therefore be a true expression of the nature of the mind that creates it. It must be in intelligence, in feeling, and in freedom, never such as an unintelligent, an unfeeling, or a mere mechanical power could effect. Indeed, the more of these great characteristics of mind, the more of intelligence, the more of feeling, the more of freedom, are put into the ideal, the richer and the higher will be the product when realized in complete form.

To laws of intelligence;—I. Truthfulness.

§ 110. More particularly, every ideal in art must conform to the nature of the mind as intelligence. It must therefore in the first place be *truthful;*—it must be such as that it may be apprehended by the intelligence through a perfect propriety in all the internal characters;—in all the relations of its parts to the whole and to one another—§ 66. Several more specific rules are comprehended in this.

Implying;—*a.* One whole;

I. The ideal must be *one whole.* It should be a unit, so as to be susceptible of being apprehended as one whole. So vital is this requisite to all beauty that, as we have seen, some writers on art have resolved all beauty into this one character—unity in diversity. Partial as is this theory it yet contains this amount of truth, that there can be no perfect beauty without the strict observance of this principle and moreover, that wherever there appears this unity in diversity there is beauty more or less perfect, and simply because it is ever a form of mind; because it is the characteristic expression of the mind as intelligence.

b. Correspondence of parts.

2. All the parts must be in such relation and keeping every way as that they may readily be recognized as complementary parts of the same whole by the apprehending intelligence. This rule looks to the relations of the parts to one another; the previous rule to the relations of the parts to the whole. Each rule, indeed, necessarily involves the other; but they may be advantageously considered separately. This second rule is founded on that internal propriety which we have discovered to be requisite, —§ 66. In the successive working out of the several parts, as in the elements of the ideal itself, in the kinds of matter, and in the methods of embodying, this necessity of a perfect harmony and congruity in all the parts will everywhere exist. And to secure it, there will be needful a careful study of each part in its relations to every other, so that not only all confusion, distraction, and contradiction shall be avoided, but also positively, so that the very harmony and correspondence of all the parts shall facilitate and help out the apprehension. This very correspondence between the parts will greatly aid the interpretation as it passes from one part to another, and thus render the whole product more perfect as form for another mind.

These two rules are more vaguely and blindly comprehended in the general direction that in all art not only must the design be intelligible, but that every part should help out the design and be meaning and significant. It can be so only so far as this fundamental condition of all intelligence is observed that there be one whole to which all the parts are strictly subordinated while being perfectly coördinated with one another.

Under these two rules, as we have already seen and shall have occasion hereafter frequently to remark, are comprehended the several regulative principles in all art — of unity, contrast, æsthetic number, proportion, symmetry, and harmony.

2. Catholicity.

§ 111. The æsthetic law of idea, as founded in the intelligence, once more requires that it be presented in art as *catholic* or *typical*,—§ 74. The principle of *kind*, of the general, rules in all nature. It is one of the highest and most characteristic functions of the intelligence to recognize what in each object is common to other objects—to generalize and classify. In all products of art the mind looks for that which thus characterizes a class. The representation in landscape painting, of a cloud that differed as far as possible from all other clouds, and showed as little as possible of the essential nature of a cloud, every pure taste would reject and condemn. On the other hand, the skill of a master in art is at once recognized in his seizing firmly such essential characteristics of the subject which he treats as are specific or general, and then distinctly presenting them, to the subordination of what is merely accidental, or belongs only to the individual. This law is founded on the very nature of idea in art as a product of intelligence, whose highest function is thought or knowledge of the particular in the general. Presented thus *a priori* by the nature of idea to be expressed, it meets confirmation as viewed from the product side of art. Thus Ruskin, in his Modern Painters, says most truly: "There is but one grand style in the treatment of all subjects whatsoever, and that style is based on the perfect knowledge, and consists in the simple, unencumbered rendering of the specific characters of the given object, be it man, beast, or flower. Every change, caricature, or abandonment of such specific character, is as destructive of grandeur as it is of truth, of beauty, or of propriety." And again: "The true ideal of landscape is precisely the same as that of the human form; it is the expression of the specific—not the individual but the specific characters of every object in their perfection; there is an ideal form of every herb, flower, and tree; it is that form to which every individual of the species has a tendency to arrive, freed from the influence of accident or disease."

This law is perfectly compatible with accuracy of detail in rendering where necessary the individual. It simply requires that the generic or specific, the catholic or universal, the proper typical, by whatever name it be expressed, be exalted to its due rank above the fortuitous and the monstrous. Even in those recognized forms of art which represent the wild, the extravagant, the irregular, the fantastic, the monstrous, known as the grotesque, the arabesque, the moresque, the highest beauty will ever be found to consist in their representing under and through these wild combinations, or strange objects or features, what is general, universal, typical,

In the Arabian Nights, which is a specimen of the grotesque in discourse, the extravagant and contra-natural only the better reveal what is common in human nature.

To laws of feeling.

§ 112. In the next place every ideal in art should express a feeling spirit;—it should have heart and soul as well as intelligence. Beauty speaks first to the heart; and can make itself heard only as heart speaks in it. Form, as already stated, is both of and for mind; the imagination has ever an active and a passive side. And the condition of all imagination, of all form, of all beauty, is a common ground of sympathy, of reciprocating sensibility, between the creative and the receptive imagination, between the revealing and the contemplating mind. This sensibility, this heartiness, this loving spirit should therefore characterize all productive art. It will appear everywhere in the character and tone of the ideal, in the nature of the material, and above all in the embodying; for here will chiefly be expressed the soul of true genius, in the tender affection, the anxious care, the persistent, patient devotion and toil which pervades its whole work.

To laws of goodness.

§ 113. In the third place, the ideal in all art should express the free personality of the creating spirit. Just so far as this appears and characterizes an object, it becomes so far graceful § 79. If we inquire now what are the specific forms in which this attribute may be most perfectly secured to any artistic product, we shall see at once that, as the free personality can be perfectly expressed only in accordance with its highest law—the law of rectitude and goodness—every ideal will be most perfect as it is in harmony in all respects with this fundamental law. The more moral in its character and in its whole expression the ideal of art is, the more perfect must be the final form and the beauty. Undeniably the more elevated and pure the character in any work of art—a painting, a statue, an epic, or a drama—the higher will be the grade of beauty. But at the same time it must be allowed that the base, the impure, the malignant, is legitimate subject of art-representation. It is to be borne in mind, however, that not the bad itself in its own shape and character appears in art, but properly the artist's conception of it. It is a most pernicious notion that the bad should properly be represented in the highest art precisely as it is, apart from all feeling or judgment respecting it on the part of the artist. The vice of this theory appears in this—that art never represents immediately its subject, but the artist's ideal of it. This ideal must, as it is marked by naturalness and freedom, be shaped and colored by the spirit and disposition of the artist. It cannot be that a virtuous soul should be in perfect, complacent sympathy with the bad; that the good should rejoice in the evil and fiendish. When a pure-minded artist therefore is called to introduce into his art a foul character, he must, in order to the highest success as an artist, render it not as it is in its own foulness, but with something of his own antipathy and loathing; as he is called in the exercise of his art by the very laws of art to represent not that which is without, but that which is in himself; not the foreign object but his ideal of that object. When a poet or a painter displays vice in expressed sympathy and complacency with it, his work so far fails as a product of art; it offends and disgusts. Its merits may be ever so great in other respects, yet its ideal so far as sympathetic love of vice appears must necessarily detract from its æsthetic value as a whole. Milton has introduced Satan as a prominent character in his great poem. He has invested him with many heroic qualities worthy of all admiration. Who ever rises from the perusal of the Paradise Lost with the feeling that sin is in it commended, or viewed by the poet otherwise than as the worst of horrors? His treatment, inasmuch as not Satan himself but Milton's ideal, which could not but color his apprehension of the fiend with the antipathies and repugnancies of his own pure nature, is presented to the reader's view, never repels, never stains, or mars to our eye, the sublime creation. How different is the representation of Cain and of Mephistopheles by two more recent poets! We may admire the power of conception and of rendering, but we are repelled and disgusted by the skepticism in regard to virtue in the one case and by the positive sympathy with vice and evil in the other. The very nature of beauty prescribes this law to all procedures in art, when treating the evil and the vicious; that while the ideal be truthful and be exactly conformed to the object, it should be, as ideal, ever characterized by the profoundest, warmest loathing and reprobation of the bad as such. "Taste," says Carlyle most truly, "must mean a general susceptibility to truth and nobleness;" it cannot relish therefore the false and the vile. Not only a living representation of evil as evil is forbidden in true art; but even a mere indifference to its moral demerit.

CHAPTER III.

LAW OF MATERIAL.

Range of selection.

§ 114. The most fundamental law in art production founded on the matter in which it is to produce its work, is that it be suited to the ideal to be revealed and to the capability of the artist. The range of selection of material meeting this demand of adaptedness is limited; yet within its limits there is an indispensable necessity of care and study in order to success.

It is true that the material is often given and the ideal and the artistic skill are to be selected with a view to that. The artist in landscape has his material given in the ground he is to beautify and the vegetable growths within his reach and suited to the peculiarities of the soil and climate. The sculptor works in stone; he must select his ideal in reference to its suitableness to be represented in stone. It is so with the other arts. Yet is there even under these restrictions wide range of selection. Thus in architecture, the character of the ideal as given in the design and object of the structure will guide to the selection of stone, of brick, or of wood; and still farther to the choice of the specific varieties of each kind of material, whether there be one single kind or a combination. If there be a combination, the adaptation of the different varieties to one another and to the details of the design will require careful deliberation and exercise of taste.

In reference to idea.

§ 115. The most fundamental division of art material in reference to the idea is that which regards the idea as a progressive action in time or otherwise. The same principle of division applies to the arts. Thus movement in time can be immediately represented only in sound, bodily action, and word;—in the arts of music and discourse, and the histrionic art. The other arts immediately represent only objects in space. If, as in painting, an event or scene is to be depicted, it can be only by some suggestion or some conventional symbol. Accordingly we seek in the first of these classes of arts, the beauty of action as predominant; in the other that of repose.

Selection in reference to mediate or immediate form.

§ 116. Another division of art material and accordingly of the arts we have recognized is into those which are immediate to the ideal or otherwise, §§ 84, 85. The artist in the case of the mediate arts will need to study not only the suitableness of that matter in which he himself embodies his ideal but also of that in which it is to be finally presented to the contemplating mind. The architect may put his elevation and design in perfect form on paper; his proper art terminates there. But before his work can be fully realized in completed art product, the materials which the mason and the carpenter professionally handle are to be shaped and worked so as to receive his design. He has need, therefore, in elaborating his design to study the material in which it is ultimately to be embodied;—the quality and color of the stone, the strength, durability of the wood; the capabilities of these materials to be wrought into the forms required for his design. So the musical composer may be no performer. But his compositions must all be elaborated in reference to the kind of sound in which they are to be rendered, whether that of voice or of instruments; and whether of voice or of instruments, in reference to the number and kind. In like manner dramatic compositions have been wisely constructed with reference to the capabilities and characteristics of particular actors. It is accordingly the duty of the artist to attend carefully to the material in which his product is designed at last to address the contemplating mind.

CHAPTER IV.

LAW OF FORM.

Method.

§ 117. The collective laws of form are founded on the third and more vital constituent of beauty and are immediately indicated by the particular attributes that are given in this constituent. Book I. Chapter V. These laws respect more directly the artist himself as he determines his own activity immediately in embodying his idea in its matter. They may conveniently be studied as they apply (1) to the artist irrespectively of the particular design in his production; or (2) in respect to the particular design; or (3) in respect to the relation he is to observe between the idea and the matter. These different views give us the three divisions of the laws of form. (1) The laws of style, which respect immediately the artist himself; (2) the laws of design, which respect the object or aim of his procedure; and (3) the laws of artistic expression.

Naturalness.

§. 118. I. THE LAWS OF STYLE.—The fundamental law governing in this department of art production is that the procedure be *natural*. This law prescribes that the artist put himself into his work of embodying or rendering just as he is. This is true style, as expressed in the French proverb: *le style c'est l'homme même*—style is the man himself. It is directly opposed to *mannerism* and to *servile imitation*, both which express some deviation from that free movement which the perfect embodiment of the idea in the given matter requires.

Opposed to mannerism.

Style is derived from a word denoting the instrument used by the Romans in writing; and *manner*, etymologically denoting what pertains to the hand, points at once to the symbol of execution. Both terms used metaphorically have much the same significance. We may speak of the style of Raphael or the manner of Raphael while meaning the same thing. Mannerism is a departure from true manner or style. It is of a two-fold character, as it either gives undue regard to some one principle of style; or makes style itself excessively predominant in the rendering or embodiment.

And to servile imitation.

Servile imitation is opposed to true style as it subjects the true rendering of an idea to a controlling endeavor to copy. The proper way both to avoid this servility, which is hostile to beauty, and at the same time to secure the excellencies that have characterized great artists, is by such a careful preparatory study of those excellencies as shall make them one's own. The conscious effort to imitate them in production necessarily causes awkwardness and more or less complete failure. The disciple of a great artist, whether orator or painter, musician or sculptor, will unavoidably catch more or less of the peculiarities of his master. He can only reach the standard of a true style by so possessing himself of them as to be entirely unconscious of their presence when producing.

Truthfulness and Catholicity.

§ 119. Style being, in a just sense, the man himself and hence having for its first and fundamental law that it be natural, that it express ever the producing artist himself, will of course be variously characterized by the various degrees and modes in which personal traits and qualities are combined. The style of every artist must more or less reveal his own personal nature and character. We accordingly find style modified by these personal diversities. As art should ever aim at perfection it is a law of style in every art that it should, as far as may be, reveal a perfect soul—perfect in intelligence, in feeling, in power and freedom.

In respect of intellectual perfection, style should be truthful, be in propriety and fitness, and be catholic. We characterize a style or manner that is faulty in these several particulars, as false, as uncouth and indecorous, or as grotesque and monstrous. The artist appears false to his nature; as a double-minded man, a man of duplicity, whose characteristics we cannot harmonize into a true soul. Or he appears in disharmony with other things and with conditions or circumstances around him, and irreconcilable with his aims or objects. Or he is a kind of artistic monster whom we cannot place in the class of rational artists. Farther, intellectual richness or barrenness will reveal itself in style. One artist is full of idea; another rendering the same object will appear barren and empty. The one style captivates; the other repels.

Sympathy. § 120. In respect to emotive perfection, style should be characterized as sympathetic. A warm loving heart should pour itself out into the work. Well has Ruskin observed in regard to the art of language, that the "secret of language is the secret of sympathy, and its full charm is possible only to the gentle." The same principle holds true of every art. The artist should have a loving heart for his work—for his idea that he is to render, for the object he seeks in rendering, for the souls that he addresses in his art. Even in painting if the soul of the artist has no capacity of being kindled into an intensive glow as he thinks of those who may contemplate his product, his cold unsympathizing style will mar his work.

Grace. § 121. In like manner in respect to the expression of power and freedom, style should be characterized as graceful. It is the grace marking the handling of an idea, the incorporating of it in the matter, that constitutes the charm of many a work of art; it is not the greatness of the subject, not the preciousness of the material, but the free and easy handling of both. And here, in the perfectness of skill which conceals all effort lies the highest perfection of art; as Du Fresnoy teaches: *Maxima deinde erit ars, nihil artis inesse videri.*

With wonderfully philosophical justness and

completeness has the apostle Paul in his second epistle to Timothy enumerated these three generic features of a perfect man as the comprehensive gracious gifts of God to form the style of a true christian—the spirit "of power, and of love, and of a sound mind."

The laws of design threefold.

§ 122. THE LAWS OF DESIGN.—We have recognized the two kinds of beauty distinguished as free and dependent. § 94. Beauty is free when the form is for its own sake; it is dependent when the form is determined by some exterior end or aim. We have in this line of gradation all grades of beauty from the mere tool to the purest form of art in a statue revealing not any real being, but a mere ideal as an Apollo or one of the Graces. Besides this, in dependent beauty wherever the form predominates only to a certain extent over the ulterior end or aim, as in architecture, we find this free independent beauty seizing upon every opportunity to assert itself and reveal its purely ideal work in the manifold ways of decoration, in divers modes of appended beauty. Proper design takes the given ideal to beer vealed, whatever it may be, and embodies it with reference to the end or aim of the revelation. If that end be a pure end of utility, as mechanical design, it prescribes that the embodiment proceed toward its end ever under pure æsthetic laws. If that end be a predominantly æsthetic end, where perhaps with a real end of utility, whether of truth or of good, yet the form presides and rules, there are then the principles of proper artistic design to be observed,

Still further, if the form be simply accessory, not self-subsisting and wholly independent, the laws of decorative design come in and prescribe a procedure modified in a peculiar way. We have thus the three divisions of the laws of design, according as it is *mechanical, artistic* or *decorative.*

Mechanical design; its nature.

§ 123. 1. *Mechanical Design.*—As man's nature is essentially æsthetic, it prescribes as a general law ever to be observed that his whole activity go out and express itself in forms of beauty. His sensibility should never be offended unnecessarily by what is rude, rough, unseemly, deformed, ugly. Even the spade with which he turns the earth that it may yield him mere bodily subsistence he requires should be in a certain fashion and finish; and the higher his culture, the higher will be his demands in this direction. As the true and the good are in nature one, they can ever as well if not better be attained as ends in accordance with the principles of a correct taste. Justly has it been insisted that no tool will lose in its fitness for its end as a mere instrument of utility by being tastefully made. In such perfect accord are utility and taste that it is claimed even beyond this that a tool will be more serviceable as a tool if fashioned and finished in taste. So it is everywhere. We require that our text books of science, which propose mere instruction, shall be in taste; that the laying out of the matter, the structure of the sentences, the printing, the binding, recognize more or less the laws of taste. So in manners, every movement should be graceful and proper, even if it be merely to cross the room, to move a chair, to render some service or aid. The rough, the rude, the stiff, the awkward, meets hindrances which an inoffensive nature misses.

The law of man's æsthetic nature accordingly prescribes that even in mere mechanical designs taste should ever preside and regulate in the shaping of the ideal with reference to the end that is proposed, the selection of the matter on which the work is to be fashioned, and the whole elaboration of the design to its last finish. Taste must yield to the end or aim; but except where overborne by that should assert its right to rule.

Artistic Design: its nature.

§ 124. 2. *Artistic Design.*—The artist, as distinguished from the mere mechanic, is governed predominantly by the form and seeks that for its own sake. But when it is said that in free art the form rules, this can never be understood absolutely. Even in the freest of arts, sculpture and music, the artist can never wholly extinguish in himself the idea that form is for mind as well as of mind; that his creation is for his own contemplating spirit if not also for others; and his production will ever be modified by this reference to its being an object for contemplation. He will work to please himself; to satisfy his own ideal; but this very aim so far will modify from that perfectly free creation which results when idea forms itself in matter with no reference whatever to any contemplation.

But farther, there are arts which we recognize as free, although they necessarily govern themselves by a reference to an end that is beyond the demands of the mere form. They are often thus only comparatively free. The ulterior end, as of shelter in architecture, of instruction in didactic poetry, is admitted to govern but so subordinately, that in contemplating we give relatively less heed to that. The form is predominant in our attention. We find here as everywhere the grand truth that our æsthetic nature is one and inseparable with our moral and intelligent nature although not in thought indistinguishable from it. For study, for improvement and culture, and for practice and execution, our finite nature requires, as the nature of the case permits, that we give prominent attention sometimes to one and sometimes to another of these divers phases of our complex being. But as they are but phases of one and the same they may ever be harmonized in art. The moral end may in it be attained with no necessary violation of æsthetic principles. These principles in their application to dependent art only need to be shaped and modified.

Regard to form.

§ 125. The two fundamental laws in artistic design are accordingly two:

First, neither the ulterior end nor the æsthetic form should ever be disregarded. Even æsthetic taste forbids that the end and object of a work should be sacrificed to the means by which it is to be realized. A discourse which was professedly designed to commend some important undertaking, but which should lose itself in poetic embellishments or spend its life in perfecting its diction, would disgust more than an earnest plea even in an uncouth and unlettered style. An edifice that should sacrifice the conveniences in use for which it was designed to beauty of architectural form would receive a like reprobation from a just taste. Nor on the other hand does any principle of our being forbid, while our æsthetic nature requires, that this ulterior end in dependent art be reached in a true æsthetic procedure throughout;—that this foreign end itself be wrought out in perfect form.

II. Must harmonize both.

§ 126. The second law of artistic design in dependent art, requires that the ulterior end and the æsthetic form be kept in perfect harmony. This is always possible as we have seen from the union of the good and the true in the same nature with the beautiful. It needs to be remembered only that forms differ as ends differ; that moreover there is a choice of forms on æsthetic grounds. The design for a religious temple should vary from that of a city hall, and this again from a private dwelling, although shelter from the elements and from the commotions of human life without, be alike the common end in all. Even when the conveniences sought are the same, as in a house of religious worship and of public instruction, each requiring only the conveniences for speaking and hearing, æsthetic invention will elaborate very different designs. It will characterize the one by every admissible feature that will bespeak the presence of the high and holy, and the other by such as will feed the spirit of docility. Thus outside of the complete attainment of the end of the structure, art will have a field open to it for extended inquiry and study — a field of æsthetic form, in elaborating its design.

Decorative Design: Its nature.

§ 127. 3. *Decorative Design.*—The laws of design have here to deal with accessory or appended beauty;—with form as not self-subsistent, but as attached to other forms which to it is main and principal form. This species of form has a range conterminous with art. In every department it finds place. In architecture it fills up blank spaces with dentils or triglyphs and connects principal members with moldings, or ends out the whole or leading parts with capitals and turrets and finials. In music it helps out the effect of simple melodies or keeps it lingering in the mind by variations, or facilitates the passage to new movements by interludes, or breaks the abruptness of the cadence with trills, or prolongs the whole effect by a lingering *coda*. So in all the arts it fills up vacancies; it smooths transitions; it softens abrupt endings.

As decoration is in its nature but appended and so accidental form, it admits of all gradations. We have accordingly modifications of style from that which is characterized as simple, chaste, severe, lean, and meager to that which is luxuriant, rich, ornamental. Decoration is best viewed as the exuberance of the æsthetic spirit that loves to pour itself out and spread itself through every opening over all its work. Its laws are given at once in this view of its nature.

Its laws: I. Must be subordinate.

§ 128. 1. It must ever be subordinate. Whenever decoration usurps attention to itself, it is in revolt against the rule of beauty. It ceases indeed to be decoration and becomes principal form. If dress draws from personal beauty and overpowers its superior attractions, it defeats its purpose, which is but to adorn, not to eclipse. So when manner runs out and loses itself in formalities or smothers kindness and sensibility to the wants of others which is its very soul in unavailing courtesies and impertinent modishness, it is no longer gentility but mannerism, or affectation, or foppery. Manners do not make, they set off the man. In the same way in the other arts, whenever decoration asserts for itself independence and hides or overbears the principal form, it offends against true taste. It yet has a wide province. The true æsthetic nature will burst out everywhere and cover everywhere whatever procedure engages it. Its luxuriance needs pruning and guiding.

II. Must subserve principal form.

§ 129. 2. A second fundamental law in all decorative design is that it not only do not overbear the principal form to which it is appended, but also positively promote and further its proper effect. It may be safely assumed that it has no place where this its positive effect may not be calculated upon. Nor need this be interpreted so as to repress a luxuriant imagination; rather so as to guide it into its highest and most efficient ministry. Stage-decoration should facilitate the effect of the performance, by its distribution of the lights, by its scenery, and its disposition of walls and seats. The variations of a melody should only seek to deepen and prolong the impression of the simple strain; to extend its reach and fill out its content. Decoration should accordingly ever be not only subordinate to the principal form but ever subservient to it. It must to this end be in harmony and in perfect keeping with it. Contrast is not necessarily a hindrance. There are discords in music that are preparative for a richer harmony. The comic may, as in Shakespeare, but serve to make the tragic more effective. But there are limits here. The contrast allowed in decoration must ever rest on a deeper harmony; and the mingling of contrary natures is ever repulsive. The moods of human feeling, like colors on the retina, linger somewhat. There is a kind of inertia in them which is opposed to sudden and abrupt transitions. Contrasts themselves thus need softening; and in managing them, decorative design has a large part of its work. They serve for relief; they prepare for reaction. They are thus serviceable to the highest effect in art.

As subservient to the principal form, decoration must not only be in harmony with it, but also be itself of the true nature of form and be expressive. It must contain idea, must be significant. In its lowest variety it will be expressive at least of the exuberance of the artistic life, whose skill and grace and insatiate love of form will spread itself, like a luxuriant vine, over and beyond its frame and deck it with a life it did not of itself demand. But still all decoration is form, and if unmeaning, idea-less, is a blot and an imperfection.

Conventionalism in art.

§ 130. It is chiefly in reference to decoration in art that the principles of *conventional* representation are to be considered. By conventional representation is to be understood a representation other than what is natural and significant in itself and is expressive only by reason of a common understanding between the representing and contemplating mind. As there are all degrees of natural representation, varying from the exactest imitation in material as well as in form of every feature to the representation in other material and of the most partial extent, so the natural and the conventional shade into each other. Further, they may both concur in the same production; and accordingly the product may be characterized either way according as the natural or the conventional happens to predominate. The distinction in essential properties is, however, clear. The conventional representation is that which is founded not on the object represented but on a common understanding between the artist and the contemplating mind. The distinction rests on the truth that, as already stated, form is *for* mind as well as *of* mind.

Some conventionalisms are proper symbols. A symbol possesses itself the attribute represented. Justice is symbolized by the scales in equilibrium, as having the common attribute of horizontal impartiality. A closed book is symbolical of mystery; they both conceal their contents. Pericles was represented by the sculptor with a thunder-bolt as a symbol of his power in eloquence. A public building decorated by a figure of Mars would be thus symbolized as devoted to military uses.

Other conventionalisms are mere signs which men have somehow come to accept as representative of certain objects or attributes. Such signs may have been symbols or have been founded on them, but have lost the attributes by which they became significant, or are merely suggestive of something to be supplied by the imagination. They may be a single part of the object thus suggested; as in architecture, in bas-reliefs, a leaf suggests a vine or some symbolical tree, as the olive or the laurel. They may serve simply to relieve from the effect of vacancy, as a simple line or dash of color on a canvas, a band, a spot even on the plain surface of a building where a full delineation of the object would be impossible or too far removed for vision. So simple tones, repeated without melody or harmony, fill up an interval and keep the sense from wandering.

All conventionalisms come under the laws of decorative design, and, moreover, as being founded on the common understanding between the representing and contemplating mind, must be such as will be readily and correctly interpreted. The sculptor who sought to symbolize Moliere's peculiar skill in mirroring life and manners by representing him as holding a looking-glass, made himself ridiculous as suggesting that the subject was a dealer in that article.

Three-fold division.

§ 131. III.—THE LAWS OF ARTISTIC EXPRESSION. These laws of form respect immediately the relation which the artist is to maintain between the given idea and the given matter. We have already recognized § 96, the three different relationships between these constituents; as being either—1, an equiponderance between the two giving to form the character of proper beauty; or, 2, a predominance of idea over matter, giving to form the character of the sublime; or, 3, a predominance of matter over idea, giving to form the character of the pretty, the comic, the diverting, the ludicrous. The laws of expression accordingly fall into the three divisions of—1, Law of the proper beautiful; 2, Law of the sublime; and 3, Law of the comic.

§ 132. 1.—*Law of the Proper Beautiful.* The comprehensive law of productive art here is that it keep both idea and matter ever in view, and maintain a perfect equipoise between them. The idea must never outspan the capabilities of the matter, nor the matter overbear the idea which is expressed in it. As the sublime suggests more than it expresses, the proper beautiful expresses all it means.

Commensurateness of idea and artistic matter.

This law implies that both these elements—idea and matter—are within limits and measure. The character of this commensurateness between idea and matter varies in different objects and in different arts. The elements in the ideal of a dwelling, so realized in material as to be pronounced beautiful, the ideas of suitableness as to condition, of comfort and convenience, are commensurable with the nature of the material as of stone or wood, in site, in size, of the whole and of the parts, the number and arrangement of those parts, and the like. The too great or the too small in the matter in relation to these ideas so far detracts from the beauty of the structure. So the beauty of dress appears in the adaptation of the material to meet the demands of protection, shape, freedom of movement, complexion, and the like. Whatever in the material goes beyond or falls short of these demands so far fails. In discourse, in the same way, the language should correspond with the thought in loftiness or in commonness, in richness or in simplicity, in all its characteristics in short that can be expressed in words. In painting, if grace predominate in the idea, the outline and figure must correspond.; color that would hide, or shading that would too feebly express, would mar the product. The famous statuary group of the Laocoon has occasioned much dispute whether it is expressive of physical or mental pain—the pain from the bite and constriction of the serpents, or the hopelessness of escape on the part of the victim; whether the open mouth expresses the outcry of bodily pain or the sigh of despair. The thorough anatomical investigation of the muscles of the face, the chest, the abdomen, shows that the sculptor has most perfectly rendered the muscular relaxation in which the sense of hopeless despair instinctively expresses itself. That emotion just fills out the entire bodily contour. It is this perfect conformity of idea with matter throughout which makes this beautiful product "a joy forever,"—the fascination and the admiration of all the successive ages of beholders. The outer inorganic matter, the marble, has its just demands of weight and cohesive force regarded in the supports and the continuity of structure; the organic, also, in proportionate size and outline of every part in relation to every other; the sentient, likewise, in the attitude, the feature, the swollen vein, the rigid, relaxed, or relaxing muscle, everywhere in exact sympathy with the inner spirit; and, once more, the spiritual ideal revealing rational sentiment of despair and sense of loss of all in all the attributes of its proper nature that such an experience makes prominent. So perfectly has the immortal artist conformed his idea throughout to the matter that the contemplation is never disturbed by any disharmony.

Of the essential nature of this relationship between idea and matter which is presupposed in the very notion of beauty, as before intimated, we know nothing. We can only accept the great fact just as it is given us, that idea may be expressed in matter,—in inorganic, organic, sentient, other spiritual being,—and that there is such a thing as right expression, true expression, which we can readily recognize, and in which idea and its matter may perfectly harmonize in their impressions on our rational imagination. The artist must needs know how this harmony may be observed in his art. He must know more or less perfectly the attributes of the idea he is to reveal, and the attributes of the matter in which he is to reveal it. He may obtain this necessary knowledge either by analytic study of the idea and of the matter each by itself; or he may obtain it by contemplation of proper form in which both are united in one single object ; or he may obtain it by the union of both methods. He may obtain it by determinate plan and endeavor in systematic study, or through habits of observation and reflection may have accumulated the required treasures of intelligence in ways and at times he cannot afterwards recollect, of which he is hardly conscious at the time. The sculptors of the Laocoon had gained in some way this requisite knowledge of the history of the scene which they were to represent, of the characters and the passion in all its intrinsic features which predominates in them ; of the nature of the different forms of matter in which this passion was to be embodied, the physical frame and the whole condition of mind and soul in which such a passion finds place. They must have acquired all this knowledge and then they must have kept in all the execution of their design the attributes of all these elements so in mind that the idea should just fill out the matter everywhere. One unintelligent stroke of the chisel that should take off more of the marble than the idea required in order to its full expression, or one chipping less than was needful for this, would have been fatal. Exact equipoise between idea and matter throughout, perfect harmony between them is the comprehensive law of artistic expression in all proper beauty.

The sublime subject to law.

§ 133. 2. *Law of the Sublime.*—In productive art, law here can respect only representative, not properly natural form—the sublime of ideal not of idea. The natural sublime in which the idea reveals itself overpowering the matter, so far as it is of human production, is well nigh above law, or better, perhaps, is a law in itself. Its very characteristic is that it bursts forth impetuously, outswelling all the fixed channels of expression. Yet the sublime is ever of a rational origin and partakes of a rational nature. It can never forget all law. Its outgoings will be in a true order and under a determinate law. In other words, the sublime is in the realm of form, and must never ignore or belie its nature. It is akin to proper beauty, and may be—as, in fact, it ever is—closely associated with it. Eloquence, that in the greatness of its passion overbears the ordinary forms of discourse and utters itself in broken words, in disconnected sentences, yet keeps itself, as if by an internal guide, ever within a certain range of order, one step beyond which would plunge it into the depths of the ridiculous. Its sublime is ever but an upheaval from a plane of beauty. So the sublime of heroism, of noble daring, of magnanimous self-sacrifice and devotion, of grand achievement, has a law of its own which has grown up in its growth. Ceasing to be rational, it becomes brutish; and the brute can reveal the sublime only as the idea of its creator grandly displays itself in it, as it does also in the forms of inorganic nature. The human sublime must ever be rational, orderly, and conformed to law, or it ceases to be human.

Its conditions: I. Subject to growth.

The only laws of the natural sublime are either that which regards its growth and development, or that which requires its outworking to be in the line of beauty. To be sublime in thought, in feeling, in action, the first grand condition is to feed and train up the spirit to its fullest, largest capacity. Only the great soul can be sublime in its utterances. And the second condition is, that its utterances be in perfect form. The sublime awes, indeed, but attracts also; never repels or wounds the tenderest sensibility. It falls as readily and as gently upon the imagination or the capacity of form as proper beauty itself.

II. To form.

Artistic representation of the naturally sublime.

§ 134. It is the representation of the naturally sublime to which the laws of the sublime in productive art more immediately apply. They are comprehensively two as they respect: (1). The idealizing, or (2) the proper representing part of the procedure.

I. Its law of idealizing.

(1). The very principle by which form is distinguished into the sublime, the beautiful, and the comic, is quantitative; and consequently the sublime is ever characterized in terms of quantity. It is the great, the vast, the infinite. But quantity is external or internal; quantity of extent, or of degree. The idea therefore to be idealized by the artist, whether one of power, or of truth, or of passion, may ever be regarded by him either in the vastness of its reach or extent or in the intensity of its degree. Power is vast in its sweep, or mighty in its inner force, and as expressed in either way becomes sublime. The ocean is sublime in its boundless extent and in the resistless might of its waves. Thought is sublime as it comprehends the immensities of the universe or as it pierces to the inmost mysteries of being and of law. Passion is sublime either as it is wide and comprehensive in its objects or as it is deep and fervid. In apprehending these ideas of the sublime for representation, there is but one course—that of deep and long contemplation, and of free and full sympathy. No art can render perfectly an object with which it is not conversant, nor particularly in the passionate sublime an object with which there is not the tenderest sympathy. If he who would make others weep must first weep himself, the artist, to stir deepest emotions, must have sunk himself by long meditation into the very depths of the passion he is to represent. The effective actor on the stage loses himself in the character he represents; drops his own identity for the time and becomes what he personates. It is the same in all representative art. Only when the soul is swelled to bursting from drinking in the greatness of the object which it has long and closely and sympathetically contemplated, can it stream out in sublime torrents, for which the ordinary organs of expression are all too narrow and too low.

2. Its law of representing.

(2.) In representing the sublime in whatever object, while the idea side is not to be overlooked and care must be taken that the object be truthfully rendered, it is yet the other side of form which comes more fully under law. It is, in other words, the imagination addressed which the artist is most to regard. The one great difficulty will be to preserve the predominance of the idea over the matter in which the very essence of the sublime consists while at the same time the matter is sufficiently given to enable the contemplating mind readily to receive and appreciate it. Nowhere, perhaps, is the perfectness of form to be estimated with more distinct reference to the mind addressed. The cultivated mind is awed by the majesty of law in the order of the universe; the uncultivated mind under the same revelation of outward phenomena remains unimpressed. In oratory, accordingly, only when the orator has brought up his hearers to full sympathy with himself, can he venture upon that broken and inadequate expression which reveals the greatness of his thought or passion. His eloquence otherwise becomes unmeaning or ridiculous. True art can never disregaıd this condition of the passive imagination which it must ever address. Its very life is in obeying

> "That instinct of our kind
> To link in common with our own
> The universal mind."

Its law must be, therefore, to give so much of matter as will enable the interpreting imagination which it addresses to grasp the idea to the utmost extent and degree possible. It will seek, so far as in its power, to arouse the passive imagination to intensest sensibility, and to expand it to its widest reaches. In Discourse, in Oratory, in Dramatic and Epic poetry, even to some extent in the Lyric, may this procedure be followed; and the success of the speaker and the poet will be most complete as he most perfectly follows it. In other arts it is less practicable.

With this address immediately to the passive imagination should be associated such suggestions respecting the object toward which the emotion is to be called forth as will lead to the highest and fullest ideas of its greatness. This suggestive work will be the crowning work in rendering the sublime.

The Gradations of the Comic.

§ 135. 3. *Law of the Comic.* This department of form we have recognized as extending from the confines of the proper beautiful, in its first gradation of the pretty, where the idea only sinks but is not overborne by the matter, to its ultimate gradation of the grossly ludicrous, where the idea is at its minimum. The best exemplification perhaps of this extreme grade of the comic is in unmeaning laughter, begun perhaps in perfect coolness by mere empty imitation of the outward laugh, but which continued and repeated by companions passes at length into the intensest ludicrousness;—the most convulsive laughter where there is nothing to laugh at.

The unintentional Comic.

We have here to distinguish the intentional and the unintentional comic. The latter species, the unintentional comic, is either the blunder or genuine humor. There are natural wits, who, without being conscious of it, much less designing it, are given to play. Their governing mind is humor, delighting in dropping the serious and in holding forth the mirthful side of life. Their discourse abounds with sallies of wit. Thought and word each gives occasion for a leap of fancy into the diverting or the ridiculous. Ideas incongruous in their elements or in their associations go out into words as incongruous for expression ; and words point to the odd or quaint in thought even to unnatural doubles in sense. So in art, genius often inclines to caricature that overrides the natural proportions of features and elements and attributes, and exaggerates here or belittles there, that it may sink just idea in form. The humorous by indulgence and by training becomes a secoud nature.

The intentional comic.

Of the intentional comic, we have the two distinctions of the original and represented. The original humorist does not blunder, does not fail in force or justness of idea. In representing, the comic artist takes for his idea the blundering, the silly, the vicious, and renders that in diverting form. The comic element may be in the ideal, or in the matter, or in the rendering, or throughout. It may in part be comic and in part serious. Ridicule on one side passes readily into satire. The epigram diverts or wounds ; it is humorous or sarcastic, according as the design is seen to be serious censure or playful entertainment. The comic does not lose its proper nature, is in itself ever the same—a form where idea is given as weak ; but the elements of the representation changing to the eye of the beholder, the form changes.

Its domain.

§ 136. Productive comic art reveals in all the proper æsthetic arts. In discourse it usurps to itself one entire field of literature—comedy—for which it legislates with undivided authority. In the humorous epigram, also, in parody, and travesty, and in all the sallies of wit in oratory, or in other prose discourse, in puns, and other kinds of word-play, the law of the comic governs. In pantomime, also, and in the histrionic art generally, in music, in sculpture, and in painting it equally finds place. As the grotesque, the fantastic, it enters also into architecture.

Its laws: I. Must not ignore its nature as form

§ 137. The nature of the comic as thus indicated in its relations and its forms, suggests its governing laws. The first is that it never forget its nature as form—which is the revelation of idea in matter. If its characteristic as a department of form be to reveal the un-reason of human experience, it must ever remember that what is not human, what is not rational, can never become an ideal in art. The simply monstrous has no form and must ever defy the attempt to represent in art. If his desire is to represent the ridiculous, the artist must not make himself ridiculous in representing by attempting the unnatural ideal or the unfit matter. He must proceed under the control of the essential principles of form. The remark of Bonhours, indorsed by Addison, that "the basis of all wit is truth" may be extended over the whole domain of comic art and be applied not only to the ideal to be rendered but to the selection of the matter and to its use in rendering.

2. Must reveal idea as weak.

The second general law of comic art is that the relatively weak in idea must ever govern. So soon as this characteristic of the comic is dropped, the form changes. As remarked, the laughable becomes sarcastic or scurrilous ; the playful becomes bitter ; humor becomes satire. In the proper comic everywhere the ideal drops the serious and the weighty ; its elements are the more superficial and the transitory of human experience.

Hence in the comic all that is associated with the idea in the rendering must be akin to it. False spelling does not constitute a considerable element in true wit ; yet the weak reason that gives character to the comic may appropriately show its weakness in its ignorance of the proper forms or of the proper uses of words. Hudibrastic humor plays with fantastic rhymes as well as doggerel verse and irrational practices and uncultivated manners. So everywhere the entire representation should be in keeping with the proper comic, in all that is incidentally associated with the product as in the essential elements of the product itself. The buffoon, while he does not cease to be a man, yet assumes a dress that ever suggests the ape ; and the monkeyish plays over all his performances.

CHAPTER V.

SPECIAL LAWS—ARCHITECTURE.

Origin.

§ 138. The noble art of Architecture had its origin in a pressing want of human condition the supply of which the æsthetic spirit took occasion to invest with its robe of beauty. Not that this is a merely embellishing or decorative art. On the contrary, it took the cabin or the cave and gave it a new being, informing it throughout with a new principle and nature. The germ of idea given to it in the felt want of shelter it has fructified and matured into one of the grandest growths of human culture.

Threefold Law

The special laws of Architecture distribute themselves readily into the three general divisions marked out in the preceding chapter—the Laws of Idea, of Material, and of Form.

Laws of Idea, Primarily to be found in provision of Shelter.

§ 139. I. THE LAW OF IDEA IN ARCHITECTURE. Architecture we have already recognized as uniting with the pure principle of æsthetic form that of an end foreign to it—as a kind of beauty somewhat dependent yet predominantly free. This foreign end in architecture, which makes it so far dependent, is primarily the provision of shelter. Shelter is the original want of human nature which has furnished the occasion and foothold for architectural art. It is, accordingly, an idea that is inseparable from it, even where, as in memorial architecture, the edifice can subserve no uses of shelter. Still that idea must be present and give character to it throughout. "The wigwam grew into a hut," says Mr. Fergusson, "the hut into a house, the house into a palace, and the palace into a temple by well defined and easily traced gradations, but it never lost the original idea of a shelter." This idea of a shelter—shelter from the elements, from the beasts, from the violence, the rudeness, the disturbance in every way of men —is the fundamental idea in architecture, and makes its governing law. But this primitive idea of shelter associates with it the ideas which enter into the regulative principles of the art. They so far give modifications of its products.

Modified by associated ideas of rest and repose.

In the first place, with the negative idea of shelter assuring safety and security, come in the more positive ideas of repose and comfort, and all the rich circle of ideas centering in these, so far as provisions for shelter could by enlargement or by modification be made to minister to these wants.

By special uses.

In the next place, the idea of shelter is modified by the divers uses for which the shelter is required. This principle of modification has given rise to a familiar division of the art. Thus we have the three grand departments of Domestic, Religious, and Civil Architecture, with their respective subdivisions, and also the less important branches of the art determined in reference to the special uses of the structure, as Memorial, Educational, Theatrical, and Commercial architecture. Besides the mere end of shelter, other ideas derived from the special uses of the structure enter into the art, and give law to it. The building must be constructed for the purpose for which it was designed ; for the æsthetic nature is not distinct and foreign from the rational which ever prescribes an end to all its activity. Rather it is itself rational, and its native impulses are repressed or crossed whenever the end or aim of a procedure is overlooked or hindered in ite Æsthetic principles themselves, accordingly, the essential principles of form, require that a building to be in the highest degree beautiful should ever express, not only the fundamental ideas given in the end of shelter, at which all architectural art aims, but also the ideas given in the special use for which the building is intended. To ascertain these ideas is the first work of the artist ; his special province as an artist will be suitably to express them.

Two procedures of art ;—to meet the ends, and to express the ideas proper to the structure.

§ 140. This province of architectural invention comprises two distinct procedures. The first is to contrive how to meet the ends of the structure, as those of shelter and those required by its intended uses. The second is to engraft on this the further expression of the ideas proper to the structure. The former procedure which seeks directly the attainment of the object proposed in the building, is truly æsthetic ;

for rational activity, even when seeking some end of mere utility, should be in perfect form. But this foreign end here governs. In the second procedure the principle of form rules ; it only grounds itself on the first and starts from it. It may harmonize with the first, for both procedures are alike from an essentially æsthetic nature. The first is under the dictate of want, and the second under that of wealth ; which as free, rising above the supply of a want, is well allegorized as the daughter of creative art and of wealth —of Jupiter and Plusia, —according to the Grecian myth. Dependent art and Free art are of one fatherhood and so ever in close harmony.

The Law of idea here is that the artist carefully apprehend these ideas which may enter into the structure, and form them into the single and exclusive ideal of his procedure.

Applied to domestic architecture.

§ 141. In Domestic architecture, after securing adequate shelter and protection from every kind of disturbance from without, the interior economical ones of the building are next to be provided for. These of course will vary in kind and in extent with the character of the family. They need to be thoroughly studied in themselves and their relations to one another and to the whole building, that their fullest demands may best be supplied. It is sufficient to say that there is here a work ot inventive art to be performed that is by no means inconsiderable in which experience, skill, and earnest labor can be put to the best account.

In the more pure æsthetic procedure, there are besides these economic ideas, others that are given at once in the general notion of family life. This class of ideas, that may be denominated æsthetic to distinguish them from the properly economic, also vary greatly. And it is the proper province of the artist here to inquire after these ideas that he may worthily express them in accordance with the economic demands and subserviently to them. The ideas of retirement and privacy, those of repose and quiet, those of cheerfulness and social affection, those of meditation and culture, and the like properly domestic ideas, find fit artistic expression, not only in the interior plans and finish but also in the external proportions and colors and adaptations. Just so far as these are fitly expressed, there is beauty in a dwelling.

To religious architecture

§ 142. In Religious Architecture there is the same distinction of economic and properly æsthetic ideas to be gathered up by careful study and to be harmonized into one ideal of the structure. The economic ideas vary from those in domestic architecture in kind and in extent, as the family differs from the worshiping assembly. The æsthetic ideas of seclusion from secular pursuits, of purity, sanctity, reverence, joyous confidence, holy aspiration, with those gathering round the special needs of convenience for all the uses of the structure, of physical comfort, and protection as well as of mental tranquillity and freedom, may find free expression here and so constitute an ideal which will satisfy all the demands of æsthetic form.

To civil architecture.

§ 143. Civil Architecture comprises several departments, each having its characteristic ideas, both economic and artistic. Of these the more prominent are those for proper political uses, as those pertaining to the Legislative, the Judicial, and the Administrative functions. In the latter department lie two leading branches of the art—Military and Naval Architecture. While in these two last named, the economic ideas more predominate, the wealth and greatness of a nation may more appropriately find free expression in Legislative Halls, in Judicial structures and the buildings designed for the various uses of civil administration. The function of the artist here is to make himself master of all the specific needs of the structure, and then to give free expression to the full extent of his means to those ideas that cluster about a nation and about that particular department of the national life whose demands the building is to meet. His work is not a blind groping for æsthetic ideas to express; nor an unquestioning obedience to the dictates of caprice or individual feeling. The æsthetic ideas lie all within the range of the relationship of the building to its special uses and to the character of the national life. His one ideal will be composed of the ideas thus given him. It may be his duty to select; to give more exclusive prominence to one than to another of such æsthetic ideas. But his work is a purely rational one, not one that is blind and at hap-hazard.

All ideas so far as regarded in form, ideas of beauty.

There are no ideas of beauty which may be taken up and wrought into a building, outside of those that are given in the relationships mentioned. These are the only ideas of beauty for use here. They become æsthetic by being suitably expressed. The enumeration of ideas "conveyable by art"—the ideas of power, imitation, truth, beauty, and relation, given by Ruskin in his admirable work—Modern Painters—starts from a fundamentally erroneous notion, both of idea and of beauty; and is fitted to mislead. All ideas from their very nature as ideas in so far as they are capable of being expressed, in so far as they may come into form, are ideas of beauty, in the only conceivable sense of this very vague expression. They are distinguished from ideas of truth only as different phases of the same. The same idea becomes one of truth as it is regarded in itself—in its own interior relations to its parts, or in its exterior relations to ideas without—and one of beauty as it is regarded merely as expressed—as mere form. The evil here flowing from this teaching of an admirable yet often unphilosophical writer, is that the artist is put upon a search after ideas of beauty so called entirely outside of the sphere of the object of his art. The ideas immediately given in the design and relations of the proposed building are the only ideas of beauty with which the architect in a given case is to concern himself. His work, to be truly artistic, æsthetic, must be thus intelligently and rationally prompted and regulated. The vices in art, the false taste in art, we may attribute mainly to the irrational search after some fancied idea of beauty, which if anything else than idea regarded as form, in distinction from idea regarded as of truth or of goodness, has no existence. If a so-called idea of power, of imitation, of truth, or of relation, be not an idea of beauty, then it was wrong to introduce these into an æsthetic work as coördinate with ideas of beauty. They are æsthetic only as ideas of beauty; that is, only as ideas regarded not in their essential nature or their object or end, but simply as expressed—in form. In other words every idea possible to a rational spirit is an idea of beauty if viewed simply as expressed or revealed.

Other departments of architecture.

§ 144. It is unnecessary to apply more specifically the law of idea to the other departments of architecture. They vary in respect to both economic and æsthetic ideas and their relative predominance. In Memorial Architecture, the ideas are chiefly æsthetic and are for the most part given in the character of the person or event to be memorialized, or in their relations to society or to history. Commercial Architecture, as applied to the uses of trade, or of business, follows more the lead of economical ideas; while theatrical architecture may pay higher regard to the more proper æsthetic ideas. The law of idea is one for all:—Find the ideas to be expressed in the designs of the structure and its relationships and let these compose the one ideal. Its perfectness will consist in its exactness and fullness as composed of these specific ideas, and in the harmony in which they are combined.

Art respects permanence.

§ 145. THE LAW OF MATERIAL IN ARCHITECTURE. It is only in respect to enduring structures that Architecture deserves consideration as an æsthetic art. Although it had its beginnings in the movable tent, the perishable cabin, or the cave that could be left at any moment of necessity without a thought of loss, it has had its growth as an art in connection with the idea of permanence. In the pyramid, the temple, the palace, architectural genius has sought to immortalize itself, and this expectation of continuance has been its inspiration to its highest executions and best achievements. The materials which have been employed under the control of this principle of permanence are chiefly stone, brick, wood, and iron. These materials have each its own characteristics and adaptations, affording to the architect a wider or narrower field of selection and arrangement.

Kinds of materials.

Further, these materials in form address the imagination through the sense of sight; and through this sense, chiefly through outline, but in a less degree through light and shade, and also through color. To each of these mediums of revelation, accordingly, architectural art must have regard.

Imagination addressed through sight.

§ 146. The use of stone in architecture can be traced back to the earlier stages of human history. In the ancient Petra, Hebrew *Sela*—both names signifying rock—the cave, with its rough walls, was gradually transformed into the beautiful temple with its corridors and pediment, its columns and capitals:—well illustrating the growth of architectural art from the primitive rudeness of nature to the highest forms

Use of Stone.

of artistic creation. So well fitted for permanence, for shelter and defense from the elements, from savage beasts and from savage men, it naturally invited to its use for all these purposes. It moreover well satisfied the various demands of the æsthetic nature, as it is susceptible of being readily wrought into the most diversified and most pleasing forms; it is thus a highly expressive material. To this adaptation to the uses of expressive art, sculpture owes its origin and growth.

While the facilities for producing this material will be a controlling principle in selecting, there will be wide room for judgment and taste in selection furnished in the different characters of hardness, resistance to elements, susceptibility of cleavage and delicate chiseling, of color also, which different kinds of rock possess. Each kind has its own characteristic expression, and consequently each its peculiar adaptation to the different departments of architecture. There is moreover a possibility of combination of different kinds of rock in the same structure, either by appropriating one kind to one part or use and another kind to another, or by combining two or more kinds in the same part.

Of Brick.

§ 147. The use of brick, either of clay simply baked in the sun *(adóbe)* or hardened by artificial heat melting its more fusible ingredients, and molded into convenient size and shape, can also be traced back to antehistoric times. Unlike the other architectural materials —stone, wood, and iron—it enters but little into free art, inasmuch as it has but a very feeble expressive power. Æsthetic art accepts it as a condition but not as its best and most perfect instrument as means of expression, and builds on or over it, covering it from view.

Of Wood. § 148. Wood was likewise ever a common material in building. Its peculiar properties as such material, to a great extent determined the leading features of Grecian architecture, as seen in the column, the architrave, and the roof. Its liability to decay naturally invites the use of paint as a protective, and thus leads to the artistic study and use of architectural coloring.

Of Iron. § 149. Iron has but recently been employed to any considerable extent in building. Its hardness, strength, permanence, capability of being molded into desirable forms, as well as considerations of economy, have been its leading recommendations. It is well adapted to express ideas of this class. Mr. Ruskin, indeed, maintains "that true architecture does not admit iron as a constructive material." But he finds it difficult to justify the sweeping principle, and after allowing exception after exception, finally comes to think "that metals may be used as a cement but not as a support." Yet his allowed exceptions are in part violations of this restricted rule. But although nature does not shelter with artificial iron as she does with her stone grottoes and her windfall cabins of wood, and therefore iron structures are no imitation of what is found in nature, yet we may rather suspect the correctness of the principle that art must ever be such imitation than accept the inconsistencies into which its earnest advocate is driven. Far more justly does Mr. Fergusson maintain that "in none of its stages is imitation an element of composition; no true building ever was designed to look like any thing in either the animal, vegetable, or mineral kingdoms." The simple question is: can iron represent fitly to us any idea? If so, it must so far be admitted to be a proper æsthetic material.

Outline. § 150. As it is chiefly through outline that architecture addresses the imagination, the leading principles of the art, so far as they regard the material, will chiefly respect the effect of figure. Hence the more capital rules of the art look to lines as continuous or broken, as straight or curved; to surfaces as geometrically regular and complete or otherwise; to dimensions and proportions.

Light and Shade. § 151. The effect of light and shade must also be carefully studied in the whole architectural design. The parts which although necessary are yet not so conducive to artistic expression will need to be thrown back or even shaded, if it may be, while the more expressive elements will be so disposed as to receive and reflect the light. Particularly in decoration will this principle require careful study.

Color. § 152. The use of color presents questions of more difficult solution to the artist. Besides the choice and disposition of materials with reference to their natural color, there comes up for primary consideration the propriety of artificial coloring and then the determination of what colors and what disposition of them.

That art should never deceive is a proposition which has some truth in it but must receive a very limited and carefully guarded interpretation or it will fatally mislead. All imitative art proposes to represent truly; but its representative products can never be exactly what its originals are. A portrait is not all that the living man is or was. A literal Chinese imitation is of less worth than an idealized representation of character. A photograph cannot in a front view present the features in their respective projection and retreat as they are partially represented in a profile. It cannot give the face in all respects as it actually is. If the artist color it to supplement the process and so give the complexion, is that to be accounted a deception that should be condemned? When the architect carves a four-leaved figure upon an elevated part of the building far removed from the eye of the observer which he intends to be taken for a *quatre foil*, a four-leaved plant, is he by the deception violating the spirit of true art? Paint on wood to protect it from the elements is allowed by the most rigid advocates of truthfulness in art. Is it required by this principle of truth that it be so applied as to represent this and only this? "If it be clearly understood," says Mr. Ruskin, "that a marble facing does not pretend or imply a marble wall, there is no harm in it." Must a work of art be approved so long as the motive of the artist is unknown, but be condemned so soon as it is discovered that his motive in choosing the material was wrong when tried before a merely moral tribunal? Must art necessarily be tried morally before it can be judged æsthetically? Although what is immoral can never in itself be beautiful, and all immorality as all ignorance and error must so far as it appears in art of necessity be a blemish and defect even as æsthetically regarded, yet art does not necessarily in essential features always reveal the moral disposition of the artist; nor can the artistic merit of its products be measured by his moral deserts. If the ideas he represents are true and right, if the material be fitted to reveal them, and if the meaning be correct, art-criticism can not go back into the heart of the artist before it can justify its approval. Even Mr. Ruskin, exacting as he is with his Lamp of Truth, which yet, it must be said, seems to burn with impure oil, confesses that painting is not such deception as he condemns.* "Whatever the material," he says, "good painting makes it more precious; nor can it ever be said to deceive respecting the ground of which it gives us no information. To cover brick with plaster, and this plaster with fresco, is, therefore, perfectly legitimate; and as desirable mode of decoration, as it is constant in the great periods. Verona and Venice are now seen deprived of more than half their former splendor; it depended far more on their frescoes than their marbles." The

* Seven Lamps of Architecture, c. II, §15.

use of paint, then, is æsthetically right. When and how to use it are questions for the artist to be solved by the fundamental principles that all art must worthily reveal just idea by fitting material. Marbled shop fronts are not to be reprobated æsthetically as if falsehoods, for they deceive no one and were never intended to deceive; they are censurable because they do not reveal any just idea of art properly. The language of Mr. Fergusson is strong, but is expressive of real truth when he pronounces color to be "one of the most invaluable elements placed at the command of the architect." While external polychromy has not been completely successful, he declares that "with regard to interiors there can be no doubt. All architects in all countries of the world resorted to this expedient to harmonize and to give brilliancy to their compositions and depended upon it for their most important effects."

§ 153. III. THE LAW OF MECHANICAL DESIGN IN ARCHITECTURE.—The Law of Form we found to distribute itself into the three departments of Style, Design, and Expression. Of these, the first and the last—the laws of style and of expression—do not call for more special consideration. It is sufficient to observe in respect to the last mentioned, that here the proper function of the architect yields to those of the mason, the carpenter, and the sculptor. Even masonry and carpentry, although proper mechanic arts, yet admit of æsthetic expression in the execution of the plans of the architect; for intelligence, skill, power, freedom, may and should mark all human effort. By enlisting these in its service, toil redeems itself from drudgery, and work puts on beauty and grace. Sculpture is itself an æsthetic art; and the most celebrated architects, as Phidias, Polycletus, Scopas, Callimachus, among the Greeks; Boschetto, Brunelleschi, Michael Angelo and others of the Italians, were eminent sculptors who, more or less, wrought out with their own hands the forms by which their structures were to be beautified. The special laws of form applicable to architecture, deserving particular consideration, are those of design which we have recognized as of three divisions—mechanical, artistic, and decorative.

Laws of Mechanical Design.

§ 154. The laws of mechanical design in architecture respect the dependent side of the art, and look to the ends other than such as are purely æsthetic which a building is to effect. The artist is here to study how best to embody these ends in the given material. He has the character of the material to consider on the one hand, and the demands of these particular ends on the other, that his embodiment of the one in the other may give æsthetic satisfaction.

1. In respect to material.

The particulars to be regarded vary, in the first place, with the kind and nature of the material. Its strength in reference to the parts which it is to support, and its weight or pressure on the sustaining parts, its capabilities of resisting outward violence, as of the elements, and its adaptations to the interior uses, are to be weighed. Stone supports vertical pressure, but is relatively weak to resist horizontal strain. It is heavy, moreover, and requires for itself firm supports. Iron supports, and binds, and also sustains from above; but its pressure is heavier than wood. Such are specimens of the problems which mechanical design is to solve when looking more at the material in reference to the ends or aims of the structure.

2. To ends of Structure.

In the next place mechanical design has to look more directly at the ends for which the building is proposed, while still in reference to the material in which these ends are to be embodied. Here the particulars vary so indefinitely as to forbid enumeration. It will be sufficient to exemplify by the mention of a few. The fundamental idea of shelter in its largest significance with its associated ideas of repose and comfort, is to be carried into the mechanical design throughout. Then the special ones of the building, comprehending all the conveniences which it should furnish, come into consideration. More specifically may be enumerated, in exemplification of what mechanical design is called to regard, the kind, the pitch, the projection of the roof; the thickness and composition of the outer walls; the general arrangement of the rooms in reference to the light and the prevailing storms; the means of warming and of ventilating, so important yet in general so illconsidered in modern architecture, both domestic and public; the provisions for ingress and egress; the acoustic and optical arrangements in buildings designed for music, oral discourse, and theatrical exhibition.

Its meaning.

§ 155. IV. THE LAW OF ARTISTIC DESIGN. — While mechanical design has regard only to the ends of utility, artistic design looks farther to the æsthetic form of a building. The rudest art may secure sufficient support to all its parts; the animal instincts of the beaver are competent to this: the æsthetic nature of man requires that beyond these mechanical demands, intelligence, feeling, moral goodness, in the fullest degree mingle in the work that contrives and executes the mechanical support. The limits are, as before intimated, those of the inventive spirit and of means, for we must ever remember that art is the daughter of Jupiter the creator, and of Plusia the goddess of wealth. Mechanical supports the artist converts into columns and arches and buttresses, that do an infinitely higher ministry than that of sustaining weight.

Law twofold:—

The æsthetic principles which rule in this department of the art are comprehensively these:—

1. Must respect ends.

1. That the ends of utility in the building, the nature of the material, and the mechanical requisites never be overlooked; but that the æsthetic procedure coöperate throughout in completest harmony with them.

2. Must respect line, light, and color.

2. That the æsthetic expression be determined by the principles of outline, light and shade, and color through which architecture addresses the imagination. The more specific rules which are immediately comprehended under these two general laws, are mainly

those of support derived from the mechanical side of the art, and those of intellectual beauty derived from the ideal side.

Emotive power. The principles of emotive beauty have, indeed, their wide application in this art. One can hardly appreciate in the lowest degree the excellency of architectural art, whether, as it is displayed in the Grecian temple, the Roman basilica, or the Gothic church, unless he discern the warm sympathetic heart that so lovingly and so patiently poured itself into the outmost details of his work, and the free, unselfish, and richly cultivated skill and power which has designed and executed all. But these requisites to successful art must be prescribed in the general rather than be elaborated in formal rules of specific practice.

Power. The elements of freedom and power have likewise their wide application here. But only one has such rank and prominence as to require distinct mention. In architecture, more than in other arts, the æsthetic character of a product depends on mere magnitude as an expression of power—of free ability. It is the vastness of such structures as the Egyptian pyramid and the Hindoo temple, the Roman amphitheater and the Christian Church, the immense area they fill, the massiveness of their walls, the loftiness of their domes and towers and spires, the infinitude of their parts and decorations, which chiefly engage the imagination and inspire the admiration of the beholder. It is grandeur which has characterized the ideal of the great architects of the world. The power which can express itself in the work, commanding field and means and skill, with a freedom as nearly as possible approximating that of the Divine architect, is a leading element in all architectural genius.

Law of support requires both actual and apparent support.

§ 156. I. *The Law of Support.* This law, as a regulative principle of æsthetic art, requires that every part of a structure appear to the eye of the observer to be adequately supported. Wherever there is a want in this respect, the eye of the contemplating imagination is offended; the building does not express its true character. Stone, brick, wood, iron, have gravity, and must be sustained, or their very nature is disregarded. It is not enough that there be support, but that the building show that such support does or may for aught that appears exist. Whenever the imagination is put upon difficult labor to fashion out in what way this necessity is met in a building, there is imperfection.

A support may be vertical or horizontal, as walls may be pressed downward or outward by unsustained weight. Vertical supports are either from beneath or from above, by direct support or by suspension. The one comprehensive law of support requires that in whatever direction the pressure or strain may come, there shall appear to the observer a possible support adequate to resist the downward pressure or the lateral thrust. Mechanical design demands the provision of the actual support; it is incumbent on artistic design, to see to it that such supports do not appear to be lacking.

The law forbids columns and pilasters, or appearances of them, which have no base; projections from walls, as oriel windows, which show no means of support for them coming out of the walls; and brackets or corbels which are designed to show such support, but have no support themselves; towers or domes at a distance from upright walls and columns, and so, as being without apparent support, threatening to crush in all below them. This is the negative or prohibitory law of artistic design.

Law of intellectual beauty.

§ 157. 2. *The Laws of Intellectual Beauty.*—The several principles of art-production which are founded in the intelligence, as a necessary organic element in every rational effort, have a greater relative predominance in architecture than in any other of the great æsthetic arts. These principles are unity, contrast, æsthetic number, proportion, symmetry, and harmony.

Requires unity.

§ 158. (1.) *Law of Unity.*—The ground of this æsthetic principle of unity we have found to be in the intelligence with which the æsthetic nature is united in one rational being. Every rational procedure must have one end, one direction, one aim. Where, therefore, as in a building, there are parts, this rational principle of unity requires that they be so grouped and subordinated that the imagination addressed, as itself also rational and able to interpret only what is rational, shall be able to apprehend all as forming one whole. Unity is not the exclusive element of beauty, as some have taught; but it is a universally necessary condition of beauty in all art.

This principle of unity is to be applied, not only to the whole structure as having one end, one design, and one comprehensive use, but also to each part, which should be wrought out as a whole itself, having all its parts so disposed that they may be regarded as one. It is one application of this principle which requires that the exterior, as in the string-courses marking on the outside the divisions into stories, should correspond to the interior—no part should belie the whole or any other part.

Contrast.

§ 159. (2.) *Law of Contrast.*— Mere uniformity and bald simplicity have only a very low æsthetic rank. Diversity, variety, richness, ever enhance beauty, as they bespeak a higher, larger, livelier imagination. But as æsthetic diversity rests upon a broader unity, it appears in art as true contrast, in which the diverse parts or elements are regarded as indeed different, yet as tied together in a true unity, as belonging to one whole. Architecture avails itself of this principle everywhere—in size, in form, in light, in color. The magnitude of a structure, of its area and of its height, can be shown only by contrast. We enter into an adequate conception of the vastness of St. Peter's at Rome only as we measure its immense reaches by some relatively small object, as the angels supporting the lavers, or the bronze statue of St. Peter, or some more integral part of the building, as a chapel or a column. The apparent greatness of a structure, indeed, depends in a large degree on the skillful contrasting of like parts. The simplicity and uniformity of a Grecian temple make it appear much smaller than a Byzantian cathedral of the same size, with its manifold domes of varying dimensions, or a Gothic church, with its multiplied parts.

So the beauty of form and of outline may be greatly enhanced by the variations from the rectilinear to the curvilinear, by diversity of curves, by combinations of the vertical with horizontal lines. In like manner, a great part of the beauty in a colonnade and in architectural sculpture and other decoration depends on the skillful contrasts of light and shade. The illimitable combinations of colors have in all styles of architecture, by the tasteful contrasting of hues, been turned to æsthetic account. Polychromy, indeed, both exterior and interior, constitutes one leading department in the art of architecture.

The fundamental principle regulating the use of contrast is, that in the diversity introduced, the unity on which it rests never be violated or obscured.

Moreover, contrast is not by any means the sole nor the governing principle in art. It must ever keep its place as in harmony with other principles, and often as subordinate to them.

Limitation.

§ 160. (3.) *Law of Æsthetic Number, or of Euarithmy.*—The eye of imagination, which architecture immediately addresses, can take in but a limited number of objects into its vision at once. Metaphysicians have variously fixed the limit of easy apprehension from four to seven. But although it may not be possible to determine the limit on any metaphysical ground, a great multiplicity of parts is perplexing and confusing, and consequently a hindrance to the experience of visual beauty. Hindoo architecture, which has manifested a tendency to run off into endless subdivisions, stands in wide contrast in this respect with the simplicity of the Grecian orders, which, presenting the leading parts in great distinctness from one another, at the same time admit but few subdivisions.

Proportion.

§ 161. (4.) *Law of Proportion.*—This law respects the special relation to be secured between the parts of a building and the whole. As architecture has to deal to so great an extent with masses, and has to rely for its æsthetic effect so much on these special relations between the members and the whole, the study of proportion has engaged a leading part of the attention of theoretical architects. Search has been instituted for some fixed mathematical principle which may be relied upon to satisfy all æsthetic demands. The analogies in the mathematical relations of position in which the germinal points in plants stand to one another and to the whole, and in the mathematical relations of musical sounds, have seemed to furnish some ground for hope that such a search might be successful. The results of these inquiries have not thus far been entirely satisfactory. The most perfectly proportioned buildings of ancient and modern construction, as even the master-pieces of sculpture, have been carefully measured and averages have been taken in the hope that the principle of all architectural proportion might be definitely ascertained. The rule of the "golden section" has been one of the fruits of these researches. This principle is the same as the geometrical section into extreme and mean ratio. A line is said to be so cut when the square on the larger of the two parts is equal to the rectangle of the whole line and the less part; or when the whole bears the same ratio to the greater part that this part bears to the less. In other words this theory of a perfect architectural proportion prescribes that lines be so cut as that the larger part shall be a little over three-fifths of the whole line or more nearly six hundred and eighteen thousandths of the whole. Another mathematical principle of proportions thus reached, is that of Hay, who maintains that the beauty of proportion depends on the visual angle. He has in accordance with this theory constructed a scale of angular proportions, taking the right angle as the most perfect angle for æsthetic effect. Mr. Fergusson, once more, prescribes as the rule of proportion for a room, that its "height ought to be equal to half its width plus the square root of its length."

Golden Section.

Hay's rule of visual angle.

The law to be found in study of ideas and material.

It is questionable whether any such rules of absolute proportion which are grounded on principles not given at once in the ideas and the material of the art, can be relied on to any extent. The nature of the material itself, as having gravity and so needing support, gives one principle of proportion, viz:—that the support be adequate to sustain the weight which rests upon it. This principle must regard the character of the material. Stone is heavier than wood, requires a stronger and so a more massive support; wood on the other hand is weaker as support than stone; while iron still farther differs in both respects from both stone and wood. The rule, consequently, of some architects, that the support should be equal to the weight, is without good reason.

Still more must the ideas expressed in the building, both the ideas originating in its end or uses, and the proper æsthetic ideas which are suggested by these ends but yet not essential in them, vary the rule of proportion to be observed in a given case. Ideas of power, majesty, stability, permanence, lead to proportions entirely different from those of the Ionic and the Corinthian.

It is thus seen that the principles of architectural proportion are to be derived not from some standard assumed from without, but from a careful study of the nature of the ideas to be expressed and the material to be employed.

Symmetry respects relations of parts to one another.

§ 162. (5.) *Law of Symmetry.*—While proportion respects the relations of the parts to the whole, symmetry respects the relations of the coördinate parts to one another. It requires that whatever dimensions are adopted in one member shall be adopted for every other like member. This law is founded on the same principle in our nature as the law of unity—the most perfect reason has but one most perfect mode of accomplishing its end in the same circumstances. No two branches of a tree, no two leaves are exactly equal; but so far as there is no ground for difference, likeness is maintained. It is thus that nature maintains the unity in a pleasing diversity. So if the weight to be sustained and all the relations to other parts, as well as to the light, the air, the surroundings generally, are the same, the law of symmetry requires that the columns of a building should be alike. Variations must be determined by differences that are actually ascertained and known. Only as these are known can the variation be justified. The keen æsthetic sense of the Greek architects deviated from exact symmetry in the diameter of the column at the angles of a building as compared with the others to obviate the different effect of light. In the Parthenon the deviation is one forty-fourth part of the diameter, in the temple of Theseus one twenty-eighth part. But the principle of symmetry still holds that, except for known cause, like members be of like dimensions. The law applies obviously to openings in walls, as for doors and windows, to all spaces as well as to columns and solid walls, to lines and surfaces as well as to solids.

Harmony requires likeness in like parts.

§ 163. (6.) *Law of Harmony.* — The same principle of reason which demands unity and symmetry enjoins also harmony. The import of this principle is that the rational grounds for adopting any one dimension, or figure, or color, should govern in the adoption of every other dimension and figure and color, except so far as the special case calls for different treatment. It is in this way that the diversity which the peculiarities of the individual part may prescribe, is harmonized by the application of the same rule to all the parts so far as there is likeness; and the æsthetic nature becomes thus satisfied with the form as perfect. This principle, in one of its applications, may be recognized in the human body. Each of every pair of members, as of hands, arms, eyes, etc., is like the other of the pair; but one is on the right side, the other on the left, and this difference in position necessitates corresponding difference in the form. The one is not the exact repetition, but rather the reflection of the other; the one is turned in one direction, the other in the opposite. But the whole expression is one. There is harmony as well as symmetry;—oneness, agreement, likeness, in essential properties, and in offices and relations, as well as in mere dimensions.

§ 164. Exemplification of the Principles of Architectural Design in the Leading Styles of the Art in History.—Every nation and every tribe has its style of building. Some genius invents what convenience, economy, taste, recommend, and the common mind, from ignorance or indolence, accepts and copies. The divers modes of life, with the diversities of wants incident to them, the character of the climate and of the soil, the supply of materials, lead to so many different styles of building. The wandering nomad erects his tent; and naturally carries over the form to which he has been wonted, into more solid structures when he settles into more permanent abodes. Chinese architecture is of the tent type. The rich agricultural plains of Babylonia led to permanent settlements, and in the want of stone and timber, the inhabitants developed a style which the abundant clay and bitumen as their most available materials prescribed. Egypt built gigantic pyramidal structures on the out-cropping rocky strata that bound the moist, yielding soil of its great river bottoms from materials supplied by its convenient quarries of granite and sandstone. Greece elaborated its noble architecture in a mild, sunny climate, on a rocky soil, with mountains of marble. Western and northern Europe availed itself of its forests and timber, and formed a style which such material invited or suggested.

Three leading styles.

Of these historic styles of architecture only three—the Grecian, the Roman, and the Gothic—need be explored for the desirable exemplifications of the general principles that have been presented. They have been significantly characterized by the modes in which they respectively roof spaces; the Greek roofs with a flat stone; the Roman, with a circular arch; the Gothic, with a pointed arch composed of circular segments. It was entirely natural that artistic genius should apply itself predominantly to this its most difficult function to provide support for coverings to doorways, to passages, to compartments, as well as to the whole interior of a structure, and to expend here the wealth of its resources. Styles of architecture arose as the chief exertions of the art were directed upon this element. Besides the three styles of commanding interest just mentioned, respectively characterized by this mode of roofing spaces, we find Hindoo architecture prominently marking itself by an arch, not radiating as in the Roman and Gothic, which is formed by wedge-shaped stones, but horizontal, being formed by stones laid flatwise and overlapping each other like inverted steps. Not improbably this simple mode of covering a space in a wall was the original of all arches. Hindoo architecture retained the horizontal position of the stones as in the rest of the wall, and thus worked out a peculiar style, beveling off the overlapping stones, and inserting corner pieces and brackets with most elaborate skill and rich intricacy of work. The horse-shoe arch, in the same way, has given character to certain styles of the art, as in Moorish architecture. In recent times the *truss* has been employed to sustain vaults and domes with characteristic effect.

Characteristic of Grecian architecture.

§ 165. 1. *Grecian Architecture.* — The Grecian style of architecture, as has been intimated, is characterized by upright walls, the space between which is covered by a horizontal beam. Its characteristic lines are right lines, not curved; its angles are right angles; the directions of the lines vertical and horizontal. The conditions of the climate, however, compelled the Greek to pitch his roof, in order to carry off the rain. The æsthetic character grounds

Its elements.

itself on these simple elements :—upright walls, horizontal ties, slightly pitching roof. The inventive genius of the Greeks had but a narrow scope within the limits of these elements; but with most marvelous activity of imagination and delicacy of taste did they fulfill the æsthetic mission allotted them. Instead of naked walls for supports, they substituted columns, and made the column the typal element of their architecture. They developed the simple flat stone or timber beam into the rich entablature, and the gable into the graceful pediment. The free art of sculpture, maturing itself at the same time, at once both aided and shaped the development of the sister art. Particularly in perfection of outline and in optical effect, Grecian art attained peculiar excellence. It calculated the effect of relative distance, and of the position of the beholder and the relation of the parts of the building to the light with extreme mathematical minuteness, giving to the column the slight swell already noticed, called *entasis*, and to projecting parts a slight pitch, thus deviating from real directness of line to secure apparent directness.

Orders.

Grecian architecture within these general characteristics diversified itself in three leading modes, called orders, from the more staid and simple Doric, to the more graceful Ionic and the more ornate Corinthian. The characteristic features of these several orders are found in the column and its capital. But variations in the form of the column occasioned variations also in the whole façade or front of the structure. This was conveniently regarded as of three parts: the column, the beam-part or entablature con-

The three members.

necting the columns and reaching from wall to wall, and the triangular gable or pediment between the beam and the roof. Each of these has been conveniently viewed as of three principal parts. The column was regarded as composed of the base, the shaft, and the capital. The entablature had for its component parts the beam proper or architrave, the frieze, and the cornice. The gable or pediment, moreover, had its base, and its cornice, and the triangular space between, called the *tympanum*.

The three members of the column.

Of the entablature.

Of the pediment.

I. Doric order

§ 166. The Doric column properly had no base; it rested directly on the stylobate or platform of the building. A pedestal, however, was in later times introduced, consisting of three parts, the base, die, and cymatium or cornice. The shaft was fluted, the flutes or channels being preferably twenty, but allowably sixteen or twenty-four in number, more shallow than in the other orders, and meeting on a sharp edge at the surface. The height of the shaft, measured in the usual way by the lower diameter as the unit of measure, varied in different structures from four diameters to six and a half. The shaft contracts with a slight conoidal curve or swell, called *entasis*, diminishing its diameter from bottom to top about one-fifth. The capital of the column was about one-half of a diameter in height, and consisted of three parts: 1, a necking of one or more annulets or circular fillets; 2, a convex quarter-circle molding, called

Shaft.

ovolo; and 3, a square stone-abacus immediately supporting the entablature.

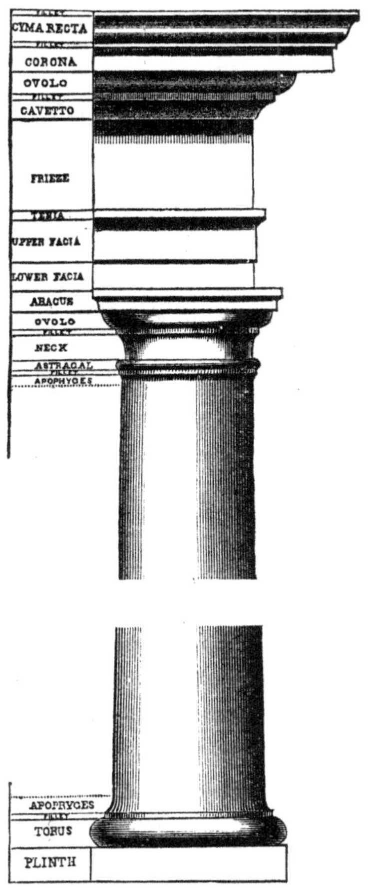

Grecian Column.

Entablature. The entablature varied in height from a little more than one diameter of the column, as in the temple at Paestum, to over two diameters, as in the temple at Selinus. It consisted of three parts: 1, The architrave, a beam with a plain surface, resting directly on the abacus of the column; 2, the frieze, having its surface broken by projections or tablets, called *triglyphs*, which were divided into three equal parts by two vertical channels or *glyphs*, a half channel being cut on each side, and were placed one over each column and one between, thus leaving spaces called *metopes*, which were sometimes richly ornamented with relief work; and 3, the cornice.

Pediment.

The pediment consisted of its base, the triangular space called the tympanum or drum which was often ornamented with statuary, and the cornice.

There were great variations within the general limits of relative massiveness and simplicity, as compared with the other orders. The proportions—in all the dimensions of height, breadth, and depth or projection—both in the parts of the building and in the spaces, the number of subordinate parts, the moldings, and the decorations, varied according to the site, the size, the means at the disposal of the builder, and his own individual taste or judgment. Among the decorations often added may be mentioned in particular, the drops—*guttae*—under the triglyphs, and the small blocks—*mutules*—attached to the under surface or *soffit* of the *corona* or chief projecting part of the cornice. These mutules were placed over the triglyphs and the metopes, and were wrought with three rows of six guttae in each.

The Parthenon.

§ 167. The Doric order is perhaps best exemplified in the famous Parthenon of Athens, built in the most flourishing period of Grecian art, the age of Pericles, a little over four hundred years before the Christian era, under the superintendence of the architect Ictinus and the sculptor Phidias. It is built of the white Pentelican marble, and stands upon a platform

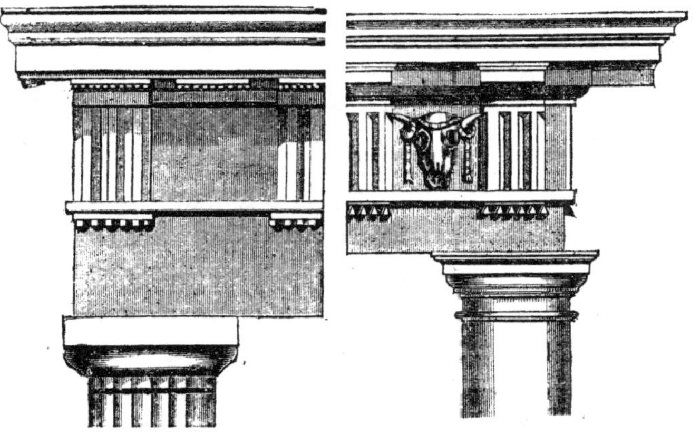

Doric Order.

or *stylobate* reached by three steps, each one foot and nine inches high and two feet and four inches wide. It is *peripteral,* that is, colonnaded all round, and *octostyle,* having eight columns on each end, there being besides fifteen columns on each side, making forty-six in all. The temple is 228 feet long, 101.33 feet broad, and 59 feet high from the surface of the stylobate to the top of the pediment. The columns are fluted, and rest immediately on the stylobate without a base. The height of the shaft is a little more than five and a half times the lower diameter, being 34.232 feet, and the diameter being 6.15 feet, and the capital is slightly less than half a diameter. The distance between the columns —the *inter-columniation*, as it is called—is a little more than one diameter and a fourth.

The metopes in the frieze were filled with sculpture in relief by Phidias, of the most exquisite skill.

The pediment had a roof pitch of fourteen degrees only. The tympanum was ornamented by statuary by Phidias.

The body of the temple within the peristyle—the cell—was 193 feet long and 71 feet wide, having eight columns on each end. It was divided into two parts, the larger of which contained the great statue of the goddess Minerva to whom the temple was dedicated. The cell was *hypaethral*, that is, it was lighted through an open space above. Mr. Fergusson, however, thinks it was lighted through openings in the upper part of the walls, making a kind of clere-story.

The bounding lines, for the purpose of securing apparent directness and sharpness against irradiation and other effects of light, are slightly curved. The platform or stylobate, thus, is slightly convex, being highest in the middle; the columns have the entasis, and those at the angles are thicker than the others by one-fiftieth of a diameter. They also dip inwardly. With such nice care did the architect labor to secure every where the appearance of perfect straightness and sharpness of outline and give the charm of distinctness and fullness of contrast, yet with no displeasing abruptness or chasm. The eye took in readily the whole as one, and passed from part to part without a leap or a stop, rising along the upright parts to the top, only to be led gently down again along the easy pitch of the roof, or to some horizontal line only to be conducted to some upright, free to turn upwards or downwards, to the right or to the left, round and round with unceasing variety, never tiring and never dropping its hold on the contemplation. Unlike the Gothic which carried the view upward and launched it into the mysterious abyss above to which it pointed, or like the Roman which kept the view confined to the single circle round which it ever carried the eye, giving it no point from which to escape its endless whirl, the Grecian kept the view, ever upon itself, yet never chained it to a single member—allowing perfect freedom, yet only within its own charmed limits, thus entrancing and delighting with a perfect beauty.

Ionic Order. § 168. The Ionic order was coeval with the Doric. It is supposed to be of Assyrian origin. Its characteristic expression was lightness and elegance.

The distinguishing feature was the capital of the column, which presented in front a double volute or scroll, the spirals of which spread gracefully each way from the axis of the column and terminated in a center or eye, sometimes flat, sometimes conical, and sometimes in the form of a rosette. The size of these volutes, the character and numbers of the spirals, and the ornamentation, varied greatly. The capitals of the columns at the corners of a peristyle required special treatment in order to maintain uniformity ; and the difficulties were met in various ways.

The shaft of the column was relatively higher and consequently slenderer than the Doric shaft, but tapered less. It was from a little over eight to over nine diameters in height. The flutes were shallower and the edges were covered by a fillet. They were

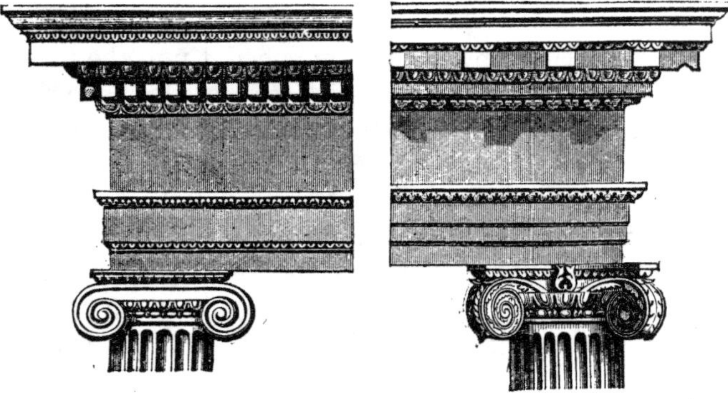

Ionic Order

continued into the capital above and into the base below by a part called an *Escape*, Greek *Apophyge* French *congè*.

The base varied. That of the temple of the Ilyssus was nearly two diameters in height, and consisted of a plinth or square member at the bottom rising about one third of the whole height of the base, a plain *torus* or semi-circular convex molding about one-sixth ; a *scotia* or concave molding with a fillet above and below of the same height ; and a horizontally fluted torus with a bead and a fillet connecting with the apophyge.

The entablature consisted of an architrave, sometimes plain, sometimes broken into three horizontal corners or bands called *fasciae* or *faciae;* a frieze also plain ; and a cornice which, like the other two parts of the entablature, admitted a greater number of moldings, plain or carved, and was sometimes ornamented with *dentils* or toothlike blocks placed upright closely together, and *modillions* or bracket-like projections under the corona.

III. Corinthian Order.

§ 169. The Corinthian was the most ornate of the Grecian orders. Its characteristic feature is in the capital of the column. This had a larger diameter and a greater height in proportion to the whole column

Corinthian Order.

than in the other orders. It had two horizontal rows of eight leaves in each row surrounding it, and other leaves with volutes over them supporting the abacus. Vitruvius narrates that the idea was suggested to Callimachus, the famous Grecian builder, by this incident. The nurse of a Corinthian maiden who had died, had brought to her tomb a basket of articles to which the maiden had been partial when alive, and placed it with a tile laid upon it over the root of an acanthus plant. Towards spring, the plant threw out stems and foliage which, climbing the basket, reached the overlaid tile, and bending over formed graceful volutes. Callimachus, as he was passing, was attracted by the form and took the hint for the capitals in the buildings he was erecting about Corinth. The Egyptians, however, had long before the time of Callimachus used the essential features of this capital.

The shaft was fluted with twenty-four channels, which were some times *cabled*, that is, were so cut down through the lower third as to present the appearance of a cable laid in the bottom of the flute.

The entablature had an architrave like the Ionic, which was either plain or banded, a frieze plain or sculptured, and a cornice with a deep projection to correspond with the capital.

This order admitted a rich ornamentation.

Tuscan and Composite Orders.

§ 170. With these three classic Grecian orders, the Doric, Ionic, and Corinthian, two others have been associated. The one, the Tuscan, is characterized by extreme plainness and solidity ; the other, the Composite, by extreme lightness and richness. The Tuscan, which is of the heaviest and most massive Doric in its general proportions, is without ornamentation; the Composite, which is of the lightest Corinthian in its general proportions, is profusely ornamented and is more precisely distinguished as combining the characteristic double volute of the Ionic with the foliage of the Corinthian capital.

Roman architecture curvilinear.

§ 171. ROMAN ARCHITECTURE. The characteristic feature of Roman art is in the use of curved instead of straight lines, which rule in Grecian Architecture. The Romans probably were indebted for this element in building to the Etruscans. Early in Roman history, in the age of the Tarquins, the famous sewer, *cloaca maxima*, called by Pliny the greatest of all works, was built of a circular form. A quarter of a mile in length of this great work from its mouth on the banks of the Tiber, still remains, 2500 years since its construction. The famous Pantheon, built, both the portico and the body of the temple according to Prof. Nibby, by Marcus Agrippa, 26 years before the christian era, was circular; and the still more famous Coliseum or Flavian amphitheatre commenced by the Emperor Vespasian and finished by Domitian, was elliptical in its general form. The immense aqueducts were supported on circular arches; and the structures which were designed in purest beauty, as temples, triumphal arches, and tombs, also availed themselves of this element of beauty and of strength. If right lines properly express order and rational aim, curved lines suggest freedom. A regular curve is the natural expression of a fuller rational nature, as it is the result and sign of a movement that has been not only in intelligence, but also in freedom. Roman art having received Grecian ideas and culture wrought this new element of expression into the Grecian orders.

Pantheon.

§ 172. The Pantheon was circular in ground plan, but was fronted by a proper Grecian portico, an octostyle of the Corinthian order, with a pediment of steeper pitch than that of the Parthenon, and having its tympanum originally ornamented by relief work in gilt bronze. The interior was about 142 feet in diameter. At the height of 75 feet rose the hemispherical dome divided into five rows of *caissons* or panels, rising one above the other and running horizontally round the dome, at the top of which was the circular opening for light of about 27 feet in diameter. The supporting wall was 27½ feet in width—necessarily thus heavy to support so vast a dome. It was broken within not only by the grand arched entrance and the arcade directly opposite where stood the colossal statue of Jupiter, but also by six niches now used for as many chapels, each one having in the wall two pilasters, one on each side, and two Corinthian cabled columns.

In this structure thus we find the circle introduced every where. The ground plan is a circle; the walls are in part supported by circular arches; and it is surmounted by a circular dome. It well deserves the name of *rotonda*, round, by which it is now popularly known. Yet the characteristic elements of the most ornate of the Grecian orders were employed in combination with the circular element, with the highest skill.

Coliseum.

§ 173. The ground plan of the Coliseum was an ellipse, a curve still more expressive of freedom than the circle. The axes of the ellipse were in the ratio of about three to two—very nearly that of the golden section. This immense structure, designed to accommodate over 100,000 spectators around the vast area, rose to a height of 170 feet by four orders placed one above the other, first the Doric, then the Ionic, then the Corinthian, each of these three having alternate columns and arches, and above all, an order of Corinthian pilasters. In each of the three lower orders were eighty arches, those in the lowest covering the entrances. It seems to be a just criticism upon this design that the columns are made to appear to support the walls above, which yet have already a sufficient support in the arches, while in fact their real service is as props to resist the outward pressure of an interior arch. Their apparent use is thus entirely superserviceable, and their real use is not that proper to a column, and is moreover discoverable only after the edifice is examined within.

St. Peter's.

§ 174. There is of course no natural antagonism between the Grecian right-lined and the Roman curvilinear architecture. The principles of unity and harmony require only that one system of support be made to predominate, and that the other, if introduced at all, be kept in subordination. If in the case of the Coliseum the columns and the arch systems seem to be put to exceptionable uses and in other cases were introduced together without subordination and consequently to the violation of unity, and if, moreover, a heavy column was sometimes made to rest on an arch, thereby making the weaker sustain the stronger in violation of the principle of support, still in a riper age of the art, architectural genius achieved a harmonious combination of the two systems, in one of the architectural wonders of the world. After the bold yet skillful design of Brunes-chelli, inspired by the study of the Pantheon dome, had lifted a smaller dome over the crossing of the nave and transept of a church in Florence, Michael Angelo, catching the inspiration from Bruneschelli's success, conceived and accomplished the bolder design of hanging "the Pantheon itself in the air;" and in St. Peter's at Rome combined the Greek and the Roman styles in harmonizing expression, as one of the proudest achievements of architectural genius. This vast dome, which at its base has an exterior diameter of 195½ feet, and rises to a height of 405 feet above the pavement, rests upon four piers which, although strengthened by Michael Angelo, were originally but parts of the intersecting walls of the nave and the transept, and finds in these piers thus strengthened adequate supports against its lateral thrust. The Pantheon, as has been already noticed, sustained this lateral pressure only by its massive walls of 27½ feet in thickness; the Coliseum could only protect the outward pressure of an interior archway by resort to a deceptive colonnade; the genius of Michael Angelo made the nave walls themselves perform this additional service of lateral support, and on a scale of most marvelous extent and grandeur.

§ 175. The dome is the crowning element in circular architecture. It was employed to an extravagant excess in Constantinople after the removal of the Empire to that metropolis. It has hence been regarded as constituting the proper Byzantine style, and characterizes as well Greek churches as Turkish mosques.

St. Sophia. The church of St. Sophia in Constantinople, the magnificent work of the Emperor Justinian, is surmounted by a circular dome of 115 feet in diameter, which receives its vertical support from four piers standing at the four angles made by the intersection of the nave with the transept—the general ground-plan being that of a Greek cross. The lateral support is from side domes, resting upon the arms of the cross. This kind of dome is called the *pendentive* dome, from the portion of it which is not supported by the vertical walls.

Roman Cross-vault. § 176. There was another use of this circular element of architectural support and of beauty devised by the Romans. It naturally grew out of the familiar employment among them of long passages or galleries covered by cylindrical vaults. If such a passage be crossed at right angles by another like vaulted passage of equal dimensions, the intersection will form at the top two curves crossing diagonally through a central vertex. These two curves will be supported virtually on the corners of the upright walls supporting the vaults, and will be propped against a lateral push by these same walls. If now these curved lines or *ribs* be covered, we shall have a vault fully supported, resting over the square space formed by the intersection of the passages, leaving the passages themselves entirely free and open. This is the Roman *cross-vault*—an element of great beauty, as also of availability as a mode of support.

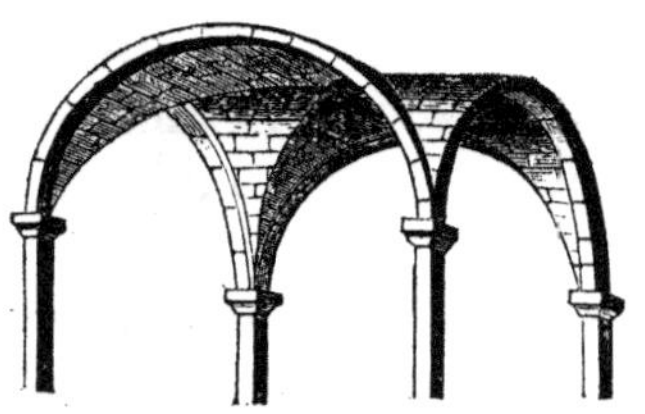

Roman Crossvault.

Pointed arch.

§ 177. 3. *Gothic Architecture.* The characteristic feature of this style of architecture is the *pointed arch.* Wherever or whenever this element was first employed, or whatever may have suggested its use, certain it is that the necessity of steep roofs in severer climates than those of Greece and Italy, combined with the higher æsthetic value of the curved line, determined the general prevalence of the pointed arch in all the central and northern parts of Europe after the revival of arts and letters at the period of the crusades. "Nowhere but in the Gothic building," says Prof. Lubke, "do we find the pointed arch made the fundamental law of the construction, and vaulted roofs, arcades, windows, and niches all executed with its assistance."

The theory of the pointed arch is perfectly simple. Two like segments of equal circles intersecting at the apex of the arch, furnished the two conditions of steepness of roof for support, and of curved form for æsthetic expression. Its origin has been in question. The probabilities are that it grew out of the mode of covering doorways or passages through walls by horizontal layers of stones, each higher overlapping that below it, as described in § 164. Simply rounding out the projecting corners of these layers, so as to form the concave surface of a segment of a cylinder, would form the familiar pointed arch.

The circular curve seemed to satisfy the eye of the designing architect, who for the most part rejected the ellipse. Yet there can be no impracticability to be found in its nature to forbid the use of this curve which, as has been remarked, is a curve of higher æsthetic expression than the simple circle, as this again is of higher character than the straight line. The ellipse was, however, tried on the continent, but rejected. In England the use of it was more successful as in the Westminister Abbey, and in some modes of compound vaulting it was a necessary combination with the circle.

The buttress.

§ 178. The high roof introduced the necessity of additional props to the supporting walls against the outward pressure. The Egyptians and the Greeks, as also the early Romans, as we have seen, relied for this protection on mere massiveness of wall. The later Romans used props, but concealed them. The Coliseum, as already remarked, used for this purpose columns that were made to appear to be designed merely to support upright walls above. The church of St. Peters covered its props in piers at the intersections of the nave and transept walls. The Gothic architecture openly displayed its prop in the *buttress*, and converted that element of support into an element of beauty. The buttress became thus a distinguishing feature of Gothic architecture. In order to support the high center walls in churches, constructed on the ground-plan of the Roman basilica with two arches on each side of the center nave but of less height than the nave, *flying buttresses* were resorted to, which were carried by arches over the aisles to rest on their pillars or walls outside.

The groine vault.

§ 179. Further, the circular dome of the Byzantine or Romanesque architecture became in the Gothic the groined vault. The Roman cross-vault, formed by the crossing at right angles of two semi-cylindrical vaults, had four groins meeting at the apex on the surface of the intersecting vaults. These groins were at first plain, but in process of time were covered by ribs. But the crossing vaults may be formed of segments less than a semi-circle, as in the Gothic or pointed style. Still further, as these groins or ribs are the supporting parts of the vault, so that all the intervening parts of the vault may, if desired, be dispensed with, if they are of sufficient strength themselves not to be crushed by the incumbent weight, and if also themselves adequately supported, they may be covered by covers resting

upon them ; and these coverings may be laid across in flat stretches from rib to rib, or may be of other form convex or concave. The whole interior appearance of the vault may thus be diversified indefi-

Groined Vault in Westminster Abbey.

nitely. Still further, more than two vaults may intersect each other, or the ribs may be of different circles, and so may arise all the modifications of what is called *fan-tracery* vaulting. The genius of architectural design thus had opened to it a field of unlimited invention. The art by its development into the use of the pointed arch and the groined vault, that is of

Fan-tracery.

an arch and a vault formed of curves of whatever number and curvature, simple or compound, of uniform or contrary flexure, while never disusing the old Egyptian right-lined or the Grecian columnar styles, reached its fullness of growth, so far as the æsthetic treatment of support by vertical pressure or horizontal props is concerned. The one principle which governs throughout is obviously this; that while the necessary mechanical support be provided, this support shall be made apparent to the eye of æsthetic contemplation. This is the first demand of the true æsthetic spirit, that the support be real, and that its reality be discernible, or at least credible. This strength of support may be in the massive wall, the incompressible arch, the solid buttress; but it must be there, adequate to resist every pressure, and it must be there so as to satisfy the contemplating eye that it is there, if it do not discern in every particular how it is provided, in order that there may be true æsthetic satisfaction. True taste forbids the use of materials in a way that contradicts their very nature. Weight presses immediately downward, and also indirectly outward. An arch supports weight only as its convexity turned upward shoulders what is laid upon it; to put weight apparently on an arch whose convexity is downward, violates the essential principle of the arch as one of support. A curve of contrary flexure is indeed, in itself, one of richer beauty than a curve of uniform flexure; but to rest weight apparently on such a curve is in false taste, for weakness at a single point in a support is weakness throughout. So the point of greatest resistance in the arch is at the apex; to rest the heaviest weight on any point below is æsthetically wrong. A stone or timber supported at one end by its principle of cohesion will support a certain weight at the other end, even although not otherwise supported. Stones or timbers projecting from vertical walls, in other words, *corbels*, of whatever kind, can on this principle of cohesiveness be allowed to sustain a certain weight. When, however, masses of heavy wall, or high towers, or columns, or roofs are made apparently to rest on such weak supports, the æsthetic eye is offended, although the mass may, in some concealed, deceptive way, be in part sustained. Weight presses heavier nearer the earth, nearer its ultimate support; to place the weaker support beneath the heavier is consequently in violation of nature, and so of sound taste. What is useless it is against reason to employ at all; to introduce what is for no conceivable use, is accordingly against correct taste, as pilasters hanging without a base against a wall. Their proper office and significance is support; but needing support themselves, in order to support other weight, without such support provided for them, their office is hindered and their significance is destroyed.

All these particulars are but applications of the universal principle of all beauty, that it is ever the expression of some idea. It must express, really and truly, or it is not true beauty. Art miserably deceives itself and fails when it attempts to create beauty without an idea to express. Its function is to grasp the idea, to begin with that; and then express that idea truly,—that is, in accordance with its own nature, its essential properties and necessary relations.

Characteristic effects of the different styles.

§ 180. It is pertinent here to indicate the distinguishing characteristic effects of these different styles of architecture on the æsthetic sense. That of the Grecian style will readily be recognized as elevated repose. The vertical lines here all run into horizontal lines, and are terminated by them, while the latter sweep round and round without end. The eye is lifted at once to the entablature, which is recognized to be in perfect support as it rests on the stable column, and is then kept in secure and quiet admiration of undistracting, perfectly simple, yet perfectly complete æsthetic form. The Roman arch that turns the contemplating eye, round and round upon itself, presenting no point from which it can break away, except simply to follow down the columnar support, suggests as its proper æsthetic effect the steadfast orderliness and practicalness of ordinary life. The proper expression of the pointed architecture is as obviously aspiration. It lifts the eye ever upward; gives it no resting place, not even at its highest elevation, nor yet when itself can reach no higher, by a gentle and smoothed bending suggests a downward return, but seems only, by its sharp ending, to bid the contemplation, with the spring it has given it, soar ever higher. The æsthetic expression of the Grecian style is thus tranquil repose; of the Roman, unending orderly activity; and of the

Gothic, upward aspiration and endeavor; while that of the heavy gloomy Egyptian and Hindoo, running ever into the expression of the infinite unknown of extent, and duration, and power, is oppression, fear, dejection.

The future of architecture.

§ 181. A boundless field for artistic invention is now fully opened to the architect in the æsthetic treatment of the several methods of support by upright walls and by columns, by arches, and by buttresses. One other element of support, already alluded to, remains as yet historically not fully developed and matured. It is that of the tie in the form of the truss. This element is available only as prop support for resistance to lateral push. But it is easily conceivable that by it architectural genius may yet design structures that shall be as original and as admirable as anything in the past ages of architecture. Its use has been hitherto subservient and retired from open view. In bridge architecture it has been summoned to a grander service.

Pendent support.

It should be added that the pendent support, consisting simply of weights hanging from the interior base of a dome to resist lateral thrust, so common in Turkish architecture, is an element which may be made available to rich æsthetic expression in western art.

To what this great art may yet develop itself lies in the secrecy of embryonic genius. In combination with the other more maturely developed principles of architectural supports, in subserviency, or in cooperation, it summons to still new endeavors of creative invention, and holds out to it the premium of triumphs worthy of lasting commemoration. Certain it is that not by mechanical copying of existing forms, or by any mere combination of them is the art to advance. Only as the artistic imagination, quickened, trained, and nourished up by the careful study of past achievements and of the processes of the great architect of nature, shall be prompted and enabled itself to create by the origination of new forms in the expression of new ideas in new ways, is there rational hope of progress.

Decoration and principal design.

§ 182. V. THE LAW OF DECORATIVE DESIGN.—All decoration we have found to be not self-subsistent, but only accessory or appended form. This indicates at once the relation of decorative design to proper artistic design. It is closely connected with it, so closely that it may be impossible to discover the exact line of junction and of separation. They run into each other, as do mechanical design and artistic design; as in fact light shades into darkness, and body into limb. We can in neither case so draw a line of separation as to be able to say on this side is the one exclusively, and on that side is the other exclusively.

Its motives.

The motives to decoration are either negative, by contrasts, by grading transitions from part to part or member to member, by relief of too strong effect in artistic design, to attemper the whole for a more pleasing contemplation; or positively expressive in revealing in some way what lay beyond the province of proper artistic design.

Means. The means of decoration are either (1.) by use of new and perhaps dissimilar material; (2.) by richer treatment of the same material; or (3.) by the introduction of entirely new form.

Diversity of material. § 183. (1.) The Athenian with his wealth of the most perfect material, the purest Pentelican marble, had no motive to mingle in a baser material into his structures. A severe simplicity thus was imposed on him in artistic consistency, from the single material given him, to be observed in all his procedure of designing and expressing. Where an inferior material is to be used, the opportunity of selection and of combination is furnished, which skillful architects in other countries have availed themselves of with the happiest results. Stone of different qualities and hues, may thus be wrought into the same walls, and relieve of the heavy effect of a single inferior material.

Paint. But the Athenian artist did not reject the use of paint, even with his marble of purest white. How far Grecian temples of the best days of Grecian art were thus painted, is a matter of dispute. But no candid antiquarian now doubts that it was used to some extent even in the purest specimens of Athenian architecture. Frescoed ceilings and frescoed upright walls, the best artistic taste admits and advocates against the denunciations of purists in art. That fresco may be employed deceptively and so improperly, may be conceded; but it has a legitimate function to perform in relieving from the glare or the deadness of blank walls and ceilings. Not only for protection, but also for allowable decoration is paint thus used in connection with the proper material of building. Bronzing and gilding are justified in the same way in decoration

Richer treatment. § 184. (2.) The same material, again, may, for decorative purposes, be more richly treated; and this in two ways, by multiplying parts or members, and by varying the outlines of principal or subordinate members.

Moldings. The introduction of moldings is a species of decoration in the first of these ways, which was early introduced and has become universal in architectural art. A base, a shaft, and a capital were regarded as essential parts of a Grecian column. Moldings were decorative parts, answering the purpose of relief to the monotonous effect of a perfectly plain column, and also of grading the transitions from member to member,—from the pedestal to the base, from the base to the shaft, from the shaft to the capital, from the capital to the architrave. These moldings have become so general in use, that the eight familiarly recognized in the art deserve to be enumerated. They are:—

1. The *ovolo*, or quarter round, called also when carved the *echinus*. It appears convex or rounded outward, and is about a quadrant of a circle or like part of an ellipse. It is commonly found under the abacus.

2. The *cyma* (wave), *cyma recta*, having its outline concave above and convex below.

3. The *talon*, *ogee*, or *reversed cyma*, having its outline convex above and concave below.

4. The *torus*, a large semicular convex molding.

5. The *scotia*, or *trochilus*, a concave molding.

6. The *cavetto*, *mouth*, or *hollow*, also called a *casemate* or *casement*, a concave quarter-circle.

7. The *astragal* or *bead*, a small torus, or semicircular convex molding.

8. The *fillet* or *listel*, embracing the flat *band*, and the circular *annulet*, a round molding used chiefly to separate other moldings.

Sir William Chambers says that of these moldings, the cyma and the cavetto were constantly used as finishings and never applied where strength is required; the ovolo and talon as supporters to the essential members of the composition, such as the modillions, dentils, and corona: the torus and the astragal chiefly to fortify the tops and bottoms of columns and sometimes of pedestals; and the scotia only to separate the members of bases, while the fillet is used for this purpose not only in bases but in all kinds of profiles.

The pointed architecture in the same æsthetic spirit covered buttresses with pinnacles, and pinnacles with finials, just as the Byzantine added dome to dome. It also clustered columns and ribs and vaults.

The severe taste of the Greeks exacted in their right-lined architecture the most undeviating straightness, not only in reality but also in appearance. Hence to counteract the effect of different light, as we have seen, they gave their columns a slightly conoidal outline. They also to secure the fullest effect of light and shade, nicely adjusted the projection of members and of moldings. Grecian art thus by the intensest effort of æsthetic invention and design, wrought into their beautiful material the most perfect beauty of form, in the utmost simplicity of material and of plan.

Again this æsthetic impulse prompted a richer treatment of the particular parts themselves. Thus the simpler Doric capital was enriched into the Ionic with its graceful spirals, and this again into the foliaged Corinthian ; and yet again this into the Composite.

To this we may attribute the carving of columns into forms of life. The *caryatides,* columns in the shape of men, a series of decorations borrowed by the Greeks from the Assyrians, were a fruit of this impulse, which to a severer taste and to one not familiar with this servile mode of bearing burdens, is by no means expressive of æsthetic ideas.

New decorative form.

§ 185. (3.) A more advanced development of architectural decoration brought in expedients to keep the contemplation fed up to completest fullness. Lest excessive blank surface should weary, the Greeks broke up the long frieze by triglyphs on the under surface of the cornice. With the same design they placed *mutules*—rectangular blocks, standing out from the plane surface.

The system of Gothic foliation is another example of this kind of decoration. Circles, or other curvilinear figures containing forms somewhat resembling a leaf, called *trefoil* if containing three leaves, *quatrefoil* if four, *cinquefoil* if five, and so on, were placed in the eyes of vaults or of arches, in angular spaces on the walls, every where to keep the imagination ever awake. So also in blank spaces the artist, giving free scope to a playful fancy, wrought in the most grotesque figures,—heads of animals with human hands and bodies of monstrous outline. Just as the Greek had carved his moldings, so the Gothic artist carved vines, leaves, trees, as place was given him, not to represent actual forms in nature, but rather to prevent the eye from being offended with mere blankness. In the same spirit the early English architect placed what are called *crockets*, consisting of projecting bunches of leaves curled back like a shepherd's crook or of leaves on a long stalk, at the angles of spires, canopies, pinnacles, and on gables and weather-moldings of doors and windows.

Decorative Sculpture.

A more developed system of decoration still than this, spread every where on every member that could receive it expressive sculpture. Sometimes in low relief as on the frieze of the cell of the Parthenon; sometimes in high relief as in the metopes on the outer frieze; sometimes in distinct statuary forms, as in the pediment. So also in Roman architecture, statues of apostles and saints, placed in niches in the walls, over the entablature, or on the roof, suggest the character of the religious temple. This system of significant decoration, which of itself represents some idea, as opposed to those kinds before mentioned which are not meaning or representative, is most fit and most happy in æsthetic effect. It opens to the artist a wide field of inventive design, in which he is free to use either natural, conventional, or allegorical signs and symbols,—in fact every variety of representation possible in architectural material.

CHAPTER VI.

SPECIAL LAWS—LANDSCAPE.

Landscape:—its name and sphere.

§ 186. The art of Landscape, more commonly designated by the cumbrous name of Landscape-gardening, is the art of shaping or forming lands, as the word, a compound of land and *shape* (Anglo Saxon *scap an*), indicates. It comprehends primarily the laying out of grounds and secondarily the treatment of these grounds by culture and the investment of them with such forms as the neds of utility or of beauty may prescribe.

Origin in want of food.

§ 187. The art has its origin and spring in a human necessity—that of food. The supply of this want gives occasion for the æsthetic nature to assert itself, which then by incorporating itself in the mechanical labor to secure the supply and by animating and guiding it by its own peculiar spirit, elevates the drudgeries of land-tilling into the æsthetic art of land-farming. It is the province of this art to spread æsthetic form over all the operations which the supply of food from the earth may occasion.

Other associated wants.

§ 188. With this primary and fundamental want of food are associated other wants to be carefully studied in the art. The wants of social inter-communication in roads, alleys, walks; of shade and shelter from heat, and cold, and storm; of diversion and recreation, and others incident to domestic and public life, are wants more or less closely connected with the need of food; and rank among those which determine the economical ends of the art.

Penetrating and investing these economical ends are the æsthetic aims which may and should be sought and which come in to direct and regulate it. This general view of the relation of æsthetics to the art of Landscape will readily suggest to us the particular laws which are to govern in it.

Law of Ideal—twofold.

§ 189. I. THE LAW OF IDEAL IN LANDSCAPE.—In all dependent art we encounter the two classes of ideas: those of utility—the economic ideas—and the proper æsthetic ideas. Every expressive art, so far as expressive, must regard both with unremitting care.

1. Economic.

§ 190. The leading economic ideas in Landscape are, as already noticed, those involved in the supply of food, of intercommunication, of shade and shelter, and of recreation. These ideas vary in their modifications in the more special uses of grounds.

Domestic use.

We have thus, in the first place, the modifications determined by domestic uses. The ideas concerned in the production of food here rank paramount to all others. Landscape predominantly concerns itself here with the garden, the lawn, the orchard, the forest. But collateral with this leading idea are those of retirement, of shade, of shelter from wind and storm, which more naturally solicit proper æsthetic treatment. There are still, besides these, the ideas connected with the demands for recreation, for walks and drives, for games and exercises of whatever kind related to a rich, well-regulated, domestic life. These economic ideas in Domestic Landscape require each its due consideration. They are paramount and must govern, or even the proper æsthetic aims must be frustrated.

Public use.

We have, in the next place, the modifications determined by public use. In Public Landscape, the economical ideas are concerned chiefly and prominently, not with the production of food, but with walks and streets and roads, with parks for recreation, with gardens for social culture and refinement, with cemeteries in which all the sacred offices which cluster about the resting-places of the departed may have opportunity of unmolested observance, with room and place also for all the diversity of civil operations.

2. Æsthetic. § 191. The ideas over and beyond those conversant with economical ends which may be expressed in landscape, are at once suggested by them. Domestic life implies, at the outset, retirement and seclusion. This idea may be expressed in the selection and disposition of the trees and of the larger shrubbery. Domestic life requires internal freedom, and the associated ideas of cheerfulness and tranquillity. It requires also, for its perfection, the expression in all the surroundings of home life, of the ideas of growth and training, of which this art may furnish the fittest suggestions; of the ideas, too, of order and of neatness; of care and forethought and watchful attention; of a perfection of character, as fashioned with grace and tenderness and symmetry and harmony; of dependence, also, on providential orderings and support, and of creaturely humility, trust, and love.

Public landscape has for its governing æsthetic ideas those of regularity and civil order, that may be expressed in the direction and construction of its walks and roads, and in the selection and arrangement of trees and shrubs and flowers; those, too, expressive of the proper spirit and character of the nation or community—its greatness, its generosity, its fostering care over its subjects, its historical achievements and experiences.

Æsthetic art prescribes that this rich field of economic and æsthetic ideas be entered and carefully explored by the undertaking artist; and that when well and richly furnished with them by this exploration, and only then, he proceed to embody them in his work, in laying out and also in investing his grounds. As he shall make these ideas rightly and clearly to appear expressed in his work, will his landscape be accepted as æsthetically perfect or otherwise.

Law of material.

§ 192. II. THE LAW OF MATERIAL IN LANDSCAPE.—The regulative principles in Landscape given immediately by an exclusive consideration of the material are either those which respect its selection or those which respect its use.

Selection.

The material here is both inorganic and organic. Of the former is the earth or the ground, the selection of which may be directed in reference to the character of the soil, and the kind and extent of rock, and of water, whether of ocean, lake, river, brook, or in fountains. Of the latter is vegetable growth, including trees, shrubs, flowers, grasses. Indirectly, moreover, animal life must be regarded. Both beast and bird, made serviceable to the divers uses of man for food or raiment or labor or entertainment, are to be introduced and provided for. In selection, there will be occasion for separating in that which is already given, that which is to be retained from that which is to be rejected. Unserviceable or unseemly hummocks or crags, unsightly rocks or trees, may need to be removed, and water diverted or drained.

Use.

§ 193. The use or treatment of the material is to be controlled by considerations given immediately by the nature of the material itself. First, it should be used ever in accordance with its own nature. Inorganic matter in soil, rock, water, as also all vegetable growth, has its own properties, which must be recognized in all æsthetic treatment of them. True taste forbids that they should ever be belied. The liability to this in landscape arises from an irrational desire to surprise by unnatural contrivances and devices. Rocks and water can be artificially placed where by natural laws they could never be found, and trees and shrubs can by artificial appliances be made to grow in uncongenial soils and in most fantastic shapes, and in this way shocks and surprises may be given; but they are offensive to a pure taste. Bold and rugged rock-work, in imitation of the wildest mountain scenery, when placed in low plains and luxuriant gardens, whether for grottoes or for miniature mountain water-falls; or shrubbery forced by trimming and training into fantastic and monstrous shapes, trees maimed and mangled to appear picturesque, are offensive because unnatural. True effective art in landscape, as everywhere, discovers itself only through nature; and natural products, whether inorganic or organic, are legitimately treated only when in accordance with their natural properties and relations.

The proper treatment of organic material in landscape must regard every where its peculiar attributes of growth and of change with the seasons. The effect of trees and of shrubs, changes with their age, and with the season. There is no beauty in the sight of a field newly ploughed, or in stubble. Most attractive is such a field when covered with springing grass or waving grain. There is little beauty in leafless trees; exceeding beauty in the same trees in full foliage and flower. An evergreen that is beautiful in a yard when but a shrub in size, may be a deformity when of full growth. Different plants have different times for blooming. The landscape changes with the seasons. The artist, accordingly, has here to anticipate and to calculate for these changes incident to growth and season.

In reference to sense addressed.

§ 194. Secondly, material in Landscape must be used in reference to the channels through which it reaches the imagination. This principle respects only the æsthetic treatment of material, and is in subserviency to the economic ends of the art. Landscape commands more avenues to the æsthetic sensibility than architecture. It addresses through the sight like the sister art—it employs outline, and light and shade, and color like that—and in addition to these uses of light, it has much more to do with perspective than that; while, besides, the use of reflected light from water surface or from land or gardens, or from groves is almost peculiar to it; and moreover depends like that on proportion, symmetry, and harmony for its æsthetic effect. But it addresses the imagination also through the ear. The singing of birds which it invites into its retreats; the divers modulations of the wind howling or gently rushing through the diversified foliage of trees, and inspiring sentiments of awe and reverence, or of cheerfulness and peace; the music too of water in trickling fountains, gurgling brooks, rippling lakes or surging sea, are all æsthetic elements to be turned to account in landscape. The sense of smell, also, through the divers perfumes of flowers, and the sense of taste in the diversified fruitage are not to be overlooked. Landscape enjoys this distinction above all the sister arts, that she commands more avenues to the imagination than any of them. The artist is required to make the best use of this advantage in the treatment of his material.

Mechanical design respects economic ends.

§ 195. III. THE LAW OF MECHANICAL DESIGN IN LANDSCAPE. — Mechanical Design here has to inquire how the economic ends proposed in the art can best be attained in the treatment of the given material. It must begin with ascertaining fully and precisely what these ends are. It must then lay out the grounds in reference to these ascertained ends: selecting and then treating the material whether soil, rock, water, tree, or shrub, so as best to accomplish them.

Mechanical design works out the farm or kitchen-garden, rather than the park or the flower garden, which are the more proper object in artistic design. There will often be conflict between these two departments of the art. Where they cannot be reconciled, it must be decided which shall in the particular case be preferred, profit or æsthetic pleasure, and how much shall be sacrificed of the one to secure more of the other.

But it should never be forgotten that a true æsthetic interest may be imparted to a farm, or a kitchen-garden, or a simple house-yard, by the skillful adaptation of the ground to its desired uses. What is needed is a clear apprehension of these uses, and a judicious adaptation of means to them. Is the farm for tillage or for grazing; is it for fruit or for forest; what parts are to be used for this and what for that particular purpose; then what partitions, what kind of fences, what roads or walks, what out-buildings; what treatment of soil, what drainage, what enriching, what rotations in products,—these are the leading questions incumbent on mechanical design to solve, the right solution of which cannot fail to return a high æsthetic satisfaction. The right expression of a rational aim is ever in itself beautiful; whatever is without aim or aside from proposed end is deformity. Every ordering in mechanical design, therefore, should have a meaning and significance. That every arrangement and disposition of the grounds and use of material has this significance, and is not from haphazard and in blindness, but has rational aim, stamps the whole work as a procedure in taste and satisfies in its degree the demands of the æsthetic spirit. Every change in the original condition of the grounds; every line of partition; every introduction of new material as well as every use of old, should have a justifying reason for it, and so far as practicable should unostentatiously display it. Mind should every where manifest its triumphant control of nature, not by abusing it, but by directing its forces and its properties to the designed ends.

Three principles of artistic design.

§ 196. IV. LAW OF ARTISTIC DESIGN IN LANDSCAPE. — The three comprehensive principles regulating artistic design in landscape are: 1. That it work in subordination to mechanical design and through it; 2. That it work in conformity to the laws of those organs of sense through which the art addresses the imagination; and 3. That it work in accordance with the principles of the rational nature.

1. Subordination to mechanical design.

§ 197. First, no landscape can please æsthetically which manifestly controverts its very design and purpose. This principle has a wide application. We have the violation of it exemplified in a very common practice of laying out approaches to the dwelling or commanding structure in the grounds. The rule of reason is that every end be attained in the directest manner; that, consequently, if a road or walk is designed to conduct to a given object, it be as direct as is admissible in the circumstances. In æsthetic procedures, the principle is that the road or walk appear thus direct. If there are apparent obstacles in the direct approach which should be shunned rather than crossed, or if there are apparent objects to be secured by a deviation from a straight course, the æsthetic eye is not offended. Serpentine walks or drives, also, in pleasure grounds designed for leisurely contemplation and for successive study of views of diversfied character, are justified by the design. But justly deserving of the criticism which Mr. Repton administers to it is the approach to his picturesque mansion, designed by the author of a treatise on the Principles of Taste, which was so winding and so blind that a direction-post was required two hundred yards from the mansion to indicate the way to it. Equally censurable is the erection of two square boxes for lodges at the entrance into a park, under a fallacious notion of symmetry. The lodge is for the residence of the gatekeeper, who, as he has but one life, does not need two dwellings. In like bad taste gardens were formerly laid out in Italy and in France, in resemblance to the human body—the great walk in the middle representing the trunk, the branching alleys representing the limbs of the body. This is an exemplification of the so frequent violations of taste occasioned by the fallacious notion that imitation of nature must always give beauty.

II. Address to imagination chiefly through sight.

§ 198. Secondly, the imagination is to be addressed in landscape chiefly through the sight, but to a less extent through the senses of hearing, smell, and taste, and is to be reached in conformity to the laws which govern in those senses. Confining our view to the optical principles which are to be observed in landscape, we shall find them to be embraced under the three which are given by the relative position of the observer, the form of the objects, and the nature of light.

Optical principles from position of eye.

§ 199. (1.) The relative position of the observer will greatly determine the æsthetic effect. The view will vary with the elevation of the eye of the observer, whether he look from the ground or from the lower or higher stories, or from the top of the mansion; from a valley or from a hill; from one point on the surface or another. In this connection is to be noticed the expedient of concealing. By judicious disposition of trees and shrubbery, what is unsightly may often be hidden from the view at any given point. Bounding fences may be concealed so as to give the effect of distance and extent; the limits of a sheet of water may be covered, changing the effect of a pool into that of a stream, or of a lakelet into that of a river; views may be opened or closed; outlines that are too straight and regular may be broken, whether they be outlines of the surface of ground or of the horizon.

From position of object.

§ 200. (2.) The divers forms in which an object may be presented to the eye in a landscape will often vary the effect. Sloping grounds and objects appear foreshortened. Undulating grounds appear more extended than plane surfaces. Strait roads or fences crossing valleys obliquely appear curved. This different aspect presented by the same object as to its form and size is an element of æsthetic effect which demands careful study of the artist in landscape.

From nature of light.

§ 201. (3.) The laws of light itself as the medium of vision require careful attention in landscape. The principles of what is called aerial perspective have here a wide application. The effect of distance on the apparent size and relative form of objects, and on their apparent relations to one another in position and in magnitude; the varying effect of dawning, midday, and evening light, of haze and cloud, of shade and coloring, all require study. For illustration, views to be taken from a southern outlook need different treatment from those from a northern; those from an eastern outlook, a different treatment from those from a western. The effect of long vistas through rows of trees may be enhanced by breaks, and also by a gradually deepening foliage. Inasmuch as we estimate the size of distant objects by reference to some assumed standard of known dimensions, the introduction of a familiar object dwarfed from its ordinary size, will enlarge the apparent size of objects whose dimensions are not known. A standard of greater than ordinary dimensions has the reverse effect. Mr. Repton mentions a colossal statue of Penn, which was placed on the roof of a building, and which consequently diminished the size of every other object around. On the same principle he recommended placing cattle of a small breed on a contracted lawn to make it appear larger. A dwarfed tree made prominent will cause trees in a forest or a grove to seem taller. Mr. Repton relates that an obelisk at Holkhorn appeared at a distance to be surrounded by shrubbery; but on approaching, these apparent shrubs were found to be in fact large trees.

Objects, further, appear smaller if placed in strong light, or when outlined against the sky or a sheet of water; they appear larger, on the other hand, when outlined upon a dark back-ground.

In a northern latitude, a sheet of water viewed from a southern outlook appears bright and cheerful; while from a northern outlook it will appear dark and gloomy. In the same way the light reflected from a low surface of water may not reach the eye, and thus a lake or stream may appear cheerless that would reflect the full radiance of a cheering sun to an eye at proper elevation. A dense mass of foliage reflects in the same way light and cheerfulness towards the sun, but shade and gloominess in the opposite direction..

Still further, Mr. Repton remarks that he has found from careful observation that all natural objects, such as woods, trees, lawn, water, and distant mountains, appear best with the sun behind them; while all artificial objects, such as houses, bridges, roads, boats, arable fields, and distant towns or villages appear best with the sun full upon them.

III. Conformity to rational nature.

§ 202. Thirdly, the ideas in landscape are to be expressed in conformity to the rational principles of our nature.

Unity.

The principle of unity requires that the grounds and the entire investiture of them be designed in reference to the dwelling or the public edifice for which the landscape is intended. Its magnitude, its style of architecture, its economic arrangements, should lend suggestions in the whole design, that through it all may be viewed as one. This will furnish the general principal of unity. Subordinate principles will be found in the more specific objects proposed, as whether a farm or a park, a kitchen-garden or a flower garden, water-scenery or rock work, forest, grove, or orchard, intended to give character to the whole or to any part.

Contrast. The principle of contrast, by which the eye is made to recognize more prominently the different, while yet the general unity upon which it rests is not obscured, has a large application in landscape. In material, in object, in size, in outline, in light and shade, and in color,—every where, this great element of beauty may be used with rich effect by the skillful artist.

Æsthetic number. The principle of æsthetic number prohibits an excessive multiplicity of divisions and of uses. It is fatal to æsthetic effect to break up into manifold fields, and put them to divers purposes as for gardens, grazing, orchards, or to multiply objects, whether buildings, clumps of trees, sheets of water, bridges, fountains, drives, or walks.

Proportion. The principle of proportion here as in architecture, requires that each part bear a due relation in extent and magnitude to the whole.

Symmetry and harmony. The principles of symmetry and harmony have their application everywhere. They require that the like parts be treated similarly if in the same relations. The abuse of these principles is in introducing what is not needed for the purpose of applying them; designing the landscape for the principles instead of simply obeying the principles when the landscape designed for its own purposes gives occasion for their control. This common perversion of a most necessary principle has been well satirized by the poet in the familiar couplet:

> "Grove nods at grove; each alley has a brother;
> And half the platform just reflects the other."

History of landscape.

§ 203. EXEMPLIFICATION OF THE PRINCIPLES OF DESIGN IN LANDSCAPE IN THE LEADING STYLES OF THE ART IN HISTORY.—Ancient life was too unsettled and warlike to allow early development in this art. Homer's imagination conceived nothing beyond the kitchen-garden of Alcinous. Plutarch tells us the practice in his times was in ornamental gardens to set off the beauties of roses and violets by intermingled leeks and onions—a rather distasteful application of the principle of contrast. Roman gardens were displays of lavish expenditure, but of the rudest taste. Only since the sixteenth century has the art begun a true growth. It has, like architecture, developed successively elements of æsthetic expression in successive styles. Of these may be enumerated the Italian and French, or the Geometric; the Chinese, or Pseudo-natural; the Picturesque; and the Expressive, or True Artistic Style.

Four styles.

I. Geometric.

§ 204. (1.) The Geometric Style is characterized by the rigid application of mathematical lines and proportions. Public roads and streets and walks must be direct; and to public landscape the geometric style has a wide legitimate application. In private landscape, also, the rectilinear disposition of grounds is often in true taste. This style indicates a step of progress into the proper domain of art; for the old Roman practice of shearing the spray of shrubbery and trees into fantastic imitations of mechanical or animal shapes can hardly be reckoned as within the province of true art. The Geometric principle is legitimate, but it has not universal application, and is relatively an inferior one in æsthetic account.

II. Pseudo-natural.

§ 205. II. The Pseudo-natural Style grounded itself on the assumption that all art must be imitation of nature. The artificial method of the Geometric style is here consequently avoided; the compass and the chain are thrown aside; and what is actually found in nature is copied so far as practicable in landscape. No matter how opposite in character, how unsightly in themselves, any objects actually met with are legitimate objects for landscape investiture. Mountain torrents in flower gardens, dilapidated buildings in lawns, broken-down walls, dead trees, were introduced at great expense, and admired because this is nature. In like manner, seeds were to be dropped at hap-hazard anywhere, and trees and shrubs were set out in careful irregularity, the highest art being supposed to consist in the widest departures from all artificial device or rule. The fundamental error in the entire school of artists who make the imitation of the real the sole principle of art lies in this: that they make the imitation to respect the results or products of the creative spirit in nature, intermingled with all the accidental and exceptional and deficient, instead of the aims and principles of the creative spirit itself. The true function of art is to create, not to copy. It should therefore imitate, not the works of another's device and skill, but the device and skill itself; seize the aims and ends, learn the means, and energetically work out those aims through those means. Then its products will be at least imitations in the more important characters of life and expression, if not in perfection of skill and richness of design. Monkeys imitate; men, as godlike, should create.

III. Picturesque.

§ 206. III. The Picturesque style took its rise from the conception that a landscape should be a picture. Hence to design a perfect landscape, a perfect picture should first be made or imagined, and the grounds should be fashioned and invested from this as a model. Mr. Price, in his treatise on the picturesque, is an earnest advocate of this doctrine. It is true that the same general optical principles regulate in painting as in landscape, and so much justification in truth belongs to the theory. But the utter impossibility of transferring the outlines, the perspective, the shadings, the coloring proper for a good painting of a few inches or feet in size to acres of extent in grounds, except only in the most general principles of vision, must doom the theory as to any important practical use to be made of it. The attempt must ever miscarry, and occasion only deformity. The simple fact of the perpetual change going on in real landscape from season to season and from year to year, is of itself sufficient to condemn the theory. A spring view is as unlike an autumn view, except in mere outline, as a view taken in the nakedness of winter is unlike one taken in the full rich dress of summer. The theory is grounded on only a very partial truth; it has been valuable only as it has led to the investigation and use of those principles which are common to both arts.

IV. The expressive.

§ 207. IV. The Expressive or True Artistic Style appears as the last stage in the development of the art of landscape. Its principle is that the legitimate effect of landscape, æsthetically speaking, is to be sought by the due expression of the ideas, both economic and æsthetic, proper to the art. The artist begins with ascertaining determinately what ideas he is to express — what ends he is to effect, what sentiments reveal, what aims accomplish. His selection and use of material are then directed in reference to the accomplishment of these clearly apprehended aims. His work thus proceeds rationally, and commands success. The skillful revelation of his ideas of itself invests his grounds with the robes of beauty—with ever diversified, ever harmonized, ever intelligible, ever pleasing form.

Extent of decoration.

§ 208. V. LAW OF DECORATIVE DESIGN IN LANDSCAPE.—Landscape, like architecture, invites decoration. It affords room everywhere for the outpouring spirit of æsthetic form to utter itself. Both in design and in execution, it may go beyond any demand for the mere attainment of economic ends or for æsthetic expression of the governing ideas of the landscape. Working in strict subordination to these governing ideas, and in harmony with the expression of them, it may bring in dissimilar material, fill in new creations of the inventive spirit, or elaborate to a higher and richer finish the governing forms.

Architecture.

Architectural decorations, of manifold kinds, as conservatories, arbors, pavilions, treillages, and the like may find place.

Sculpture.

When in keeping with the general character of the landscape, sculpture, also, in statues, relief-work, is not inadmissible; yet one can hardly regard with quiet satisfaction finely chiseled marbles exposed in open grounds to the deforming and destroying influences of untoward climates.

Vases.

Vases and other provisions for supporting small shrubs and flowers rank among the most common decorations of yards and gardens.

Fountains.

Fountains, too, and jets, also find place. An almost limitless variety of decoration is thus placed at the service of the landscape artist. If governed by a correct æsthetic judgment, and especially curbing all tendencies to excess, he will be able to enrich his grounds with divers charms which a simpler treatment might dispense with.

CHAPTER VII.

SPECIAL LAWS—SCULPTURE.

Sculpture a free art.

§ 209. With sculpture we enter the realm of free beauty, in which the aim of the production is not to satisfy some want the supply of which gives occasion for beautifying art to exert itself,—not to create some form that shall minister to some utility, but to create form for its own sake. Here the end in the art is form. If some utility in any case may be reached by it, yet this result is only through the form which ever governs in the entire art-process.

Sculpture accordingly belongs to the class of the so-called liberal arts, fine arts, æsthetic arts, phonetic arts, in distinction from the class called variously dependent arts, useful arts, mechanical arts, technic arts, in which the utility governs and form is subservient.

Origin.

§ 210. The art had its origin in the spirit of worship, of pious gratitude or hope, or religious desire. A grateful sense of favor received prompted the erection of some memorial that should be a lasting witness and remembrancer of the kindness rendered, and also of the gratitude felt. It was at first simply a stone or a pile of stones, upon which perhaps a sacrifice could be offered to the interposing deity.

The rude rough pillar of stone was afterwards shaped into some form that would at least evince a larger gratitude than the mere setting up of a stone in some conspicuous place, if it did not also suggest some attribute of the favoring divinity, or otherwise indicate for whom the offering was intended. Character thus came in for expression in the progress of the art, and so the art was perfected. The motive which should lead to the exercise of the art, came to be separated from the essential nature of the art. However prompted or occasioned, the procedure in the art itself properly began with some idea to be expressed; and the art concerned itself simply with embodying that idea in the given material.

Realm of idea.

§ 211. I. LAW OF IDEA IN SCULPTURE.—The range of idea allowed to the sculptor for his selection is wide as the realm of idea itself. Theorists, indeed, have laid down boundaries and prohibited excursions into this or that field of idea; but both on *a priori* and also on historic grounds—both from the nature of the art, and also from the actual achievements of the art,—we are constrained to reject all such teachings as one-sided and partial. What idea apprehensible by the human spirit may not in some way be more or less directly, more or less perfectly, outlined in marble or in bronze? What class of ideas has not actually been entered and from it some one taken by the artist and revealed in stone for the mere sake of the expression—for the form's sake alone? Egyptian sculpture loved to image in stone even the infinite itself, however rudely, however faintly—the infinite in extent of time and space, the infinite in power, the infinite in one or another attribute of power. Hindoo sculpture lost itself in its elaborations of this idea. All the specific shapings of creative wisdom and power in the inorganic and the organic world as also in the realm of rational spirit, have also been in different branches of the art, in different schools, delineated in stone or metal, or wood, or ivory. Even the monstrous itself, ideal creations made up of the most unnatural unions and combinations, have been revealed in sculpture. Centaurs representing the intelligence of man united with the fleetness of the animal, giants with human heads and busts terminating in snakes to express the union of reason with malignity ; mermaids and other fish monsters ; unions of human or of animal forms as superior and governing with the natures of fish as subservient and executive, have found place in the art, and in its higher development.

Yet the nature of the art as determined by the material with which it has to do and the instrument—the chisel—with which it chiefly and characteristically has to work, impose certain limitations, so far at least, as to render it necessary for the artist to select his ideas with considerate care in order to his highest skill and success.

Ideals either original or derived.

§ 212. Ideals in art are either original with the artist and are his own creations, or are given to him to be copied and rendered in his assigned material.

Original ideals in sculpture may be constituted, as we have seen, out of any of the ideas within reach of the human spirit. The Greek sculptors delighted to combine the characteristic attributes of one or another of their divers deities. Their rich mythology furnished them with a most suggestive field of ideas for subjects. The attributes of spirit, exemplified in their highest and most perfect forms in the divine nature, combined in divers ways and with divers modifications for forming special types of character, are of the highest order of elements for ideal subjects in art. One attribute made governing and characteristic, and combined with other attributes only as subordinate and as necessary for its own perfectness, becomes a meet subject for the sculptor; or a combination of more or fewer attributes uniting so as to form a more or less perfect ideal in conformity with the essential nature of each, may worthily engage his skill. It is obvious that the diversity of character thus conceivable is limitless. Power, intelligence, feeling, in their manifold modifications, may be combined to form innumerable diversities of ideals. Farther, art ideals may be founded on limitless products or states of these divers attributes of the spirit; but out of the infinity of the products of the divine creative power in inorganic and in organic being, combinations are possible beyond all assignable limit. In like manner, the products of human activity, the specific workings of human intelligence, human passion, human purpose, in all conditions and circumstances, furnish elements of ideals.

The field of actual subjects offered to the sculptor to be represented in his material is as wide as that of original creation. Real characters and real scenes, persons and events of every character, are fit themes for sculpture. Even from the animal and vegetable world it takes its subjects for representation. These subjects it may seek to imitate in all points directly imitable in sculpture, in outline, and in visible figure, giving the same dimensions, the same proportions, the same contour, the same relief to the projecting parts, the same depth to the retreating members, varying only so much as may be necessary to counterbalance the different effect of different material ; or it may seek to represent only the leading characteristics, giving them prominence and suppressing the others—may seek to idealize more or less the character of the given subject.

Three classes.

We may thus recognize three distinct classes of subjects : pure originals, imitated subjects, and idealized subjects.

Pure origina's.

§ 213. In the first class the ideal is the mere product of the active imagination as the creative faculty. It acts here in inventing ideals, not as a mere faculty of combination, taking only what is already in the memory, analyzing it, and recombining selected parts into new wholes. This has been a very prevalent doctrine, but it is superficial and narrow. The inventive spirit of man, developed and trained, it may be, through the study of actual products of divine or human art, comes to the knowledge of power and of law—of power working under the law pertaining to it. It may, therefore, with no previous study of any particular product, acquire the ability to forecast the form and shape which powers working under their laws, as modified by other forces and in divers conditions, may produce. He may acquire the ability to use existing powers, existing things, with their respective attributes, and by subjecting them to wholly new conditions, produce himself entirely original forms, which are in no true sense results of mere combination. The human spirit he may imagine to be placed in circumstances unlike any that have ever before been united, and so to work out under the laws of its own nature a character that shall be anything but a recombination of parts of character already realized in history. He may, as we have seen, even produce ideal monstrosities; and in fact no true artist ever invents by culling forms from his memory and then reconstructing them into an ideal. No genuine work of art was ever such a patch-work of combination.

Subjects from observation.

§ 214. The sculptor, in the legitimate exercise of his art as a free art, may imitate actual subjects. His function here is, first, to apprehend exactly the subject given him, and then to represent it so far as may be in his material. Here his chief art will lie in making his material, which is different from that of the original subject given him, reveal as closely as may be the exact features of that original. If thus he is to represent a personal subject, inasmuch as flesh, with its blending hues and soft yielding surface, reveals differently from marble, with its hard, lustrous surface of pure white, he will need carefully to determine how in the marble he shall secure the effect of the shading, the coloring, the soft but slightly uneven surface of living flesh.

Idealized subjects.

§ 215. Midway between these two classes, connecting the two, are idealized subjects. The artist here begins with an actual subject, and by suppressing entirely or by only more or less repressing certain features, by amplifying others, or even by introducing entirely new features, he creates a new ideal, neither real, nor purely imaginary, but one grounded on the real yet transformed and made new. A ruling trait of character in a real person is thus often brought out to stand alone and dissociated from other traits. The Grecian mythology revealed a Jupiter of divers not to say ill-sorted traits. The sculptor separates those of majesty and power and incorporates them only into his marble, that he may represent simply the king of the gods. By thus presenting real but only partial traits in a given character, the artist may elevate it above its true merits or depress it below and caricature it, according as his selection turns upon the noble and worthy or on the low and contemptible.

§ 216. With this wide field of subjects open to the sculptor which he may freely enter, the nature of his art as determined particularly by the character of the material to which he is limited, offers to him certain preferences. His highest ideals are those of character divine, angelic, or human, which may be exhibited in the forms of being, as in statues of the gods or of men, or in the forms of achievement, as in the representation of historic scenes or events. But in elaborating such spiritual activities in marble or in metal, where the muscular tension and relaxation which the given activity occasions in the living body are to be rendered, it is obvious that intense passion and strenuous exertion may in their natural expression occasion muscular contortions and tensions that in themselves are offensive to the eye. Hence for highest æsthetic effect, fixed character or habit is preferable to individual act; as repose generally is preferable for expression in sculpture to actual exertion. So the result or effect of exertion, the state or condition which comes from it, is preferable for a subject in the art to the effort itself. For the same reason the traits comprehended in the intelligence are deemed more fit for sculpture than those lying in the sensibility; the calm of intellect than the ebullitions of passion.

Choice of material.

§ 217. II. LAW OF MATERIAL IN SCULPTURE. Here, as in every art, sometimes the idea will be given to the artist and the material left to his own choice; or the reverse of this, the material be given and the idea to be embodied in it more or less free; or still further, a certain range may be allowed in each with more or less limitation. The principles of selection will be found in the greater or less adaptation of the

Guiding principles.

material to embody the idea, the genius and skill of the artist, or the ultimate design and disposition to be made of the product. The delicate lineaments of the human countenance find better expression in Parian marble than in sandstone or in granite; while an Egyptian sphinx may be better rendered in the latter material. One artist may render more skillfully in bronze, another in stone, a third in ivory. A coarser, harder material is more suitable for remote contemplation and atmospheric exposure, while a gem for close inspection demands a compact yet delicate texture.

Diversity of material.

Under these several guiding principles the sculptor has a widely diversified variety of materials for his selection. In stone for carving he has the hard and enduring although coarse granite, porphyry, basalt, sandstone, in which Egyptian sculpture reveled; and the finer and softer marble in which Grecian art achieved its principal successes; alabaster, too, both that harder variety, the calcareous, obtained from stalactites or stalagmites, and the softer variety, the gypseous, out of which ancient Egyptian and Jewish art wrought boxes for ointments and perfumes, and modern Italian art shapes vases, candelabra, statuettes, and manifold other articles of *virtu*. In still softer materials he has clay, stucco, plaster, and wax. The different woods, also, particularly the harder, as ebony and box, are fit materials for his art. The metals, gold, silver, iron, tin, copper, and compounds of simple metals, particularly bronze—an alloy generally of copper and tin, sometimes of these metals and zinc—have entered largely into the service of this art. Ivory, too, must be embraced in this catalogue. Phidias wrought his famous colossal statue of Athene, representing the goddess in the cell of the Parthenon and his statue of the Olympian Jupiter at Elis, of ivory and gold; the uncovered parts of the person being of ivory, the robes and sandals of gold.

Color. § 218. Coloring has also been employed in the best styles of sculpture, and by artists of the severest taste. Phidias not only used gold with iron, but there is reason to believe that the sculpture on the pediments and the frieze of the Parthenon were painted. Purists in taste seem to think that the one charge of deception in the use of paint suffices to secure its condemnation and utter rejection. But the charge does not cover the whole ground. To use paint for the purpose of deceiving may be condemned on ample grounds of reason; to use it for the purpose of perfecting the representation, for preventing a false impression, does not appear to come within the sweep of the censure, so far as it has reason. In stone, which does not from its very nature admit of being wrought so as to represent fine wavy locks of hair, in which consequently the best that the most ingenious sculptors could do was to carve in wrinkles or corrugations, can one on the ground of deception condemn the gilding? Or where, on the principles of light and shade and of perspective, mere outline in marble must give false proportions, false relative dimensions, can coloring which shall prevent this false representation be reasonably censured? If the proper function of art be to represent truly, how can it be maintained that it should not use those means which are necessary to enable it so to represent? The charge of deception certainly does not lie here, for deception looks to the intention. The use of paint to perfect the representation can be condemned only on grounds upon which the use of dead matter to represent living body should be condemned—on grounds upon which all representative art should be rejected.

Laws of use of material.

§ 219. In the use of the material the general laws are of an imperative character, the rigid observance of which is indispensable to true æsthetic representation.

1. In accordance with its own nature.

1. The material must be used in strict accordance with its own nature and properties. The material of sculpture, in its highest forms at least, is solid body; it is subject to the laws of gravity consequently, and must have support. Moreover, in order to æsthetic effect, this necessary support must appear; at least if it cannot be discovered in the contemplation how the support can be furnished in the case, the contemplation is disturbed, and the taste is offended. For this reason bodies in motion, in flight, or in leap, cannot well be represented in sculpture. In like manner, members of the body—the arms and limbs—cannot be represented in such positions as would in the living body be impossible as permanent positions, or only in momentary transition.

Stone, too, has little cohesion; heavy weight, therefore, should not be made to rest on slender reaches, although in life an extended arm may by muscular and tendonous cohesion be able to sustain large weight without difficulty. The sculptor may to some extent devise expedients by which he may meet both demands—that of the idea or subject, and that of the material. Thus, for example, the drapery may be made a support to an extended arm. Marble, moreover, demands a smooth polished surface. To this demand the exact imitation of slight unevenness in flesh must be sacrificed, and the softness of hair must be symbolized in plaits or corrugations.

The criticism of Sir Joshua Reynolds here is eminently just: "The folly of attempting to make stone sport and flutter in the air, is so apparent that it carries with it its own reprehension; and yet to accomplish this seemed to be the great ambition of many modern sculptors, particularly Bernini. His art was so much set on overcoming this difficulty that he was forever attempting it, though by that attempt he risked everything that was valuable in the art."

2. In accordance with laws of light.

§ 220. 2. The material must be used in strict accordance with the medium through which it reaches the imagination. This medium is light, and through light as affected by outline, by light and shade, and perspective. As in Architecture, and still more in Landscape, we have seen that both absolute and relative distance affect our estimate of the dimensions, the relative positions, and the forms of objects, and as the estimate is affected differently by different surfaces, it is seen at once to be necessary to use the material in sculpture considerately in reference to this principle. A smooth surface reflects light thus differently from a rough surface; a soft surface differently from a hard surface; a dull from a polished surface. Size, shape, relative position, accordingly appear different from the natural appearance in living flesh when the light that reveals them comes from a hard, smooth-polished marble surface. A metallic surface reflects light, too, differently from stone; and white marble differently from colored sandstone or granite or porphyry.

Law of form respects chiefly artistic design.

§ 221. III. THE LAW OF FORM IN SCULPTURE. We have here almost exclusively to consider the principles of artistic design. As a free art, sculpture has not properly to take into view any foreign end of utility as we found to be the case with Architecture and Landscape. Sculpture may be enlisted, indeed, in the service of worship or of grateful remembrance. It may be called to represent character so that it shall be recognized to be revered or remembered with gratitude and affection. But it subserves these outer, remoter ends through form, and accomplishes these foreign objects best and most perfectly as it accomplishes its own end as a free art and presents as its proper achievement a pure form. With mechanical design, it hence has little or nothing properly to do, except to use it where needful for its own uses. Mechanical design, as in architecture and in landscape, for its own end in some utility, sculpture does not employ. This principle is fully compatible with its enlistment of all needful mechanical devices and appliances in the attainment of its proper ends. The sculptor, proposing a statue in marble, for exemplification, first prepares his model in clay. To work this incohesive material, mechanical supports and scaffolding, as also mechanical tools and implements may be serviceable. When his model in clay, upon which his chief artistic skill is expended, is brought to completion, its transfer to marble may require little more than mechanical skill and effort. He may leave the work in fact to the mechanic, except in the general oversight and superintendence as far as to the last touches of the chisel.

There is as little room for proper decorative design in sculpture. The large spaces in architecture and in landscape may invite if not even demand of art to go beyond its own commanding object and end in order to help and guide the eye of contemplation as it moves from one part to another, and to keep it awake by presenting perpetual objects of study. But no such demand arises here in the limited productions of the sculptor. The grand corruption and degeneracy in the art, indeed, have ever arisen from the tendency to dwell on details, and to elaborate these so as to draw away attention from the principal design. Still decorative design has a place however limited. Symbolical decoration particularly is often tributary to the fullest æsthetic effect. Phidias in true taste placed a figure of Victory in the right hand of his colossal statue of Olympian Jupiter. The helmet, the breast plate, the shield, and the sandals of his Athene in the Parthenon were richly decorated. His sculptures, esteemed the matchless products of the art through all the ages, which once adorning the Parthenon now enrich the British museum, were in the spirit of decorative art. Indeed, every where sculpture enlists decoration. The beautiful little cast of Longfellow by Rogers is worthily, tastefully decorated with the bust of Dante.

§ *222.* The law of Artistic Design in Sculpture divides itself at once into the law of medium and the law of intelligence in form;—the law founded in the principles of light, and the law founded in the principles of the rational intelligence.

I. Optical principles.

I. The artist in sculpture must, as has been already intimated, regulate his whole procedure in conformity with the optical principles of perspective and light and shade. The particulars to be observed in this optical law of the art are summarily these:—(1) placing the parts in light or shade according to their relative importance; (2) the effect of relative distance in determining through the visual angle the estimate of size, shape, surface, and relative position; and (3) the effect of distance on the sharpness of outline and rounding of figure.

These particular laws will moreover have a various application according to the size of the work and the specific method of representing in it.

There are readily distinguished three different kinds of sculpture in reference to size. We have thus the colossal, the life-size, and the statuette. It is obvious that the optical principles mentioned will vary with these different kinds.

Proper statuary. § 223. The art, moreover, employs widely different processes, and thus works out widely different products. Its chief and most characteristic product is the statue—either single form or a group, colossal, life-size, or statuette—but detached from supporting wall, and standing upon its own base. Proper statuary embraces several varieties, determined by the nature of the material, and consequently by the process of production. Its truest form, perhaps, is the work of the chisel, and is wrought in stone from models in clay. Master pieces of statuary are found also in wood. Metallic sculpture is cast in molds from clay models. Beautiful statuary as well as relief work has been produced from the most ancient times, in *terra cotta*, being first fashioned in plaster-clay of suitable quantities for this use, and then burnt to stone-like hardness, or simply dried and hardened in the air, with colors put on, dried or burned in, or in-gilt.

Relief. § 224. A second kind of product is relief or raised work. This work is attached to a supporting wall, and according to the degree of projection from this supporting background is distinguished into the three varieties, of high relief *(alto relievo, haut-relief)*, middle or half relief *(mezzo relievo, demi-relief)*, and low relief *(basso relievo, bas-relief).* In high relief the figures are barely attached to the supporting wall. The head and limbs may be entirely detached; but still the whole work is referred to the plane back ground, which circumstance determines the character of the work. Figures that can be represented as in the same plane, as in processions, are peculiarly fit subjects for relief. In half relief work, the figures project by one half of their depth from the supporting background. In this variety, as in high relief, the rules of light and shade have a much larger application than in low relief, in which the figures barely project from the supporting surface.

High Relief.

Half relief.

Low relief.

§ 225. Of an opposite character to this raised work and constituting a third variety is *intaglio* or sunk work, in which the figures are cut or cast in the material and thus instead of being raised above the surface are sunk below it. In deep *intaglio*, the principles of shading have application. One variety of *intaglio*, is that which may be called *relieved intaglio*, in which the figures are left on the surface plane by cutting out the surface around them.

Intaglio.

Exemplifications of raised work in the smaller products are found in *cameos*, of sunk work in *gems*. Etymologically a cameo is a raised gem, the latter word being the genuine word for all sculptured jewels whether in relief or *intaglio*. Stones consisting of two or more layers were selected for cameos, the lower layer being the supporting wall of the figures. Shells, particularly of the *coneta,* having two layers of different hues, are wrought in the same way. The success of the artist in this department will depend on his judgment in selecting material having the layers of suitable thickness and of suitable colors, and on his skill in adapting his subject to the material and in rendering.

§ 226. The several principles of beauty founded in the intelligence have extensive and various application to sculpture. The principle of unity forbids attempts to bring into the same product of art either attributes or members that cannot be in their nature conjoined in imagination. In grouped statuary as also in relief work the subjects introduced should be all brought under some one principle of unity; or if the governing principle be departed from, the departure should be only in subordination. The subjects of a group should be one in time or one in place, or one in pursuit, or one in experience;—one in some respect that shall not be difficult for the contemplating mind to recognize. So likewise unity in nature is necessary to the highest æsthetic effect. The attempted union of rational forms with the shapes of animals, of birds, or of fish, can hardly be admitted to be of the highest style of art, even when interpreted symbolically. So too the attempted combination of opposite attributes in the same subject, as of the highest masculine vigor with the highest feminine tenderness can hardly be counted a success, although marked by highest skill in rendering.

Unity.

Contrast.

§ 227. Contrast, the representation of the different, also has an obvious part in sculpture. It should be the aim of the artist to present any two objects of the same kind in such way that the difference between them shall readily engage the attention.

Æsthetic number.

§ 228. The principle of æsthetic number, controls all true procedures in this art as in architecture and landscape. The nature of the material forbids the ready union of many subjects in one piece. The eye seeks to discover singleness in the block of marble or of stone for full sized, free, standing statuary; and it would be difficult to find suitable material of sufficient size for large groups of subjects. The group of the Laocoon, as stated. is in six pieces, indeed, which shows the possibility of uniting in one work of art several different pieces with good effect. But there is an obvious limitation here. In relief, however, especially in work on an extended pediment or frieze, or other large surface, complicated scenes may be represented. Even the movement of a long procession, or complicated battle scenes find place in relief; but the number of distinct objects to be grouped in one view must be limited, and if large numbers are introduced recourse must be had to subordination in groups or to distribution into departments.

Proportion.

§ 229. The law of proportion has been a prominent study with sculptors. The attempt has been made to find the proportions fixed in the nature of things between the parts of the human body, in order to its most perfect beauty. All such attempts overlook the consideration that the highest criterion of beauty being perfect expression of idea according as the ideal in sculpture is energy and force, or tenderness and grace, the proportions must vary. Hercules cannot be truly represented with the same proportions as Jupiter, as muscular force implies a broader frame than intellectual power; Apollo, as the impersonation of muscular grace, must in like manner differ from Venus as the type of feminine beauty.

Symmetry and Harmony.

§ 230. The demands of symmetry and harmony are as imperative in sculpture as in any province of art. Such of its products as are for close inspection, as is all proper statuary except colossal work, particularly require that any two like members be in exact symmetry, unless there be clear reason for variation. The statue of a smith might perhaps appropriately represent the right arm in larger form than the left; or that of a Benjamite have the left larger than the right. So to counteract the optical effect of perspective, in order to apparent symmetry the real dimensions in the two members may vary. Winckelmann has remarked that the retired leg in the Apollo Belvedere and also in the Laocoon, is longer and proportionately larger than the other.

History.

§ 231. EXEMPLIFICATION OF THE PRINCIPLES OF FORM IN SCULPTURE IN THE HISTORICAL PROGRESS OF THE

ART.—Sculpture dates back to the earliest periods. Polytheism and idolatry at once prompted and required in their service the exercise of the art. Old Egyptian sculpture wrought out in a rude, clumsy way, but on a scale truly prodigious, representations of their religious ideas in caverns and also in vast detached blocks of stone. It wrought also in bronze free standing statues as well as relief work. Miles of walls around old Thebes, famous for its hundred gates, were covered with bas-relief. It used moreover wood and clay as material. It cut its hieroglyphics in *intaglio*. It delighted in the mysterious, the grand, the monstrous. The sphinx is a characteristic product of Egyptian sculpture, innumerable relics of which are still found, and of all magnitudes to even over a hundred feet in length. It is a monstrous union of a human head and breast, generally feminine, sometimes masculine, sometimes both, with a lion's body, and sometimes also with wings. It is diversely conjectured to have been an astronomical representation of the signs of Virgo and Leo, and a symbolical representation of the union of the spiritual and the animal. It startles, perhaps attracts, at first, by its strangeness; the continued contemplation turns away in dissatisfaction, not to say disgust.

Egyptian sculpture.

§ 232. Grecian genius may have been kindled from an Egyptian altar; but it soon reached a noble independence and grandeur, and in no department of art did it attain a higher perfection than in sculpture. In-

Grecian.

deed, it seemed here to have reached the very *ultima thule* of human attainment. Four periods, marking as many styles, have been recognized without, however, very precise philosophical demarkations. The first is named the period of Dædalus, himself a mythical character. It is the first stage of a rising art.

Four periods.

The second period begins with Phidias—an Athenian who died 444 B. C. His great works were the chryselephantine (gold and ivory) colossal statues of the Athene in the Parthenon and the Olympian Jupiter in Elis, a Pallas in brass at Athens, a Venus, Nemesis, and an Amazon designed to combine manly strength with womanly grace. Besides these free standing statues, to him belongs the glory of the marvelous work in relief on the Parthenon, so often alluded to, now known as the Elgin marbles in the British museum. Of these masterpieces of art, the British artist, Haydon, remarks: "Every truth of shape, the result of the inherent organization of man as an intellectual being; every variation of that shape, produced by the slightest variation of motion, in consequence of the slightest variation of intention, acting on it; every result of repose on flesh as a soft substance, and on bone as a hard, both being influenced by the common principles of life and gravitation; every harmony of line in composition, from geometrical principle, all proving the science of the artist; every beauty of conception proving his genius; and every grace of execution proving that practice had given his hand power, can be shown to exist in the Elgin marbles."

Polycletus, who carried the art of high relief to perfection and excelled in balancing figures on one leg and in the symmetry of his parts; Myron, who executed those colossal statues upon one pedestal, and wrought out with great skill athletic figures; and Pythagoras, who is supposed to have executed the original of the famous Apollo Belvedere, are placed in this second period. It is the period in which sculpture attained full manhood.

The third period is the period of finish, of grace and delicacy in expression. To this period belong Praxiteles, a native of Paros, about 350 B. C., who executed, among other subjects, all of a more delicate cast, the famous Venus of Cos, and also the Venus of Cnidos, and the Niobe; and Scopas, also a native of Paros, who erected the famous mausoleum, or sepulchral monument of king Mausolus, and executed many noted works both in marble and in bronze. This stage of the art, in place of such subjects as Jupiter, Juno, and Minerva, in which the preceding period delighted, selected in preference Venus, and Bacchus, and Amor.

The fourth period of Grecian sculpture is the period of decline. It is characterized by excessive elaboration of details. In this period are placed Lysippus, a native of Sicyon, about 324 B. C., a painter as well as sculptor, said to have executed 610 statues, some colossal, some equestrian; Chares, a pupil of Lysippus, the artificer of the Colossus at Rhodes; and Agesander of Rhodes, who with his sons Athenodorus and Polydorus, produced the famous group of the Laocoon.

The Laocoon

Modern.

§ 233. Modern sculpture took its rise in northern Italy. Its progress was slow from the time of Boschetto in the eleventh century, the architect of the cathedral in Pisa, to that of Michael Angelo in the middle of the sixteenth. Nicolo and Giovanni da Pisa in the thirteenth, Donatello of Florence in the fifteenth and his contemporary Ghiberti, who executed the famous bronze gates of St. John's Baptistery in Florence, "worthy," in the judgment of Michael Angelo, "to be the gates of paradise," are sculptors who have made themselves illustrious in the art. Others of less distinction appeared from time to time in northern Italy. And in the most recent times the art has greatly flourished, rivaling in boldness and originality of design and in perfectness of execution the old Grecian art. Canova, born in the Venetian territory in 1757, produced many works worthy of the classic age; and Thorwaldsen, who was born in Copenhagen in 1771, and died there in 1844, surpassed his great contemporary, if not in grace and finish, in majesty of conception. These last are the two great names in modern sculpture. But in France, in Germany, in Great Britain, and in America have arisen many artists of great power and skill, and the present age is one of richest promise in every department of the art.

CHAPTER VIII.

SPECIAL LAWS—PAINTING.

Origin.

§ 234. The free art of Painting owes, if not its origin, at least much of its early vigor and growth to a want. The desire to transmit intelligence of men and events from one to another and from age to age prompted the delineation of those objects in bark, or stone, or metal, or other available material. Picture-writing thus naturally introduced hieroglyphical and proper alphabetical writing. "The earliest people," says Goguet in his *Origine des Lois,* "wrote by objects." Painting, like every other true art, thus begins with something to be expressed, begins with the idea.

Range of Subjects.

§ 235. I. LAW OF IDEA IN PAINTING. In wealth and diversity of idea, Painting even surpasses the sister art of sculpture. The entire realm of idea is open to it, even purely spiritual subjects and relations allowing representation through it indirectly and symbolically. Landscape it represents as freely as persons or animals, which sculpture can hardly handle with effect and only in low relief in which department it borders closely on painting.

Its subjects, like those of sculpture, distribute themselves, in respect to invention, into three classes: real subjects, idealized subjects, and original subjects.

Departments. § 236. In respect to essential character of subject they distribute themselves into four classes, constituting so many departments of the art, as in portrait, historical, landscape, and *genre* painting.

Portrait. Portrait painting comprehends both human and super-human subjects. In rare instances even the divine has been attempted. But, inasmuch as the human is the highest and most perfect embodiment of spirit known to men, the divine can be represented only symbolically through the human. So the angelic appears, except by symbol as with wings and the like, only through the human countenance. The representation of character, whether copy of the actual, or idealized from the actual, or wholly of original invention, has been the highest aim and achievement of the art.

Historical. Historical painting, or the representation of actions or events, constitutes a leading department of the art. In it are found many of its master pieces.

Landscape. Landscape painting, or the representation of earth and sky, of land and water, of mountain and valley, field and forest, ocean and river, more recent than Historical and Portrait painting, originating, indeed, in the elaboration of back grounds in historical pieces, has in the last two centuries won a large and worthy place in the art.

Genre. Genre Painting, although likewise of modern origin, has attained a wide celebrity. Its characteristic subjects are the scenes of actual and more especially of familiar and domestic life. Its ideals are not necessarily persons, although the highest art seems to require ever the presence of some human interest, and therefore persons are not excluded; but human character or persons are not the only subjects of this species of painting. Neither are its ideals properly transactions or historic achievements, although the familiar events of domestic life are common themes with the cultivators of this department of painting. It is a department which connects with historical and landscape painting, and often seems to trench upon their proper domains. But it represents characteristically the real and familiar scenes of life into which the human, the animal, the utensils, all the surroundings of common life enter.

Still life. In this department properly belongs a field of art which has recently been extensively and worthily cultivated, denominated *still life.* Its subjects are things without life, as lifeless animals, birds, fish, instruments, utensils. Flowers and fruits belong rather under Landscape painting; they belong to the outdoor world; while the subjects of still life are rather from indoor life. Persons are excluded; yet the objects which make up a picture of indoor reality are just those which cluster around the experiences that enter into the deepest feelings of the heart; they suggest persons, and interest only as they concern persons.

Light. § 237. II. LAW OF MATERIAL IN PAINTING.—It is the peculiarity of Painting that it represents on a surface by means of light. All its objects are thus in fact placed on the same ground and in the same plane; while by means of the diversified light in which they are represented, they are made to appear projected forward or backward from that common plane, and thus to have depth as well as surface and so appear as solids. The one means by which this effect is produced is light.

Gradations:—Outline. § 238. Three gradations in the use of light are to be recognized. The first is simple outline. Forms of objects, their dimensions, both actual and relative, both to other objects and to the eye of the observer and their distances relative to other objects and to the observer, are effectively represented in ink or in pencil.

Shade. The second gradation is that denominated technically *chiaroscuro*, or light and shade. To outline is added here shading, which is effected in three ways:—by lines parallel to the governing outline; by dots, called *stippling;* and by cross-lining called *hatching*. These two gradations are effected in pure or undecomposed light—by the use of white or black, which is accepted as the absence of light. The effect of shading is given also by intensifying the color.

Color. The third gradation is in the use of decomposed light or proper color. If a beam of light from the sun be transmitted through a triangular prism of glass, it will be separated into divers rays, having respectively colors which cannot be further decomposed, and are hence called primary colors. Of these primary colors Newton enumerates seven, violet, indigo, blue, green, yellow, orange, and red; Brewster, three, blue, yellow, red; Herschel says all colors can be compounded of three with the addition of white.

Treatment. § 239. The use of light in these several gradations is diversified both in respect to the instrument or the means by which it is used, and also the surface to which it is applied. The pencil in drawing, the brush in coloring, the burin in engraving, are characteristic instruments in these several departments of the art.

Means. In respect to the means by which the color is applied there are distinguished also, divers departments; as Oil Painting, when the color is applied in oil; Water Color, when prepared in water; Elydoric when prepared in water and oil; Distemper Painting, when prepared with size or other glutinous substance. Still other substances have been used from time to time as vehicles of color for some purpose or another, and the æsthetic effect of the work has been accordingly more or less modified. Still further distinctions arise from the varied use of heat in the application of colors. The ancients used colore mixed with wax which were applied with a hot graver. This variety of painting was named from the Greek *encaustic*, burnt in. In Enamel painting the different colors are obtained from different metallic oxides which are also burnt in after having been applied. Mosaic Paintings are formed of small pieces of artificial stone or glass already separately colored. A frame is first prepared and the surface being covered with mastic, the colored design or cartoon is imitated by placing in it these type-like bits of colored stone or glass. When the mastic or cement is dry, the surface composed of these many pieces is polished as desired.

Surface.

§ 240. The diversified nature of the substance to the surface of which colors are applied, also diversifies the art. Bark, wood, paper, canvas, metal, ivory, in truth, any material yielding a smooth, permanent surface, the art has made available to its different uses and purposes. One prominent department, perhaps the oldest of the art, Fresco painting, is denominated from the character of the surface—fresh plaster—on which the colors are applied. As the colors are intended to sink into the plaster while still moist, and to dry with it, great celerity is requisite in the artist, as well as great exactness and precision in every movement, for the nature of the work allows no retouching or correcting. The designs for this reason are often first wrought out on pasteboard, *cartone*, and are transferred to the wall through copies taken on tracing paper.

In Engraving, the design is first executed in some hard substance, as wood, or stone, or metal, to be afterwards printed on paper or canvas in outline, chiaroscuro, or colors. There are various departments of this great art named from the material or the mode of working. Thus we have Xylography or wood engraving, copper and steel engraving, and the like. In etching, the metal is covered with a preparation of wax; the design is worked in that with a delicate pencil, cutting lines through the wax into the metal; and then these lines are bitten into the plate by an acid. *Aquatinto,* water-tint, and *mezzo tinto,* half-tint, are varieties of the art.

Twofold law.

§ 241. In the use of the material, the artist in painting is subject to the two comprehensive laws which were recognized in the art of sculpture. The material must be used in conformity with its own nature and also in conformity with the nature of the medium, light, through which the art addresses the imagination.

1. Conformity to its own nature; 2. To nature of light.

Effects which are practicable through the brush it may be unwise to attempt through the burin or the pencil. Each instrument gives its peculiar characteristic to the work. So the surface, according as it is wood, or ivory, or canvas, or metal, demands a different treatment and for peculiar uses. The same is true of the divers processes employed in the art. Light and color also have certain laws which must be recognized. Light, thus, moves in straight lines. Farther, light, impinging on certain objects, is more or less reflected and more or less absorbed. It is all reflected from no object; such light from the sun would be pure white light. But no object appears as pure white; the whitest snow absorbs a part of the sun's rays that fall upon it. Whatever light is reflected is subject to the law that the angle of reflection is equal to the angle of incidence. So no object absorbs all the light that impinges upon it; were this the fact in any case, the object would be of course invisible. Farther, light impinging on some objects is in part received and transmitted through them; and in passing from one medium to another it is subject to the great law of refraction, that the different rays are bent out of their course, and this in different degrees. The order of refrangibility, beginning with the least refrangible, is, red, orange, yellow, green, blue, indigo, violet. In landscape painting, in which distant objects are represented as sky and cloud, or distant mountain, water, or tree, this law of light becomes of vital importance, as one principle of aërial perspective.

§ 242. III. LAW OF FORM IN PAINTING.—As its sister art, sculpture, the free art of painting has no end of utility to subserve, except what it attains through its own free product—pure form. Nor is there much more occasion for formally considering decorative design than mechanical design. It is true that the filling up of back ground may not be absolutely necessary for the perfect revelation of the main ideas of the work; but it stands in much closer connection with it than the sculpturing of the blank spaces in architecture, or the ornamentation of landscape. So the human figure, which land-

zhong'r

scape or genre painting may introduce, in order to invest the representation with a proper human interest, enters into the essential nature of the work, and cannot in strictness be deemed decoration.

Twofold law.

§ 243. The law of artistic design in painting is twofold, as it is founded more directly in the medium through which the artist reveals, or in his own spiritual nature.

1. Of treatment of light.

1. Not only must the artist in painting use light in conformity with its laws, as that it moves in right lines, is variously reflected, absorbed, transmitted, and refracted, according to the nature of the object on which it impinges, but in actually revealing his idea through this medium in accordance with its laws, there are certain principles which he must recognize and observe.

Linear perspective.

§ 244. In the first place, there are the principles of Linear Perspective and Projection to be observed in all representation of visual objects. These principles require first, that one point of view be fixed, from which all the objects represented are to be viewed. Next, we have the great law of Linear Perspective, that the dimensions of objects are measured by the visual angle which they subtend; the greater the distance a given object is from the eye the smaller it appears, and also if turned obliquely to the view it will appear less. Then come the laws of Graphic Projection, which require that all objects be reduced to the one plane on which the representation is made.

Graphic projection.

Shading.

§ 245. In the second place, there are the principles of shading to be observed.

Direction of light.

First, the source and direction from which the light is to be represented as coming upon the various objects, is to be determined, and the light and shade managed in accordance with the determination. The solar rays are sensibly parallel, but they may come from near the horizon or from the zenith, and they alight upon this or that side of the object illuminated, leaving the other in the shade, and cast shadows accordingly. Light from a luminary near at hand moves in divergent lines, and casts shadows in the direction in which it moves and in widening lines. Cross-lights from different sources modify all these representations. Then we have the gradations of shade, the principles of half-tint regulating the tone of shade to the varying distance of the object from the assumed point of view—gradations varying more rapidly as the object comes more directly in front. Still farther, in addition to the principles of shading from the source and direction of the light and the relative position of the object, we have those principles which are furnished in the effect that the medium through which the objects are seen has upon their appearance—the principles of Aërial Perspective. Smoke, vapor, mist, common air when even relatively clear, modify the effect of distant objects on the eye, absorbing the light from them and so dimming

Tone.

Aërial perspective.

them, obscuring and thus softening sharp outlines, as well as imparting to them a different hue. Here is found a chief excellence in landscape painting, which tints sky, clouds, distant objects on land, as their appearance is modified by being seen through the atmosphere as clear, or hazy, or smoky.

Color.

§ 246. In the third place, there are the principles of color to be regarded. Here we find the law of complementary colors. For illustration, upon the theory of but three primary colors, red, yellow, and blue, by the various combination of which with white and black all different colors may be formed, this æsthetic principle teaches us that any one of these colors or any combination of them will please best if placed side by side with its complementary color or colors; that is, with such as, if combined with it, would form white light. Red, thus, is most pleasingly associated with yellow and blue, or with green; yellow with red and blue, or with violet; and blue with red and yellow, or with orange. The explanation of the ultimate ground of this remarkable æsthetic law it may be difficult to give; of the prevalence of the law there can be no question.

Chevereul's law of contrasted colors.

Here also we find another law of equal prevalence. It is called Chevereul's law, and is thus announced: "When the eye sees at the same time two contiguous colors, they will appear as dissimilar as possible, both in optical composition and in height of tone." The artist accordingly, rendering in color, must in order to the best æsthetic effect, not only observe the law of complementary colors, but must also regulate himself by this law of contrasted colors in its divers applications. For example, in order to strong and brilliant effect, he must seek to bring the most dissimilar colors in close juxtaposition, so that both shall strike the eye at the same time. In order to softened effect, the gradation of colors must be without abruptness and sudden transition to opposite hues. If he wish to give a certain color predominance and significance, he should seek to set it off by placing its complementary in immediate proximity. If he wish, on the contrary, to prevent any color which truth in representation may oblige him to introduce from impressing the eye because of its disagreeableness or for other cause, he will accomplish his aim best by grading off with colors but slightly dissimilar.

It is to be borne in mind, moreover, in the use of colored light, that depth of color is virtually shade; the deeper tints of the same color are shades to the fainter. Ruskin has correctly taught: "Every light is a shadow compared to higher lights, till we reach the brightness of the sun; and every shadow is a light compared to other shadows, till we reach the darkness of night. Every color used in painting, except pure white and black, is therefore a light and a shade at the same time. It is a light with reference to all below it, and a shade with reference to all above it." Thus it is that some of the best efforts in painting are achieved by gradations of tints.

Law of expression in color.

Here we find, still farther, the law of expression in color. We have before recognized the fact that figure or outline is the more natural expression of intellectual characteristics; while color more naturally expresses those of feeling. Why one feeling should be symbolized by one hue and another feeling by another, it may be as difficult to explain as it is to determine the ground of the laws of complementary and of contrasted colors; but that such is the fact is a matter of familiar experience. The principle, as regulative in art, is twofold: first, each leading color has its own peculiar expression; secondly, intensity of feeling is expressed in depth of hue.

Intellectual principles.

§ 247. 2. Æsthetic design is also subject to the principles which preside over all rational activity. We have recognized these as of the twofold character of intellectual and moral.

The several æsthetic principles founded in the intelligence, already enumerated, of unity, contrast, æsthetic number, proportion, symmetry, and harmony, have their obvious application to painting.

Unity.

First, the law of unity requires singleness in the idea to be represented and singleness in the general mode of representation. So far as diversity of idea is introduced, the diverse must be in such relation of subordination that all may be apprehended as one whole. The lines of light, and the shading and coloring in kind and intensity of hue, should be not only compatible with singleness of object or of scene, but also all point to the governing object represented.

Contrast. Most painting may avail itself of a high degree of the proper beauty of contrast. In the idea and in the material, it is admissible almost indefinitely. The objects themselves in all the diversity of their attributes and the light and color in all the multiplicity of their modifications admit of contrast. It is the duty of the artist to diversify, and in diversifying to present in contrast—ever exhibiting the different, while making prominent the same in the diversity—the unity in the variety. DuFresnoy, while disallowing the close union of extreme opposites, yet lays down the doctrine unqualifiedly that diversity of objects will ever please.

Æsthetic number. Further, the law of æsthetic number limits the representation in the number cf objects presented. When a large variety must be introduced, grouping with subordination becomes indispensable. In historical painting, especially in battle scenes, in genre and also in landscape painting, there is a peculiar liability to introduce an excessive multiplicity of objects which distract and disturb the contemplation.

Finally, the other æsthetic principles founded in the intelligence, of proportion, of symmetry, and of harmony, have their several application so obviously that it is unnecessary to enter into details or specifications.

§ 248. Exemplification of the Principles of

FORM IN PAINTING IN THE HISTORICAL PROGRESS OF THE ART.—In Egypt, the mother of arts, we find the origin of the art of painting. At a very ancient period the Egyptians painted sculpture and then painted walls. They painted the walls of temples and of tombs; they painted their mummy wrappings; they painted papyrus rolls. But their art, under a most despotic restriction confining the practice of the art to families and forbidding all innovation, only rose to literal imitation in outline and in color. They, however, represented ideas symbolically.

§ 249. Grecian art sprang from Egyptian seed. It at first painted sculpture and ministered to that art. But it soon broke from this servitude and became independent. Polygnotus of Thasos, who came to Athens a little after the middle of the fifth century before our era, is to be regarded as the true father of Grecian painting. He elevated the art to a noble independence and freedom. He threw life and character into his paintings, and inculcated a truly moral spirit by the idealized subjects which he represented. But his art was meagre in material. Towards the end of the century, Apollodorus developed light and shade, and was, as Pliny says, the inventor of tone. Zeuxis, his pupil, advanced the art to its perfection so far as respects rendering in outline and in light and shade; but up to thetime of Apelles, who flourished in the period of Alexander the Great, only four colors were used, white, red, yellow, and black. Apelles is the prince of Grecian painters, if we may judge from the descriptions given by writers of his productions, for unfortunately not an original work in ancient painting remains. By untiring and loving practice he acquired a skill in rendering, which gave a matchless grace to his productions. From him we have the maxim so indispensable to all eminence in art, *nulla dies sine linea.* Pausias, of Sicyon, his contemporary, acquired great fame in encaustic. The Grecians also worked in distemper.

§ 250. Roman art achieved no distinction in painting, and did nothing towards the perfection of the art.

Byzantine art, from the seventh to the thirteenth century, contributed nothing. Its subjects were religious, and gave to the art what little inspiration it had; but the style was lifeless and smothered with conventionalisms.

Florentine.

§ 251. Modern Painting properly dates from the thirteenth century. It took its rise in Northern Italy. Giovanni Cimabue, born in Florence in 1240, is accounted, with perhaps some overdue praise, the father of modern painting. He broke from conventional servility and in the spirit of true art like Polygnotus made expression of idea or character the great aim in painting. Giotto his pupil caught the spirit of his master, and far surpassed him in rendering idea. He is accounted the first great modern painter. His subjects were religious. He introduced natural coloring and wrought in fresco. In the following century, Pietro della Francesca and Paolo Uscello developed perspective. Masaccio, born in 1402, in the brief period of his life, as he died at the age of 27, brought to the art the freshness and vigor of earnest studies from life. Leonardo de Vinci, born in 1452, introduced a wonderful richness of design, and applied in masterpieces of art the principles of expression founded in the rational intelligence. His great work, the Last Supper, was wrought in fresco. He is the prince of the Florentine school. Michael Angelo, born in 1475, with his characteristic boldness and grandeur wrought in the true spirit of Leonardo de Vinci, exemplifying the principles of unity, contrast, and the kindred intellectual principles of the art in his sublime frescoes on the ceiling of the Sistine Chapel in the Vatican.

Roman.

Raphael Sanzio d'Urbino, born in 1483, profiting by the study of the Florentine painters, raised through several noticeable stages of progress to the highest excellence, all the elements of the art, idea, material, form, so far as these elements had been developed in his age. His genius in inventing, his skill and grace in rendering, are unsurpassed. The pupil of Perugino, he won a distinct glory for the Roman school, which numbers among its artists the great names of Giulio Romano, Caravaggio, and Andrea Sacchi.

Bolognese.

The Bolognese school furnishes the equally illustrious names of the Carracci, Domenichino, Guido Reni, unsurpassed in grace of outline, Lanfranco, Albani, and Guercino.

Parmese.

In Parma, Antonio Allegri, familiarly known under the name of

Correggio, born in 1493, perfected representation in Chiaroscuro; and the school of Venice in which we find the great names of Titian, and Tintoretto, and Paul Veronese, elaborated to equal perfectness representation in color.

Venitian.

Thus in the various schools of Italy the several elements of the art, idea, material, rendering, were gradually elaborated. That true art consisted in expression of idea; that outline, light and shade, and color must be all under the perfect command of the artist; and that grace in rendering is equally indispensable were principles most fully and triumphantly brought out and established in these schools in Italy in the thirteenth, fourteenth, fifteenth, and sixteenth centuries. The continued advance of the art was thus to be limited chiefly if not entirely to the enrichment of these constituent elements. The idea had been almost exclusively religious and historical; the material, although far more fully elaborated, still invited study and invention in variety of hues, in means and appliances of applying, in surfaces too upon which light and color were to be applied; and of course a boundless field was opened in the essential element of art—execution, rendering,—in which if not richer merit in skill and grace, yet enviable distinction could be won.

Landscape.

The end of the sixteenth and the beginning of the seventeenth century witnessed the introduction of landscape as subject. Peter Paul Rubens of Antwerp, born in 1577, Nicolas Poussin, born in Normandy in 1594, Claude Lorraine, born in 1600, Salvator Rosa, born in Naples in 1614, were successful cultivators of this department of the art.

Genre.

Rembrandt von Ryn, born in 1606, with a remarkable fertility of invention as well as exactness of representation, enlarged the field of subjects for painting; and Teniers of Antwerp, born in 1610, laboring in the same direction came to be accredited as the father of proper genre painting.

The most recent art in Germany, France, Great Britain, and America, thus has had the whole realm of the art already explored and open to them in finished models exemplifying its divers principles in their divers applications: and its proud roll of successful artists shows that it has been fully awake to the calls of the age in which it is privileged to flourish.

CHAPTER IX.

SPECIAL LAWS—MUSIC.

§ 252. The free art of music takes us into a field of study very far removed from that which we have explored hitherto. Both in idea and in matter it differs essentially from the arts as yet considered, It claims antiquity of origin unexceeded by any of them. In the earliest stages of history the native propensity to the expression of feeling easily led to single-voiced song; and the susceptibility to impression from musical sound invited to the use of sounding instruments for its gratification. The feelings called forth in religious worship, the excitements of festal joy, and the enthusiasm of battle, all strong, sustained feeling shared in by numbers, found an instinctive utterance in music. At first, undoubtedly very simple and rude, mere prolongation, perhaps, of the ordinary sounds of articulate speech, or mere beating of noisy instruments, the æsthetic spirit fondly nourished up the art thus feebly beginning to be, through the various stages of melody, and rhythm, and harmony, to a maturity most marvelously rich and beautiful.

Origin.

Rank. Music now admits no superior in the sisterhood of the arts, save only perhaps that of Discourse and Poetry, to which it has from its origin been the loving and most serviceable minister and companion. As the art whose exclusive prerogative it is to express feeling, whose very idea to be expressed is æsthetic form in its large technical sense of sensibility impressed, it indeed comes nearer to the heart than any other art. Music is sensibility immediately impressing sensibility through the medium—sound—common both to the active imagination addressing and to the passive imagination addressed. In this art soul is brought into closest contact with soul, feeling with feeling. In painting, some object presented is first taken up by the imagination and then expressed by it, and the aim of the artist is to bring this object before the sensibility addressed. But in music it is not some such foreign object itself, but his own soul as impressed by it, which he aims to communicate. No art therefore so directly touches and moves the sensibility as music. Its supremacy in the arts lies precisely here, that it thus commands the inmost access to the heart, while other arts wait at an outer door.

Feeling. § 253. Law of Idea in Music. The grand distinctive characteristic of music is that it is the immediate expression of feeling. In the exactest nomenclature of mental science the idea in music is *form.* That is, it is the human soul as impressed, as passive consequently and shaped, not as impressing, not as active and shaping. This kind of idea in distinction from ideas of knowing and willing, from cognitions and volitions, it is the prerogative of music to take as its content and to express. This is the fundamental and all-governing law of music that it expresses immediately and only feeling.

§ 254. Feeling is diversified in two different ways—in kind and in degree; music accordingly is variously shaped and determined in these two ways by its idea.

Kinds of feeling.

1. Feeling is diversified by the constituents that enter into it. In its simplest and lowest form it is mere sensibility awakened or stirred by some object coming in from without or coming forth from one's own experience. By these objects it is variously colored. The comprehensive hues, are those of joy or sorrows of pleasure or pain; but they are shaded from the almost colorless serenity of an unmoved soul, up through the gradations of cheerfulness, gladness, to the brightness of ecstatic joy, or down through sadness, gloom, to the deepest sorrow. But it is mere unmixed sensibility, modified only in respect to the object which addresses and moves it. There is the serenity of a self-complacent spirit, and the serenity of a soul in harmony with the universe around it. Thus there is sensibility subjectively awakened and sensibility objectively awakened and running through all the gradations indicated. There is penitence, for example, or feeling stirred by sense of personal wrong-doing; there is sorrow for

Simple feeling.

suffering that another is seen to experience. So the innumerable objects addressing the soul from without itself or bodied forth from its own experience by an ever active imagination, each colors with its own proper hue the feeling which it calls forth. With an inexhaustible richness of idea is the art of music endowed in these countless modifications of the mere sensibility.

Sympathy.

§ 255. But this sensibitity may be modified, may be enlarged and enhanced by the admission into it of a true sympathy. Often objects move us, they excite our joy or move our grief, while our spirits do not look out upon them ; they are passively and blindly affected by them to pleasure or to pain. But as having a common origin and parentage with the universe around us, our natures are sympathetic in their very essence. Our awakened sensibility tends to go out and to respond to the calls by which it is awakened. A new element thus enters the excited feeling. It is feeling in sympathy or, it may be, in antipathy toward its object. There is accordingly music that is merely sensitive feeling ; and there is music also that is more than this; that expresses a true sympathy; a yearning to be united with the object that has stirred it or that it would itself stir. There is a music that expresses more than pleasure or joy; or more than pain or sorrow; that breathes forth in addition a joyful complacency or a sympathetic grief; a glad satisfaction and contentment or a displeasure and discontent ; a fond affection or a repelling anger and aversion ; love or hate.

Hope and fear.

§ 256. Still a third modification of the sensibility emerges when there appears not only sympathy with the object but actual desire and longing for it; when sympathy or antipathy passes into hope or fear. And here we find all the intermediate gradations between the most confident and assured and exulting hope on the one hand down through mere hopelessness and despair of good to the deepest fear of evil and the stormiest terror and shock of alarm.

Degrees of feeling.

§ 257. 2. All these divers modifications of the sensibility are susceptible of higher or lower degrees of intensity. As already intimated, joy intensifies from a simply bright serenity to the highest ecstasies of rapture; and sorrow from the merest sadness to the deepest anguish.

In this unlimited diversity of feelings in kind and degree, the art of music has an unbounded wealth of idea to express.

Music must express feeling as its one idea.

§ 258. The law of idea requires that the artist in music find that which he is to express in his art in this large but well-defined field of idea. It is his province to express not the object of a feeling;—not that which may have awakened the feeling in his own bosom, but the feeling itself. The terror which he aims to express may be differently colored in some respect according as it is awakened by an earthquake or by a thunder storm; by the assault of a raging beast of prey or an outburst of human passion; by alarms from without or from within. But it is the so colored feeling in his own imagination, not the coloring object itself; it is the quaking, shuddering soul, not the quaking, shuddering earth or storm which he is to set forth in music. To attempt to imitate the tremblings of the earth or the reverberations of the rolling thunder is to go out of the prescribed field of idea in music; it is to violate the fundamental law of the art; it is certain to be more or less suicidal. That there are sounds in nature which musical art can in a true literal sense imitate, can repeat both in respect to relative, perhaps in some cases, in respect to absolute pitch and volume, and quality of sound, and quickness of succession, is certainly true. But music, as the art whose governing idea is feeling, must represent that, not the object which awakens it. So far as these musical sounds in nature are expressive of certain feelings, and they are all to be interpreted as thus expressive, the art of music expressing the same feelings through the same medium of sound will of course use the same movements in quality, pitch, volume, and velocity; but it is still the feeling which music is to express, not the object which expresses the feeling. Not the caroling bird, but the feeling of which its carols are the natural expression, is that which the musical artist is alone concerned to embody in sound.

This law of idea in music must not be interpreted as if the artist must lay aside his intelligence or his voluntary activity. Feeling is but one side of a feeling, thinking, willing spirit. All feeling is ever intelligent and free, even although it so predominates in the experience as to eclipse to our view those other coördinate constituents of the human soul. Never must it be forgotten that all feeling is the affection of a rational spirit, which never lays aside its essential character. Yet it remains that a true artist in music, a true Mozart, breathes into his sounds only the modifications of his own feeling soul. It is his duty to put himself first into a pure mood of feeling by free surrender of his sensibility to the object which awakens it, and to suffer his own soul to be moved freely undistractedly to its proper feeling, and then reëcho in song or instrumental strain the feeling thus awakened and shaped. He may need to bring in the aid of all other faculties and resources to keep his soul under the impressing power of its object; he may need to recur to memory, to imagination, to help him to sustain this feeling; but never, as some unsuccessful artists have done, attempt to render any thing in sound but the modifications in kind and degree of his own feeling soul.

Condition of musical culture.

§ 259. Hence the fundamental condition of culture in musical art is the feeding and training of the sensibility under the laws of its nature. It is effected only by freeing the soul to the full and legitimate impression of right formed, of proper æsthetic objects from without, and particularly of sounds; by the development of sympathy through loving intercourse with whatever is lovely; and by the exercise of all true human affection.

§ 260. LAW OF MATERIAL IN MUSIC.

Sound.

The art of music addresses the ear through sound. Not all sounds, however, are to be regarded as musical; only such, indeed, as are caused by uniform vibrations of the air reaching the ear. All the different effects of music are produced by divers modifications of these vibrations.

Fourfold variation of sound.

§ 261. There are four different ways in which vibrations in musical sound may be varied. First, they may be varied in respect to the velocity, or the number of vibrations in a given measure of time.

Pitch.

Such variations give the different degrees of musical *Pitch*. While different ears vary in respect to their susceptibility to sound, no human ear can be sensible of musical sound,if the vibrations of air that fall upon it are slower than at the rate of thirty in a second; or as sound moves at about 1125 feet in a second, if the waves are less than about thirty-eight feet in length. Nor can a sound be heard, if the vibrations are quicker than at the rate of two thousand in a second. The musical note denominated middle C in the treble clef is the effect of between two hundred and fifty and two hundred and sixty vibrations or waves of musical sound in a second—the pitch of this note varying of course with the standard which is slightly different in different countries and for different purposes.

It is found, now, that the relations of different musical sounds are in an almost exact correspondence with certain mathematical ratios, which even nature, as if musically constituted, observes. Thus a string or cord tensely drawn, as in the familiar Æolian harp, so that the air may suitably put it in vibration, will as the force of the wind varies give a certain succession, sometimes a simultaneous combination of sounds which is exceedingly agreeable to the ear. If a string, moreover, vibrating at its full length, give forth a certain note, and then be divided into two equal parts, each half of the string will with the same tension and the same force applied to it, vibrate twice as many times in a second and produce another note which has an agreeable musical relation to the first. If the string thus at full length vibrate 255 times in a second, and produce middle C, each half will vibrate 510 times and produce a note called the octave of C and in perfect accord with it. Vibrating through one half of this, or 1020 times a second, it gives a note an octave above this and so on. Farther, between any note and its octave, there are intermediate divisions of the string with corresponding rates of vibration at which sounds are produced agreeable to the ear. Some of these intervening sounds are such as the string will give forth as it variously divides itself and so varies its vibrations with the varying force of the wind. The principle is this: that any two sounds are in more perfect accord as the different vibrations of air which produce them, coincide in the greatest frequency. Thus two vibrations, one of which moves twice as quick as the other, will coincide in each of the slower vibrations and each alternate one of the quicker. If, instead of double or as two to one, the time of the one vibration be to that of the other as three to two, the coincidence will be only in every second of the slower and every third of the quicker; the combination of these sounds is agreeable to the ear, but not as perfectly so as the former.

Diatonic scale.

§ 262. Thus it is found that there are, between a given note and its octave, six notes which are in a special musical relation to one another. They constitute what is called, the *Diatonic scale.* The vibrations producing these notes are severally proportioned to the first note called in this relation the *key note,* as follows: the number of vibrations in a second of time producing the second note in this scale, rising from the key note to its next higher octave, is to the number of vibrations producing the key note as 9 to 8; the third, as 5 to 4; the fourth, as 4 to 3; the fifth, as 3 to 2; the sixth, as 5 to 3; the seventh, as 15 to 8; the eighth or octave, as 2 to 1. In other words, if the first note in the scale be produced by 240 vibrations, the second will be by 270; the third by 300; the fourth by 320; the fifth by 360; the sixth by 400; the seventh by 450; the octave by 480. It will be seen that the coincidences in the vibrations or waves of the octave with the vibrations of the key note—the first or prime—are more frequent than with those of any other. Next comes the fifth; then the fourth. And the coincidences with those of the seventh are less frequent than with those of any other note.

Major and minor intervals.

§ 263. Further if we compare these numbers with each other we shall see that the ratio of the vibrations producing the first to those producing the second, 240 to 270 or 8 to 9, is the same as the ratio between those producing the fourth and fifth or 320 to 360, and also the sixth and seventh, 400 to 450, each being as 8 to 9. The ratios between the second and third, 270 to 300, and the fifth and sixth, 360 to 400, are also the same—9 to 10. Here accordingly are two classes of intervals, each class differing from the other, yet so slightly as compared with the others, that they are all denominated *major intervals* or *full tones*. The difference, however, is too great to be disregarded in musical composition. The ratios between the third and fourth, 300 to 320, and the seventh and eighth, 450 to 480, are the same with each other—15 to 16—but much greater than the others. These two intervals are called in distinction from the others, *minor intervals* or *semi-tones*. Technically all these intervals from one note to the next above or below are termed *degrees* or *steps*.

The same relations exist between the intervals in the second or next higher octave. The numbers designating the proportionate vibrations will only be double those of the first or lower octave. They will be, 480 ; 540 ; 600 ; 640 ; 720 ; 800 ; 900 ; 960.

Chords.

§ 264. On the relations of these intervals as thus determined between an assumed key note or prime and the other notes mentioned is founded the science of Harmony in music. It distinguishes the intervals into *Consonances* which stand in a relation to each other that satisfies the ear, of which the octave, fifth, and as maintained by some the fourth, are *perfect* or *complete*, and the third and sixth are *imperfect* or *incomplete*, and *Dissonances* which are the second and seventh. Moreover, the intervals are distinguished as *major and minor*. A major second thus consists of one full tone or two semi-tones; the minor second of one semi-tone; the major third of four semi-tones, the minor third of three semi-tones, and so on. The Harmonies or Chords which are found by combining tones from different intervals for musical effect are 1. *independent*, as *major triads* formed by the combination of the prime or fundamental note with the major third and fifth together with the *minor triads* formed of the first, the minor third, and the fifth, or 2. *not independent*, as the chords of the seventh which are formed by the addition of a seventh to a triad. These intervals may be varied, by raising or lowering the prime or any other note in the scale a half of a tone interval. The chords also receive divers modifications, according as they are founded on the key note or *triad*, when we have the *Tonic Triad*; or on the fifth, giving the *Dominant Triad*; or on the fourth, giving the *Sub-dominant Triad*. Each of these is still further modified by changing the relative position on the scale of the three constituents, giving rise to the distinction of *primitive* and *derivative chords*. These three triads are distinguished from triads founded on the second, third, sixth, and seventh degrees of the scale;—the former being called *primary*, the latter *secondary* triads. The chords of the seventh admit of analogous modifications.

Modulation. § 265. Moreover the tonic itself may be at any point in the scale; and in a musical movement, this point may be changed. This digression from one key to another is now called *modulation*, or to distinguish it from the progressive arrangement of harmonies for a given melody, *digressive modulation*. This change can with musical effect often be accomplished only with proper preparation and gradually, imposing laws which the artist must strictly observe.

Skips and slides. § 266. Still more, changes in pitch can be effected either by a *skip* of the voice from one tone to another—*discretely*, or by a continuous *slide—concretely*. The voice can effect this change in pitch in either way; the pianoforte only discretely.

Counterpoint. § 267. If now we suppose to be given a melody or a succession of musical sounds the nature of such sounds requires that any addition to it of one or more parts, so as to form chords or harmonies with its several notes, should be made in certain ways that musical science indicates and prescribes. This part of the science called *Counterpoint* directs what chords may be used in succession and how they may be introduced and treated. Thus the musical ear demands that a musical composition begin and end with perfect concords; that discords be introduced only in transition; that perfect concords of the same degree never succeed one another; for example, that consecutive fifths or simultaneous movements through a fifth in any two of the parts of a harmony be avoided because such movements being on different tones cannot perfectly harmonize.

§ 268. As a mood of feeling to be expressed in musical sound must be presented as prolonged and while thus prolonged as necessarily subject to certain specific modifications which shall yet not destroy its general character, if this mood of feeling be introduced as a subject or theme for musical composition the nature of sound as musical prescribes certain principles for regulating the prolonged expression. Hence arises the department of *Imitation* in musical science which directs how this theme is to be taken up successively by the different parts; while the doctrine of the *Fugue* fills out the entire treatment of a theme for two or more voices, as to character, length, mode of imitation, and the like, so far as the mere nature of musical sounds in relation to each other in respect to melody or harmony is concerned.

Imitation.

Fugue.

2. Force.

§ 269. Secondly, musical vibrations may vary in respect to their extent; as a pendulum, swinging at the same rate so many times in a second, may swing through a longer or shorter arc. The longer the vibration, the louder the sound. This relation of musical sounds to one another gives rise to the distinction of *Force*. It is a constituent that enters largely into music. The various modifications of sound in respect to force as combined with other elements furnish the matter of the department of musical science called *Dynamics*.

3. Quality. § 270. Thirdly, musical vibrations may vary not only in respect to their velocity and extent but also in regard to their form, giving rise to the distinctions of *Quality*, French *Timbre*. The quality of musical sounds having the same pitch and force thus varies with the body which by vibrating produces the sound. Wood, metal, glass, each gives forth a peculiar quality of sound.

The quality of the sound varies also with the mode in which the sounding body is put in vibration. Musical instruments are distinguished in this respect into the general classes of Wind Instruments, as the Flute, the Clarionet and others of wood, and the Horn, Bugle, and others of metal; Stringed Instruments, as the Harp, the Violin, etc.; and Instruments of Percussion, as the Cymbal, Triangle, Tambourine, Drum, etc. There are moreover modifications of these general modes; as in the case of Wind Instruments the quality varies according as the vibrations are caused directly by the breath as in the Flute or through a reed as in the Clarionet. In Stringed Instruments, the quality varies according as the cord is vibrated by friction or by the bow of the violinist or by traction as when the harpist and occasionally the violinist pulls the string out of line to give it motion, or by percussion as in the pianoforte, or as the violinist occasionally strikes the strings with his bow. The skilled player varies the quality of sound by a still more special mode of putting the body into vibration. Paganini would draw from the same string a great diversity of sounds by divers ways of drawing his bow. The human voice especially is susceptible of giving forth a great diversity of sounds in respect of quality, and it is in the power to produce these different sounds with facility and fitly that excellence in vocal music greatly consists.

The quality of musical sound varies, further, with the character of the bodies on which the vibrations or waves of sound fall. Even the state of the atmosphere to some extent affects it. If the vibrations are made to pass through confined spaces, as these passages are tubular or not, as they swell and contract or otherwise, as they are smooth or not, their quality is so far modified. If, still more, the vibrations are reflected, the quality will vary with the character of the reflecting surface. A lining of silk thus over the chest of keys in a melodeon gives it a peculiar quality very different from mere wood. The quality of a pianoforte depends to a great degree on the character of the sounding board; two instruments made by the same artisan from the same material, after the same style and with the same skill and care, being often so very unlike that one will be condemned as poor while the other will be accepted as of remarkably sweet and mellow tones.

Quantity.

§ 271. Fourthly, musical vibrations may vary in respect to the time of their continuance. There arises hence the distinction of long and short notes, or musical

Quantity and also that of slow and quick movements in the succession of notes. Combined with force, this element of time constitutes the department in musical science denominated *Rhythm*.

Twofold law of material.

§ 272. The two comprehensive laws of material in music are accordingly the following:—1. Sounding bodies must be used, each according to its own proper nature and for the peculiar expression to which it is fitted. 2. Musical sound itself, as produced by vibrations of air, must be used as medium of expression according to its own properties.

§ 273. III. LAW OF FORM IN MUSIC.—The free art of music, like painting, has lent a most beneficent ministry to other ends—to those of religion, of warfare, of sport and recreation; but it ever retains its proper freedom and ministers only as pure form. In order to its perfection, therefore, the art must never look out of itself, but only seek to express its idea through its appointed medium in its most full and perfect form. There is consequently no proper occasion for mechanical design in the exercise of the art itself.

Decoration enters more freely than in painting. Yet so closely does it ally itself with the expression of the main idea that it would be difficult, at least it would be inexpedient, here to draw an exact line of discrimination. Feeling is characteristically exuberant; it surges and sinks, it swells and ripples, it rolls and dashes, it masses into driving, whelming flood, or breaks into yielding foam or misty spray, like the ocean tide. Its ripples and its spray yet move on in the same tidal direction with the swell and the billow. Whatever be the mood of feeling to be expressed in music, it will ever seek to pour itself out and fill all offering channels of outflow.

§ 274. The Law of Artistic Design in Music, as in Painting, is modified in a twofold way, according as it respects the medium through which the expression is made or the feeling to be expressed— the sound-side or the idea-side.

Rhythm.

1. In the use of sounds for the expression of feeling, there are certain principles to be observed. In the first place there is the necessity of observing the principles of *Rhythm*, which rest on the combination of Force of sound with Time. Rhythm may be defined as the union of force and time in the succession of musical sounds so that the variations of force shall correspond with the measures of time. Rhythm varies accordingly (1) with the *accent* or the degree of relative force between the successive sounds, giving accented and unaccented sounds in a given measure of time; and (2) with the ratio in number between the accented and unaccented sounds, giving the varieties of Double, Triple, Quadruple, and Sextuple measure.

Rhythm is probably the earliest mode of musical expression. It is the only element in the music of the simplest kind of instruments of percussion, as the drum, the cymbal, the tambourine. Savage life employs it in the dance and also in the ministries of religious rites. The most ancient instruments of Egyptian music were purely rhythmical, as the triangular lyre, the kettle-drum, and the sistrum. The most cultivated music builds on it as its fundamental element, but cannot dispense with it in any part of the superstructure.

Melody. § 275. In the second place, the principles of *Melody*, founded on the relative pitch of sounds, are to be observed in musical expression. Melody may be defined as pitch in succession. It has two grand divisions, the *major* and the *minor scales*, according as the semitone occurs in the fourth and seventh or the third and sixth degrees from the tonic or key-note. The one is characteristically bold and exulting, the other is tender and plaintive. Rhythm expresses the strength or intensity of feeling; melody the moods of feeling, especially as continued and prolonged.

Harmony. § 276. In the third place, there are the principles of Harmony founded on the contemporaneous union of sounds to be observed. It is a combination of different melodies in rhythm united on the principles of the chord.

Dynamics. § 277. In the fourth place, there are to be observed the principles of musical Dynamics, founded on the variations of sound in respect not only of volume or force but also of number of melodies and of instruments. A single tone may be relatively loud or soft; it may continue uniform in volume or swell with more or less suddenness. The number of melodies combined may be more or fewer; and the number and diversity of voices and instruments may be greater or less. Musical Dynamics regulates all these modes of varying the expression. The musical composer needs to be practically familiar with all that it prescribes in order to attain to the fullest and largest power of expression, and to give forth its exactest shade and color.

§ 278. The laws of Form, that look rather to the idea-side of musical expression and are founded on the vital relationship of feeling to the other departments of our rational nature, have here the same application as in the other arts, but specifically modified.

Unity.

The Law of Unity requires not that a given musical composition should be confined to a single emotion, but having a broader foundation in the unity of the feeling soul, only requires that the parts which wake up the whole change of feeling to be expressed be such as can subsist in harmonious succession in the human soul. Feeling is proverbially changeful. As the sensibility is touched from without, it responds in the exultations of joy or the depressions of wo, according to its divers interpretations of what is intended in the object that addresses it. The tears of sorrow become at once the outflow of joy as the address to the feelings is apprehended to be not a message of evil but of good. Fear in the same way almost instantly changes to hope as the passive imagination passes from its contemplation of the cloud to the bow that rests upon it. So love and hate alternate as the voice is varied as that of a friend or foe. The finite nature cannot interpret infallibly what is addressed to it; and its responses in feeling vary with the various interpretation. The law of unity which is peremptory for all art, must therefore in its application be recognized as requiring only what is possible in the changing experiences of any single soul. In dramatic musical composition, in which different characters are represented in their diversity of feelings, the principle of unity has a larger interpretation Generally it may be said that the law of unity in music is determined by the compatibility of the possible objects which can awaken the feeling with one another in the order of nature and of event. It embraces thus the two requisitions: first, that the changes of feeling represented be such that the human soul can, in the supposed circumstances, experience them; and secondly, that they can be awakened in such a soul by possible objects addressing it.

The specific working out of this principle of unity is exemplified everywhere in musical composition;—as in the necessity of ending with the triad of the tonic; of resolving all discords, even he chord of the seventh; of presenting the theme in every successive movement in Imitation or in Fugue; and the like. The one idea to be rendered must never be lost from view.

Æsthetic Number.

§ 279. The law of æsthetic Number requires that the changes in the mood of feeling represented be few. Three tones are, perhaps, the least number that can form a theme; which, on the other hand, should not extend beyond two or three measures. The first allegro in Beethoven's Symphony in C minor is from a theme or design of four notes—three eighth notes on G and a half note on E. In an oratorio or an opera, this law of number is the same as that applicable to dramatic composition generally.

Contrast.

§ 280. The Law of Contrast has in music perhaps a wider application than in any other art. The contrasts in rhythm, in melody, in harmony, in force, in instruments both in number and kind, with their manifold combinations, are so various as to allow the utmost latitude for diversification in expression. The principle requires that on the firmly maintained ground of unity, the different be prominently exhibited as different.

Proportion.

§ 281. The Law of Proportion is as exact in music as in architecture. The like parts must in respect to time and force and measures bear a like proportion to the whole.

§ 282. The Laws of Symmetry and Harmony, requiring that the like parts should be similarly treated, are also of equal force in music. A major and a minor strain bearing the same relation to the whole, should vary only as the natures of these two moods require. They are as right and left to each other. The principle is the same as applied to all like parts of whatever kind—to the parts of a measure, to the parts of a period or a strain.

Moral relations.

§ 283. The æsthetic principles determined by the relation of feeling to the moral nature have a close and also an extensive application in music. The moral sympathies are the deepest and strongest in the soul of man. The most moving strains are those that religion has inspired. Next to this, love of country, of political freedom and independence, has most warmly expressed itself in music, as in national songs and in martial airs. The music of the merely social character, as that of the dance, while lowest of the three great departments of music, yet obviously bears a true moral aspect. Richter in his Titan has not overlooked the place of music in this moral relation :—" Music has something holy ; unlike the other arts, it cannot paint any thing but what is good.". So we should anticipate from the very nature of music as the expression of form itself, that is of the soul as impressed and shaped by other souls. For soul is essentially and characteristically moral ; and the most natural and hence the freest and fullest intercourse of soul with soul is that of one moral nature with another. It is in this deep insight into the secret abysses of our experience that that most devoted student of nature, Richter, is led to speak of the personality in the beauty and sublimity of the natural world, when he represents beautiful nature as caressing and holding like a mother, and sublime nature as standing like a father in the distance.

The particular requisitions of this principle are, first, that the artist in music seek chiefly to represent the finest feelings of his being, since they are the deepest and strongest and most quickly find entrance into the hearts of others ; and, secondly, that he seek not only to pour out his own feelings, but see also that his utterances shall come with a benign, a truly refining and cheering influence on others. Music, as moral in its source, even when most purely but the outflow of an impassioned soul moved from within, cannot sever itself from its lineage, and must at least in this outflow have some regard to the sensibilities on which the utterances shall fall.

History.

EXEMPLIFICATIONS OF THE PRINCIPLES OF FORM IN MUSIC IN THE HISTORY OF THE ART.—§ 284. Music, although earliest of origin among the æsthetic arts, has been longest in reaching maturity. The fact is a striking witness to the nobility of the art; as generally we observe that the richest perfection is conditioned on the slowest growth. Soon after the original creation of man, in the earliest history of the race, we read of Jubal as "the father of all such as handle the harp and pipe." Rhythm and simple melody were probably the limit of musical attainment for a long period. Instruments of percussion are in use among savage tribes where no other department of musical expression is known; and are found everywhere in union with those that give distinctions in pitch, and thus are capable of melody. The sacred historian aimed, it would seem, to attribute to Jubal the invention of melodious expression by means of instruments. It was a stage beyond merely rhythmical skill; but was undoubtedly itself subsequent to vocal melody. The native love of rhythm prompted the invention of a

Antiquity.

great diversity of instruments of percussion. The ancient Egyptians had the triangle, the kettle-drum, and the sistrum or timbrel. The Jews, who cultivated music to the highest degree in their religious life, had besides these the cymbal also. The early Chinese used gongs and plates of metal. Bells, plates of glass, and strips of wood even, have been used in later times.

Melody was cultivated in its simpler form of succession of musical sounds, with no nice discrimination probably of the exact relations between the different degrees of pitch, by the Egyptians and the Jews. A great diversity of wind and stringed instruments were in use among them.

Greece.

§ 285. The Greeks carried the art to a higher level. Terpander, nearly 700 years before our era, wrote melodies for the harp. Euclid reduced musical intervals to mathematical ratios. The Greeks also introduced the chromatic scale and distinguished the major and minor intervals in the diatonic scale. They invented even an enharmonic scale with degrees of only quarter tones. But there is no evidence of their having cultivated harmony to any extent. This department is of comparatively modern origin.

Italy.

§ 286. In the sixteenth century music was cultivated with great devotion and success in Italy. Oratorios, or musical representations of events, with divers characters, but without dramatic action and scenery, originated in this century; and towards its end the proper opera, with full dramatic representation, was introduced. Operatic music culminated in Italy in Rossini of the present century.

Germany.

§ 287. The German art was rooted in the Italian. Its great originator was Gluck, 1714–1787. He first propounded the principles that operatic music must fasten itself on a truthful narrative or historic action, awakening certain determinate moods of feeling; that it must directly express these feelings; and that the instrumentation must be auxiliary to the vocal representation. After Gluck followed the three great princes in musical composition, Haydn, Mozart, and Beethoven—standing in relation to modern music much as Æschylus, Sophocles, and Euripides to the Grecian drama. Besides these great names, Handel, Weber, and Mendelssohn rank in the highest place as musical composers.

France.

§ 288. In sympathy with the progress of the art in Italy and in Germany, music was successfully cultivated in France, whose leading composers are Auber, Meyerbeer, and Halevy, and also in England, whose most eminent names in the history of the art are Purcell (1658–1665) and Dr. Arne (1710–1778).

England.

CHAPTER X.

SPECIAL LAWS—DISCOURSE, POETRY.

Antiquity and rank.

§ 289. Discourse, as it was the first in origin, so it must be acknowledged to be the first in rank among the æsthetic arts. The physical man could subsist indeed without discourse, without communicating to another mind, while he could not subsist without shelter or without food. But the primitive man received the supply of these physical wants, as does the infant now, from a truly parental, even a providential care. To speak was his own first proper act, after the first survey and contemplation of the new world around him and of himself and the first trial of his outer limbs. Then, as the great poet says, "to speak" he "tried and forthwith spoke."

Word.

§ 290. The one element of all speech is the *word*. The word is the revelation of thought in sound. It is accordingly the type-form of all beauty. Its matter is sound—sound, distinguished from noise, in implying uniformity of successive vibrations; vocal sound, distinguished from sounds by other instruments than the voice; musical sound, inasmuch as every word and every syllable in a word is embodied in a sound having a determinate interval that may be measured by the degrees in musical pitch. Not so much consequently in respect to the material in which they reveal as in respect to the content—the idea—which they reveal, do discourse and music differ. Music reveals feeling ; discourse reveals thought. A word has thought for its content.

Moreover, the thought that makes the inner content of the word is properly discursive thought as it is called. That is, the words in speech are to be regarded as in their essence forms of the highest function of the intelligence—the judgment or comparative faculty. Hence the nature of the word, the forms of words, as also the nature of language generally, are to be explained and understood only from the nature of the judgment. Words are not properly names of "percepts" or of "representations," or of the relations of these forms of the intelligence, but of subjects and attributes and of their relations. They are properly to be regarded as the embodiments in sound of thought in its strictest, highest import — of the discursive intelligence.

Origin.

§ 291. Discourse had its origin in an instinct of man's rational nature—in his desire to communicate to another mind. Originally, therefore, like architecture and landscape, Discourse proceeds from a want, and thus becomes subject to an end that lies beyond the mere expression of thought in sound. It is, thus, like those two arts, a dependent art. But the progress of human culture has, in the higher attention given to discourse, effected a familiar and well-

Oratory and Poetry.

received separation between the two departments of the art; and has named the one which is dependent *Oratory*, and the other which is free *Poetry*.

We have thus given us the ready distinction between these two great departments of Discourse. Oratory expresses idea with reference to a foreign end which governs throughout in the construction of all oratorical discourse. This foreign end is the production of an effect on another mind—to inform, to convince, to excite, or to persuade. The special law of oratory is accordingly this: that it ever keep this designed effect in another mind in view, and move with undeviating steadiness towards it. History, philosophical literature, and other prose discourse generally, is but a derivative from proper oratory and a modification of it. Oratory is the subject-matter of Rhetoric.

While Oratory represents for the sake of effect on another mind and is dependent, Poetry, on the other hand, represents for the sake of the form itself, and is free.

The special laws of æsthetics, as applied to discourse, distribute themselves, as in architecture and landscape, into the two departments thus indicated as applied to oratory as dependent, and to poetry as free. Both are properly to be regarded as æsthetic arts; for oratory as poetry is revelation of idea in matter, and must ever proceed æsthetically.

Inasmuch as oratory is so familiarly expounded as to its nature, its forms, its processes, its laws, generally in rhetorical treatises, it is unnecessary to consider it here in formal detail. For this more detailed and formal exposition the author refers to his Art of Discourse as exhibiting its principles in general accordance with those of the present treatise. Incidentally, however, its more prominent æsthetic aspects will be noticed in the treatment of poetry.

Dismissing Oratory as the dependent department of discourse, we have then to consider only the free art of Poetry, in which æsthetic form is the governing law.

§ 292. I. LAW OF IDEA IN POETRY.—The proper idea to be revealed in poetic art is thought, as in music the idea is feeling. The realm of poetic idea is as wide, consequently, as the realm of thought. Themes, subjects in poetic composition, poetic ideals, are as manifold and diverse as the forms of thought itself. There are thoughts which relatively, indeed, we characterize as poetic in distinction from others which are unpoetic; but this is only a distinction in degree not in kind. There are "thoughts that voluntary move harmonious numbers;" they are of a nature which is of a kin to the spirit of art and at once wake and warm it to creative life. They are emphatically and by preëminence poetic subjects. There are thoughts which are farthest removed from the capacity and from the faculty of poetic form; they are of the purest, baldest forms of the intelligent spirit; mere abstractions from concrete realities; bare relations between ideas; they are emphatically, by preëminence, unpoetic. They are so, however, only relatively and in comparison with others which are more clearly allied to æsthetic form.

Subjects. § 293. Thoughts, regarded as subjects for poetry, are distributed into three great departments, and by this distribution give rise to the three great departments of poetic composition. Those of the first class are ideas of *truth*. Here, not feeling, not action, but simply what is true, makes up the content of the poet's thought. It is the governing idea in the field of Didactic Poetry, embracing in its divers modifications the varieties of Descriptive, Pastoral, Satirical poetry.

1. Ideas of truth.

Didactic poetry.

2. Ideas of feeling. § 294. The second class consists of ideas of feeling, in which the thought embraces a form of the sensibility, and is characterized as a sentiment. This kind of poetic idea has given rise to the department of poetry denominated Elegiac. It embraces the two varieties: the Lyric, adapted to music, comprising the Ode and the Song, as well as the Sacred Lyric; and the proper Elegiac.

Elegiac.

Ideas of action. § 295. The third class consists of ideas of action, in which the thought embraces some activity of spirit either spontaneous or voluntary. This kind of poetic idea has originated the department of Epic Poetry, which includes the two varieties of the proper Epic in which the poet himself is the speaker and the Dramatic

Epic and Dramatic Poetry.

in which the actor himself is represented as the speaker. Under these grand divisions are still other subdivisions. The Epic comprises the higher Epic—the Epic by preëminence—and also the poetic Tale. It embraces also the Heroic, a serious Epic, and the Burlesque or Mock-Heroic. Dramatic Poetry, in the same way, includes the Tragic, which represents the higher and serious life, and Comic which represents the playful and diverting in common life.

Poetic idea must be treated as one of thought.

§ 296. In whatever province of idea the poet may find the subject of his representation, the law of idea in his great art ever exacts of him, in order to success, that he treat his subject as essentially an idea of thought. His subject must be handled throughout as of the nature of thought, as having the proper attributes of thought, as controlled by the proper laws of thought. If his theme be a sentiment or an act of heroism, his first duty is to bring it into his intelligence, to shape it under the laws of his thinking nature. His conception of it must be clear and distinct; it must be clearly defined and separated from all other conceptions; it must be also clearly distinguished in respect to all its constituent parts. Dimness of vision, vagueness, confusion of idea, are fatal to poetic creation.

Skill in poetry does not presuppose necessarily logical any more than grammatical proficiency. But a poet may as well hope to succeed who ignorantly tramples on all the principles of grammar, as one who tramples on all the principles of intelligence. Poetry may appear in the infancy of knowledge; a true poet may break in upon the world from other spheres than those of the university or other halls of learning. But he must know his theme however his knowing power may have been developed. A Purcell may have composed anthems and a Mozart well harmonized melodies in their early boyhood and before they had mastered the most elementary technics of musical composition; but they had feeling and they had skill to embody this feeling in sounds that were in accordance with musical principles, as truly if not as perfectly as in the days of their maturer development and training. However he came by it, whether by school-discipline, by private tuition, by solitary contemplation and reflection, every true poet must know his theme and be able to handle it in accordance with its own nature; that is, in accordance with the principles of human intelligence or thought. The more perfect his conception of his theme, the more definite his apprehension of it, the more full and rich his discriminations of its contents, the more perfect and more replete with poetic beauty will be his product.

The grand law of idea in poetry is that its subject, being thought, must be apprehended and treated as thought, in clearness and fullness of light, in accuracy and affluence of discrimination.

Word-sounds.

§ 297. II. THE LAW OF MATERIAL IN POETRY.—Poetry, we have seen, embodies in word as its revealing matter; and word is thought embodied in sound. The outward body of poetic expression is accordingly sound as modified in word. The law of material in poetry is founded in the doctrine of word-sounds in their essential properties and their relations.

As already observed all speech is musical, inasmuch as every syllable in a word in its utterance passes through a determinate interval on the musical scale,—a semi-tone, a tone, a third, a fifth, or an octave, or a combination of these intervals—and all the skips in pitch, as the voice passes from word to word, are also through like determinate intervals. All thought expresses itself in spoken language thus in strictest conformity to the principles of music, and all discourse must proceed in conscious or unconscious obedience to their dictates. It is the proper function of the art of Elocution to enumerate and describe these musical principles in their application to discourse; and poetic discourse must observe them, and avail itself of them to perfect its embodiments.

Prosody.

§ 298. But there are special modifications of these elocutionary principles as applied to poetic expression. Thus they furnish the principle subject matter of Prosody in its two leading departments of Assonance lying in the quality of the sound, and Rhythm lying in the stress of the sound.

Assonance Initial and Terminal.

§ 299. As Assonance in poetry may be at the beginning of a recurring form of expression or at the end, we have the two varieties of (1) initial assonance or Alliteration: and (2) terminal assonance or Rhyme.

Alliteration or Initial Assonance.

Alliteration is a common element of poetical expression. It occurs in successive words in the same sentence; or at the beginning of successive verses or turns of expression.

Rhyme or Terminal Assonance.

Rhyme or terminal assonance appears at the ends of verses or turns of expression. It is perfect when like vowel sounds in the last accented syllables are followed by like and preceded by unlike alphabetic sounds. It is distinguished also as single, double, or triple; and as successive, alternate, or interrupted.

Rhythm founded on accent and quantity.

§ 300. Rhythm is founded immediately on accent, more remotely on stress of sound combined or not with time. Classic poetry distinguished these two remote elements of rhythm ; modern poetry founds rhythm on the impressive force of articulate sound, whether consisting of mere accent or of accent combined with syllabic quantity or time. Rhythm consists of measures or of a recurring uniformity of one accented combined with one or more unaccented syllables. The recurrence of a number of similarly constituted measures forms a poetic *verse*, which may consist of one measure—a *monometer;* or of two, or a *dimeter;* of three, a *trimeter;* of four, a *tetrameter;* of five, a *pentameter;* of six, a *hexameter*, etc. According as the combinations of the one accented with the unaccented syllables vary, we have different varieties of poetic measures called poetic *feet*. Thus we have the accented syllable

Feet.

preceding one unaccented, or the *Trochee;* or preceding two unaccented, or the *Dactyl;* or following one unaccented, or the *Iambus;* or two unaccented, or the *Anapest;* or occurring between the two unaccented syllables, or the *Amphibrach;* or combined with three unaccented syllables, or the *Peon,* which may be of four forms, according to the relative position of the accented to the unaccented syllables. Other varieties also occur. Greek invention especially was affluent in the distinctions of poetic feet.

It should be carefully observed that these so called poetic feet occur as truly in prose as in poetic discourse. And in this fact we recognize a proper æsthetic characteristic in all good prose composition. There is a rhetorical rhythm generally as well as a poetical rhythm. It characterizes the style of Milton, of Addison, of Macaulay, of Irving, of every superior prose writer, of every superior orator. The distinction between rhetorical and poetical rhythm is exactly analogous to the distinction between mere noise and voice; to the distinction also between a vocal and a musical sound. Voice, as we have seen, differs from mere noise, inasmuch as it consists of a continuous uniformity of vibrations; a musical sound from a mere vocal sound in its continuous uniformity of pitch; a poetical from rhetorical rhythm in its continuous uniformity of feet.

Melody.

§ 301. On these elocutionary principles is founded also the doctrine of melody in discourse. Rhetorical melody thus, respects the successions of pitch which must be given in the proper pronunciation of discourse. To show the relations of the thought as well as the intensity of feeling that enters into it, there must be variations of vocal pitch by which the parts of a sentence, or of a paragraph, or of a whole discourse, are shown in their relations to one another. A good style is melodious as well as rhythmical.

Harmony.

§ 302. Still further these elementary principles determine the doctrine of harmony in discourse, which, like assonance in particular words, is founded on the quality of sounds. But it is this assonance in successive sentences or parts of sentences which rhetorical harmony more immediately regards. Poetical melody and poetical harmony are grounded in this general rhetorical melody and harmony, which, with rhythm, constitute the oral properties of style in the general art of discourse.

Words as symbols.

§ 303. But a word is more than sound however modified; it is more than thought, however diversified in its nature and relations; as material in poetry, it is thought *formed* in sound. The exposition given of the nature of beauty, of æsthetic form, will have prepared for the doctrine that the word is medium of communication between communicating minds. As human minds can communicate only through the outward sense, words are sounds addressing the sense of hearing; but they are mediums of thought shaped in them in such way that the speaker and the hearer alike use and receive them. Words are consequently in their origin ever sounds associated, identified in some way with the thought to be communicated in the minds of both speaker and hearer, and so expressive of that thought. They are thus associated or identified in the minds of both through the common nature so far of the sensible universe around us and of our spirits within us. Words are thus originally symbols; they express thought through forms of sense. In this lies the foundation of what is called imagery in discourse. In all rhetorical imagery, which forms so large an element in all discourse, whether prose or verse, we have a kind of æsthetic form. In the use of it the active imagination of the speaker or writer shapes his idea in the material taken from the outward world—in the objects or scenes that address the outward eye, or the ear, or the other senses of the mind he addresses as well as of himself, and so communicates to the passive imagination of his hearer or reader. Such is the primitive nature and origin of all language; and however spiritualized or abstract it may become, or however unconscious or ignorant of this the speaker or writer may be in his use of it, the laws which this, its essential nature, imposes upon it, can never be trampled on without suicidal effect on style, while the fuller acquaintance with them is necessary to the highest skill in all discourse.

Rhetorical imagery.

There is of course a rhetorical as well as poetical Imagery; and the more detailed and formal presentation of it belongs more properly to the general art of discourse than to the special province of poetry.

§ 304. III. LAW OF FORM IN POETRY.—The principles which regulate the embodiment of thought in language, whether for some foreign end as in prose or for the sake of the form itself as in poetry, have a twofold outlook. They regard, on the one hand, the word-side, and on the other hand the idea-side of the process.

Use of Language as oral and as symbolical.

1. The poet must regard the nature of the word in which he is to reveal his idea. This we have discovered to have also a double element, the sound or oral element and the symbol element or imagery. The diverse nature of the idea to be embodied finds a diverse adaptation in the diversity of the several oral properties of discourse. Even the lowest of these, assonance both initial or alliteration, and terminal or rhyme, admit a distinct poetical expression. The nature of the idea sometimes bids to the use of alliteration, sometimes shuns it; sometimes the current of poetic thought leads to the use of rhyme, sometimes turns from it. The calmer and more even moods of poetry invite the bonds of alliteration and rhyme; the more impetuous and free seek a looser utterance. It is incumbent on him who would master all the means of poetic expression, so to possess himself of the true expression of these properties and bring them into such ready control that he shall not only sagaciously use or pass them as shall be needful, but shall, without the hampering effect of a conscious labor for them, have them true helpers to his poetic effort, just as one finds his familiar vernacular

speech helpful, but a strange dialect in which he has to labor to call up words repressing to his thought.

Use of Melody.

§ 305. The element of melody is a more vital one to the poet's success. It has a far more diversified expression than even rhyme. In rhymed poetry, poetic melody has but a limited range, inasmuch as the necessities of the rhyme at the end of each verse lead at once to a more simple, sententious structure, while melody appears more in the complex sentence. Poetic thought, in its diversified shapes and hues, goes out in preference sometimes in a simpler, sometimes in a more multiplex melody; sometimes in one more abrupt, sometimes in one more gentle and flowing. The ear needs to be trained to these diversities of melody that the idea may obtain its fittest embodiment. Certainly the essential principles of melody in discourse cannot be violated, to which there must be great liability in one who ignores their importance, without detriment to poetic expression. Faults in melody are not infrequent even in our best poets. The following passage from Cowper, for instance, cannot be pronounced so as properly to exhibit through the voice the relations of the thought with satisfaction to the ear:

> "As one, who, long detained on foreign shores,
> Pants to return, and when he sees afar
> His country's weather-bleached and battered rocks
> From the green wave emerging, darts an eye
> Radiant with joy toward the happy land;
> So I with animated hopes behold,

And many an aching wish, your beamy fires,
That show like beacons in the blue abyss,
Ordained to guide the embodied spirit home
From toilsome life to never ending rest."

Use of Harmony.

§ 306. The oral property of harmony, which requires that the expression suit itself to the particular quality of the sounds in vocal speech, is one which the poet must make serviceable to his aim while seeking the fittest embodiment of his idea. Let one compare the passages between Gabriel and Satan in the fourth book of Milton's Paradise Lost with Adam and Eve's Morning Hymn in the fifth book, and he will find an admirable exemplification of the happy observance of poetic harmony—the rough, harsh, impetuous force in the one, the calm, gentle, reverent love in the other, expressed in the very quality of the word-sounds in the two respectively.

Use of Imagery.

§ 307. The word, as we have noticed, is originally and essentially a symbol, an image; and from this its primitive nature springs that great element of Imagery in discourse. In Poetry, imagery characterizes both the entire cast of the poem, the whole method or conduct of the work, and also the more particular elaboration of the details, of the characters, objects, scenes, truths, which make up the body of the poem. The entire poem may be formed in proper imagery. We have in this case the Allegory. The Allegory is of divers varieties, distinguished in reference to the particular kind of imagery employed. In Spenser's Faery Queene, thus, we have an exempli-

Allegory.

fication of proper epic allegory, in which the perfect heroic character in its several constituent virtues is imaged in the achievements and experiences of chivalrous life. In the following little poem of Coleridge on "Time—Real and Imaginary," is an exemplification of another widely different variety:

> "On the wide level of a mountain's head,
> I know not where, but 'twas some faery place,
> Their pinions, ostrich like, for sails outspread,
> Two lovely children run an endless race,
> A sister and a brother.
> This far outstript the other;
> Yet ever runs she with reverted face,
> And looks and listens for the boy behind:
> For he, alas! is blind.
> O'er rough and smooth with even step he passed,
> And knows not whether he be first or last."

Of the imagery which appears in the details of a poem, the particular ideas which make up its body, general exemplifications abound everywhere in poetry. It is of the essential nature of poetry that it utters idea in image or form. It casts its chief end and design in imagery; and as well shapes all its particular utterances in symbol. In the following verses from Wordsworth's "Sunset" this imagery nature sparkles throughout:

> "The leaves that whisper in delightful talk,
> The truant air, with its own self at play,
> The clouds that swim in azure, loving heaven
> And loving earth, and lingering between each,
> Loth to quit either; are not all alive
> With one pure, unalloyed, consummate joy?"

Use of idea.

§ 308. 2. The poet must regard the idea side of his process and conform it ever to its own proper nature and relationships. The idea in poetry, as we have seen, is thought; but thought either as unmodified—mere fact or truth—or as modified by feeling or purpose. The intellectual principles of art, founded in the intelligence or faculty of thought, have a readier application here, perhaps, than elsewhere in art.

Intellectual elements of beauty.

The idea of a poem must be one. If it be an event, an action, it must be apprehended as a single event, as a single action. The general unity of an epic poem lies here, as also does that of a tragedy or a comedy. The further limitations which critics, particularly classic writers and some modern European schools, have prescribed to this broader unity, the best and highest poetry of the later times has wisely disregarded. The unities of time and place, so called, which the ancients so sacredly observed, can be enforced so far only as they enter into the unity of the general idea of the poem. Shakespeare, in the freedom rightly belonging to his art, transports us from place to place, from country to country, from year to year, without offending against our demands for such a unity as will bring his action within the grasp of our intelligence. The poetry of sentiment is more liable, perhaps, to looseness. The true principle of unity here lies in the oneness of the mood of feeling which comes in to modify the thought. All diversity that can thus concur in any one condition of human feeling is within the allowance of the law of unity.

Of the other æsthetic principles founded in the intelligence in their application to poetry, it is unnecessary to speak. They are all indispensable here. Of the principle of contrast the importance is well exhibited in a remark of Wordsworth: "Similitude in dissimilitude," he somewhere says, "is the source of pleasure in poetry." The remark is but partially true, indeed, for this is but one of divers constituents of poetic beauty; but it shows how high it stood in the estimation of one who gave to the culture of poetry a life of thoughtful study and of prolific production.

Emotive elements.

§ 309. All true art, we have everywhere discovered, is but the work of the æsthetic imagination. The truth gives law to all poetic work, that it must proceed throughout in conformity with the nature of feeling—of the sensibility or the imagination both active and passive. Another remark of Wordsworth's, alike partial as the one just referred to, yet alike important, that "poetry is the spontaneous overflow of powerful feelings," illustrates the force and authority of this principle. The Apostle Paul, as before cited, enumerates, with a profounder insight and greater philosophical exactness and completeness, the comprehensive features of the religious spirit which are identical with those of the artistic spirit—"power, love, and a sound mind." The ground of these requisitions, that all art must move in conformity with the nature of our active, feeling, and intelligent nature, has been sufficiently set forth in another place.

Hebrew poetry.

EXEMPLIFICATION OF THE LAWS OF POETRY IN HISTORY.—§ 310. Hebrew literature preserves to us the earliest productions of the poetic spirit. The song of Lamech in the fourth chapter of Genesis—the "sword-song" as Herder styles it—is the most ancient on record. It is essentially Lyric, and so prefigures the general cast of Hebrew poetry. In this department no nation has surpassed the Hebrews. The songs of Moses, recorded in Exodus and in Deuteronomy, of Deborah in Judges, and of David in the Psalms, are of the highest order of lyric excellence. In the Prophets, also, here and there, are scattered lyric strains that, like those mentioned, still command the wonder and delight of the world. Nowhere has the lyric spirit uttered itself in greater majesty, boldness, purity, in higher sublimity or sweeter beauty. The life of the Hebrew was pre-eminently religious—a life of immediate dependence on the God of gods, in immediate communion with the Lord Jehovah, whom it reverently yet boldly recognized as the almighty Sovereign who "*inhabited the praises* of Israel." With comparative meagerness of outward embodiment in word-sounds and verse-forms—in assonance and rhythm—it was rich in the interior elements of idea which was diversified in manifold ways, and shaped in highest conformity to the principles of unity, contrast, and the other æsthetic principles founded in the intelligence, and also breathed the most passionate and purest moral and religious sentiment. With no regular rhyme or rhythm, there was alliteration, word-play founded on the sound of the word, and a true rhythmical choice and arrangement of words in

Lyric.

respect to their accentuation. Parallelism of divers varieties is a characteristic of Hebrew poetry, determining a uniformity or regular recurrence of verse-form in reference both to the thought and the diction. In this particular of correspondence between the idea and the word-material, of proper embodiment, Hebrew lyric is unsurpassed. All the moods of poetic feeling that can appear in lyric are exemplified in high perfection. The imagery is equally fit and expressive, while most natural and chaste. The twenty-third psalm breathes in the most charming numbers, and the most engaging images, the deep unruffled peace of a soul reposing its trust in God. The tenderest grief and sorrow find the most touching utterance in many dirges and songs of mourning and wo. The lament of David over Jonathan, the songs that bewail national disasters, of which the seventy-third and one hundred and thirty-seventh psalms are instances, the penitential hymns, as the fifty-first psalm, go down to the bottom of human grief. The songs of praise, the anthems of victory and triumph, the strains of exulting hope and confidence, the fervent prayers for help and comfort and blessing—all the poetic utterances of joy and hope and desire are exemplified in this wonderfully rich collection of lyric poetry. The allegory as well as the imagery of thought generally is employed with great poetic skill, as in the "proverb against the king of Babylon," in the fourteenth chapter of Isaiah.

Didactic Poetry.

The department of Didactic Poetry was also cultivated to great perfection among the Hebrews. The Proverbs of

Solomon are a good exemplification of this kind of poetry conveying moral instruction in brief, pithy, poetically turned sentences, which have given the name of *gnomic* to this variety of poetry. The book of Job is another example, designed to treat the great moral lesson of the unfathomable wisdom and the righteous sovereignty of God in the administration of human affairs. Probably the earliest extended poem, it is one of the richest, and loftiest, and purest in idea, in imagery, and also in diction.

Of the Epic and the Dramatic there are no clear instances in Hebrew literature. Some critics, however, have thought they have discovered a truly dramatic structure in the Song of Solomon.

Hindoo Poetry.

§ 311. In the Hindoo Literature, the Lyric department received the earliest development. Of the four Vedas, the most ancient collections of Hindoo literature, the principal one, the Rig Veda, is made up of religious lyrics, of which there are over one thousand in number. Their date is uncertain, but goes back over a thousand years before the Christian era. They are metrical and broken into verses. The later Hindoo lyric is pastoral and erotic in idea.

Epic poetry is represented in the Ramayana, the subject of which is the descent of Vishnu to avert the destruction of the world by the demon Ravana, and the Mahabharata, the subject of which is a contest between two rival powers for the government of Hindoostan, the Kurus and the Pandus, and in other poems of less distinction. The poetry is characteristically wanting in unity, and loose in construction.

Didactic poetry appears in the two forms of proverbial or aphorismic—the gnomic of the Hebrews—and of the fable. The fables of Bidpai have been rendered into European tongues.

The Drama was richly cultivated by the Hindoo mind. The Sakuntola by Kalidasi was translated into English by Sir William Jones in the latter part of the last century. Other dramas have since been rendered into European languages. The subjects are legendary; the catastrophe happy; the form partly verse, partly prose.

Grecian Poetry.

§ 312. Grecian art, with its marvelous fertility of invention combined with matchless delicacy and purity of taste, carried every department of poetry to a perfection that is proverbial; to be classic is to be artistically perfect.

Lyric.

Lyric poetry in all varieties of subject and of verse-form, and characterized by the severe taste of the Greeks in respect to unity and precise shaping of theme, chasteness of imagery, and exactness of rhythm, as well as purity of diction, is represented in the Odes of Sappho, of which two only remain complete, of Pindar, the most celebrated of which are the triumphal odes, and of Anacreon; in the plaintive elegiacs of Mimnermus; and in the pastoral Idyls—literally, "little things of beauty"—of Theocritus. The Greek added to the Hebrew Lyric a richly varied rhythm, and thus contributed the most important element to the oral body of poetry.

Epic. Epic Poetry leaped forth into instant maturity from the fertile brain of the Greek in the immortal poems of the Iliad and the Odyssey. The subjects—"the Wrath of Achilles" and the "Wanderings of Ulysses"—clearly, distinctly, truthfully apprehended; the represented characters, diverse, natural, engaging; the imagery, simple, chaste, expressive; the rhythm, which is the majestic hexameter, exact yet flowing, and shaping itself as its variations of feet and of cæsural pause will admit, to the variations of the sentiment; the diction, plain yet apt and musical—all features are those of an already perfected art.

Dramatic. Dramatic Poetry, the growth of a later period than the Epic, attained a somewhat corresponding rapidity of development. The great tragedies of Æschylus, Sophocles, and Euripides, and the comedies of Aristophanes, are characterized by the same Grecian features of unity and definiteness of idea, truthfulness of event and naturalness of character, simplicity of imagery, richness of rhythm, and purity and significance of diction. In its poetry, as in architecture and painting, Greek art was rapid in its growth, objective and therefore simple and material in its general character; and while rich and expressive, yet ever of the exactest, even severest taste, that repressed all wild luxuriance and shunned all tawdry adornments.

Roman.

§ 313. In Rome, poetic art made no progress upon the Grecian models. In the Lyric, the odes of Horace; in the higher Epic, the Æneid of Virgil, and in the lower narrative the pleasing metamorphoses of Ovid, poetic renderings of mythological legends; and in the Dramatic, the comedies of Plautus and Terence, are all conceived in Grecian spirit and cast in Grecian molds. In its transition from Greece to Italy all art passed from a simple, natural objectiveness, to a labored, artificial, subjective character, marking decline and corruption.

Modern poetry.

§ 314. In modern times poetry has flourished in sympathy with all art, and has marked itself with generally similar characteristics. The advance has been in loftiness and breadth of ideal, as compared with classic art; in diversity and exuberance of imagery, in both these respects resembling more the Hebrew poetry in its religious exaltation of idea and its love of natural imagery; and in the great expansion and development of all the oral elements of expression—rhythm, melody, and harmony.

Italian.

Italy led in the awakening of modern art. In the thirteenth century Dante produced the masterpiece of Italian epic, the Divina Commedia, written in iambic pentameter catalectic with alternate rhymes, and in the next century, Petrarch, the father of Italian lyric, his numerous sonnets, songs and odes; in the sixteenth century appeared Ariosto, the composer of a romantic epic, the Orlando Furioso, and Tasso, the writer of a serious epic, the Gierusalemme Liberata, both in eight-versed stanzas of iambic pentameter catalectic, rhymed. Not till the eighteenth century did dramatic poetry attain great distinction. Then appeared the tragedians, Maffei, Alfieri, and others of inferior name; and the comedian, Goldoni, with others.

Spanish. § 315. In Spain, the eminent lyric poets were Herrera and Leon, both of the sixteenth century. In 1562–1635, lived Lope de Vega, a most prolific writer of dramas and other poems.

Portuguese. § 316. The one great poet of Portugal is Camoens, 1524–1579, the author of the Lusiad—a poem designed to commemorate the achievements of the Portuguese—the Lusitanians.

French. § 317. French poetry originated with the *trouvères*, composers of lyrics, and the *troubadours*, who wrote poetic romances. Corneille and Racine in tragedy, Voltaire in his epic, the Henriade, and Beranger in lyric, are the leading names in the different departments of the French school of poetry. This school is characterized by its servitude to conventional rules in art, which shackle genius and so hinder the growth of art generally as well as individual excellence.

Teutonic. § 318. In the Teutonic nations of Germany and England, modern poetry has made its best progress. The characteristic spirit in both is the so-called *romantic* disposition, which, originally engrafted on the Teutonic spirit of freedom, readily imbibed the oriental love of nature, as exemplified in Hebrew poetry, and its fondness for wild adventure and bold speculation, as brought to it in the Hindoo and Arabic philosophy and literature, and at the same time chastened and tempered itself by its converse with classic and particularly early Italian models. The age of chivalry, which was penetrated with large streams of influence from the oriental and European literatures and civilizations, was most favorable to the germination of a new poetic spirit. The prevalence of Christianity exalted and enlarged poetic ideas, and bathed them in a deeper, warmer feeling, as well as animated them by a higher motive, and at the same time purified and attempered the whole outward embodiment of them, leading to a chaster yet richer imagery and diction.

German.

§ 319. The true lyric spirit has predominated from the first among the proper German tribes. As early as the twelfth century, the minnesingers, love-minstrels, frequented the palaces and castles of princes and nobles, like the *trouvères* and *troubadours* in France. Christianity, especially after the Lutheran Reformation, elevated and expanded this native propensity; and the richer civilization of modern times has given to lyric poetry an infinitely diversified extent and richness of idea and of form. No one lyric poet, nor few, can be named who will more fitly represent the art in German literature. In respect of idea, there are love songs of every variety, martial songs, festal songs, religious hymns, exultant odes, and plaintive elegiacs; and in respect of material, they are equally diversified in respect of verse-form, rhythm, and rhyme.

In epic poetry, Klopstock's Messiah is, perhaps, the best achievement of German art. The epic spirit has devoted itself rather to the prose novel than to proper poetry.

Dramatic poetry reached its highest culmination in the dramas of Schiller and Goethe, who tower high above all other German composers in all the great departments of poetry.

English.

§ 320. English poetry ranks easily foremost in the literature of modern times. Its beginnings were nourished in the forms of that romantic minstrelsy which was the first product of the modern poetic spirit. Love and chivalry were its inspirers, and shaped its ideas and its imagery. The narrative in the metrical romance was a coeval form. The first great poet in the language was Chaucer, whose best poems are his Canterbury Tales. Like the Germans, the English poets have confined themselves to no one particular department of poetry, but have generally cultivated all, yet with unequal success and in unequal degree.

In Lyric poetry, the love sonnets of the earlier age and the sacred hymns of the more recent, have won the highest distinction.

In Epic, the Paradise Lost of Milton stands side by side with the Iliad of Homer, the Æneid of Virgil, the Inferno of Dante. Its subject lifted the poet into the highest regions of thought and speculation; it brought in the divinest and the most fiendish in immediate play with the manliest and sweetest of human feelings; it called for the richest imagery and a dignified, sustained, yet flexible diction; the inspired poet has met all these divers demands. A grander theme, vaster ideals of character, a bolder, more varied imagery, a freer diction, it justly claims above all its great rivals.

Didactic poetry has received its highest culture since the seventeenth century. Pope, Young, Thomson, Cowper, Wordsworth, are the names of but few that have attained great excellence in this province of poetry.

The Drama has its chiefest and best representative in Shakespeare—the great dramatist of universal literature. In idea, with a firm and steady grasp he held his ideal, both of action and of character, throughout the most complicated development, with unswerving fidelity and truthfulness. The whole realm of dramatic idea he commanded with equal facility, tragic and comic. Foreign and domestic history alike supplied event and action. He swept through the gradations of feeling, from the sublimest and holiest, to the lowest and most diabolical in the human bosom, unfolding the tenderest sentiments of love with the same accuracy and fullness as the utmost violence of hate and revenge; depicting domestic security and cheerfulness as truly as national strife and commotion, and private despair or joy. Whatever character came across his view he caught and reproduced in lines of living light. The perfect naturalness in all the manifold personages of his dramas — prince or peasant, old or young, hero or maiden, human or elfish, living men or ghosts of the departed — is as astonishing as is the power with which he wields whatever historic theme he takes. Through systematic truth and history alike he moves, disturbing no system, distorting no received opinion, tripping never in theology and law and natural science when his path leads him through these fields of knowledge. The natural world is equally familiar; he has studied the clouds, has marked the winds, and watched the dewdrop; he has observed the life of plant, of bird and beast, as well as of rational spirit. An inexhaustible wealth of idea, such perhaps as has never fallen into the possession of any other poet, was his, and he used it as lavishly as it had been bountifully heaped upon him.

He had also great wealth of material. His serious renderings are in heroic verse; but he drops to prose as scene, or character, or aim requires. He has little occasion for rhyme where the stately but free heroic verse occurs. But in his lyrics with which he enlivens and beautifies a more solid structure, he makes a free use of this element. His sentences are not unmelodious; but are too direct and simple for the richer forms of rhetorical melody. His imagery is simple, natural, popular.

It is however in rendering, in embodying his idea in word, that Shakespeare's chief distinction as a poet lies. Idea never overbears the outer body in which it is to live; nor is it overborne on its part and obscured in the material. The fit word to the fit thought, fit body to fit idea, characterize his style. Well has it been said that you cannot change a word or sentence but to mar. He repudiates the shackles of conventional unity as it respects the mere accidents of time and place; while he never violated the true unity of action and of aim. The principle of contrast he turned to greater account than any other dramatist. While he did not disdain verbal antitheses, he did not make so much of them as of the higher antitheses of thought, of action, of character, of dramatic effect. His characters are indeed revealed as much almost in the oppositions of other personages as in their own light; and he knew how to alternate earnestness with play, majesty with delicacy, firmness with tenderness, mirth with sadness, as few others. With especial adaptation in selection of theme, in disposition of scene, and working of plot, in choice of character, in verbal style, to the age in which he lived, to the manners, intelligence, taste, even humor of the court for whose entertainment he wrote, yet no less for all countries, for all ages, for the race, are his immortal dramas fitted to instruct, to entertain, to please, to refine. In them the true taste finds unfailing matter for its enjoyment, admiration, and culture.

CHAPTER XI.

INTERPRETATION OF BEAUTY.

What. § 321. We have distinguished the laws of beauty into the two classes of those which respect the production and those which respect the interpretation of beauty. The former class look to the communicating mind; the latter to the receiving mind. The former are the laws of the active imagination; the latter are the laws of the passive imagination. Beauty, form, as we have seen, is the intermediate; it is common to both. But it has one aspect to the producing, another to the receiving imagination. We have considered the first class of laws; we turn now to the second class—the laws of the interpretation of beauty; the laws of the passive imagination; the laws which apply to the reception of form or beauty.

Method. § 322. The comprehensive question which we are to solve is simply this: How can we best—most accurately, most fully, most intensely—apprehend beauty? We shall obtain the answer by first analyzing the passive imagination which is addressed in all beauty that we may more distinctly see what in it is to be reached, or in other words, what in it is to be brought into communication with the beauty addressing us; what is the function which each of these analyzed parts is to perform, and how our apprehension of beauty may vary in degree and in fullness by the different degrees in which these functions are brought into play; as also how we may keep what is liable to be mingled with our experience of beauty separate and distinct from the pure form itself and its legitimate impression. Our solution may then be tested and illustrated by its application to the several constituents of objective beauty as already ascertained.

Of sensibility.

§ 323. I. THE SUBJECTIVE LAWS GOVERNING THE INTERPRETATION OF BEAUTY.—The essential element of the passive imagination is sensibility. But sensibility belongs to a spiritual nature that has other endowments and characteristics; and the passive imagination is diversely affected by this complex spiritual nature to which it belongs. The sensibility itself cannot receive in its fullest perfection and degree the forms that address it except as aided and determined by these other endowments. The consideration of the sensibility in itself and as related to the spiritual nature generally in its divers endowments will guide us at once to the conditions of a perfect interpretation of beauty.

Conditions of æsthetic sensibility.

§ 324. The comprehensive law or condition of a full interpretation of beauty founded in the receiving mind is, thus, a true sensibility to form. In order to experience beauty the first and indispensable requisite is a sensibility that can be impressed by it. And it is obvious that the more impressible the passive imagination, the more immediately and closely it is brought into communication with the addressing form, and the more entirely the sensibility is surrendered to the impression, the more full and pure and perfect will be the experience of beauty. We have thus given us at once the conditions of beauty founded in the sensibility itself.

1. Impressible.

First, it must be impressible. There is great diversity in different persons in this respect; there is great diversity in different conditions of the same person. Age and use, it is commonly believed, dull and blunt the sense. So far as the mere outward, the proper physical and animal sense is concerned, this opinion may be correct. But the human sensibility which is addressed in beauty is more than mere animal, physical sense, however closely related to it, and connected with it. The outward organ dims with age; but the mind, the spirit, there is reason to believe, becomes by use more and more sensitive to these outer impressions. If the bodily nerve is less impressible, the soul that takes its impressions from these nervous agitations becomes more and more alive and sensitive to them. Thus is explained the common experience that the cultivated spirit grows ever more tender and sensitive to beauty, even although the outward organ becomes more dull. The phenomenon can be fully accounted for, perhaps, only by supposing that the active imagination, answering ever more and more readily with exercise to the impressions on the sense, comes in more freely to help out the full apprehension of form. But whatever the explanation of the phenomenon, certainly within certain limits the sensibility becomes more capable of fulfilling its high function of bringing beauty into the experience with advance in culture. And the law remains that as beauty first addresses the sensibility, and addresses immediately that only, in order to the experience of beauty, a tender, impressible sensibility is required.

2. Closeness of communication.

§ 325. Secondly, the more closely the sensibility is brought into communication with the addressing form the more perfect will be the experience of beauty. It is possible that there may be a certain sense of beauty which is moved through the intelligence; that beauty may be reasoned out, or be reached through analysis or other intellectual process. So it is undoubtedly true that the feelings which it is the province of music to communicate may be stirred simply by reading the written notes on paper. Assisted by his active imagination, a trained musician may feel more music from perusing such written characters in a given composition, than a tyro from hearing the composition rendered in proper sound. Yet after all, the sense of music is immeasurably enhanced even to the trained musician when his inward ear receives through the outward organ the immediate vibrations of musical sound. Beethoven was able to bring his soul immediately into communication with music even through the sensations of fingering the keys; but how lamentably did he bewail his loss of hearing as the immediate organ of musical form, as so far deadening his sense of its richness and beauty. No reasoning, no analysis, no imagining, no skill or past experience, can but partially supply the need of a sensibility brought into immediate contact with the addressing form. As therefore we approach at the greeting of beauty and seek to apprehend the full import of her address, we need to unveil our eye to her form and turn our ear so as to catch the full tones of her voice. Beauty addresses sense, and the more immediately, the more impressively.

3. Entire surrender.

§ 326. Thirdly, the more entirely and exclusively the sensibility is surrendered to the impression from beauty, the more perfect will the experience of it be. Just so far as we occupy our minds otherwise, just so far will the impression be indistinct and obscure. If, while we seek to feel, we try to reason, to criticise, to reflect and follow trains of suggestion, we hinder the proper effect of beauty on us. This observation, however, should be interpreted only in subordination to the conditions of beauty which are derived from the relationship of the sensibility to the other endowments of our being, and in harmony with them. Thus understood, the principle that imposes entire surrender to the impressions of beauty as a condition to its highest experience is self evident.

Belonging to an active nature.

§ 327. 2. The sensibility which in its elementary nature is simple passivity or impressibility, simple capacity of receiving impression, is however not a dead, lifeless passivity. It belongs to an essentially active nature,

As an endowment of spirit, it is of a spiritual nature; it participates in the essential characteristic of such a nature, which is activity. There can be no full apprehension of beauty except by such a living, active sensibility. It may be difficult to set forth in language, perhaps impossible to conceive fully in thought, the precise nature of this modification of the sensibility. But of its reality and its importance in the right interpretation of beauty, there can be no question. The spirit moves as it is impressed. There is ever activity answering to impression. The chords of the soul vibrate when struck; they are elastic and reäct. There is in a true apprehension of beauty not only susceptibility, but playfulness, responsiveness—a stir and motion in which the whole soul participates.

Sympathetic. § 328. 3. The sensibility in order to the full apprehension of beauty must be sympathetic. This element enters into the spiritual nature of man to which the sensibility belongs. There are divers degrees and modifications of sympathy as modifying the æsthetic sense. There is the lower degree of the mere sympathy of being with being, life with life, spirit with spirit. There is the higher degree of loving sympathy which draws the soul out in warm affection towards the object which addresses it. We are not readily impressed by that which has no hold of our hearts, to which we are indifferent. Hate may stir feeling, but not that kind of feeling which is favorable to æsthetic impression—which extends only to the form. Even love that carries the soul beyond the contemplation of the form to the being that addresses it, is unfavorable to the proper experience of beauty. But that loving sympathy which keeps the love in steady, satisfied contemplation, is the condition of the richest experience of beauty. Farther, there is the sympathy which goes out to the source of the impression, the being that addresses us, which as just observed may hinder, or as in right degree may aid æsthetic effect. There is too the special sympathy with the kind of form which presents itself. The musician sympathizes with the forms of melodious and harmonious sound; the painter with the outlines and hues of visible form. But of whatever degree or modification, this sympathy, this loving sympathy, must enter into every full sense of beauty. The appreciation of beauty, the enjoyment of beauty, the proper effect of beauty, depends on the degree of sympathy with which it is contemplated. Ever in beauty heart addresses heart, and the livelier the sympathy, the warmer will be the glow and fervor of the communion.

Intelligent.

§ 329. 4. The sensibility in apprehending form is not only active and sympathetic but intelligent. It participates in a nature which is essentially intelligent; and can never lay aside this relationship, any more than the arterial system can separate itself from the muscular system of the bodily framework. In truth the connection is more essential and intricate than this. We may as well imagine a right side of the body with no left side, as sensibility without intelligence. We may think of either side abstractedly from the other; but in actual being the one cannot be without the other. It is an intelligent sensibility that is summoned to receive the addresses of beauty. The very notion of beauty as we have proved it involves this. There is no beauty where there is no idea; and all idea is as truly for the intelligence as for the sensibility. The true is only another phase of the beautiful. Like the sunbeam, idea is light to the eye of the intelligence, and heat to the warmth-sense of the heart. The interpretation of beauty, the reception of æsthetic form is, other things being equal, ever in proportion to the intelligence which characterizes the sensibility to which beauty or form addresses itself. The animal has no sense of beauty in its proper sense. The child's sense of beauty is very limited. The gaudiest, most glaring colors entertain it more than the most finished paintings. Its physical sense is pleasantly affected, and that pleasure is elevated and enhanced by the little of true rationality that its undeveloped nature is capable of imparting to its sensations. The adult mind that has only the ordinary knowledge of art enjoys comparatively little as he perceives comparatively little when an art product is presented to his view, compared with the expert artist. To the one the object is vague, dim, little more than a blank; to the other it stands out in bold, distinct relief, in full light, and crowded with expression. The one passes his eye over it and leaves it carrying away little though he has exhausted all the treasures it has for him. The other lingers, and weary with a natural weariness of study and enjoyment returns to repeat his study, sees beauty after beauty rise, and finds his prolonged and busy contemplation over-laden with the richest treasures of æsthetic enjoyment. It is because his intelligence in regard to what there is of art in the object, his practiced eye, his enlarged view, his sharpened vision is able to interpret more, apprehend more in it. The ideal is more fully perceived, the material is more perfectly understood, the rendering too is more perfectly recognized in all its elements of justness of adaptation, of skill in embodying, of power to wield idea and material, to surmount difficulties, to enforce his aim to the happy result, and of love and patience and care poured into the labor of his hands. The apprehension of beauty is as the intelligence characterizing the sensibility that would apprehend it

Moral.

§ 330. 5. The highest form of sensibility is that which characterizes it as moral. The æsthetic nature is but a part or a phase of the rational nature whose highest form and characteristic is the moral. The moral nature, as essentially free, is in its normal condition only when moving in goodness and rectitude. The sensibility which participates in this moral nature is in its best condition to exercise its proper function of apprehending form or beauty only when it is thus morally affected in rectitude and goodness. Only then can it be in sympathy with the highest beauty; only then can it fully and perfectly apprehend such beauty; only then consequently can it fully appreciate and enjoy it.

A proper æsthetic sensibility, we may then summarily characterize as active, sympathetic, intelligent, and moral.

II. THE OBJECTIVE LAWS GOVERNING THE INTERPRETATION OF BEAUTY.—§ 331. The laws governing the interpretation of beauty which are founded in the object that is presented—in the addressing imagination—ought to be the exact counterpart of those which are founded in the subject of the experience of beauty, the passive imagination—the mind addressed. We shall on investigation find this exact correspondence between the nature of objective beauty and the nature of a true experience of beauty.

In the first place, we have found beauty to be essentially and characteristically revelation—addressing form. Just as in sight there must be a visible object and a visual organ, in exact correspondence each with the other, so in the experience of beauty, there must be an object of beauty and a sensibility to beauty in exact correspondence. As we have all along seen, in all experience of beauty an active imagination addresses a passive imagination. There is beauty produced, there is beauty received. There is, to speak more technically, form mediating between impressing mind and mind impressed—form the same in itself but having a two-fold aspect, an objective and a subjective. Beauty to be felt implies thus a sensibility to be impressed. The more tender, that is the more impressible the sensibility, the more deeply will the object impress it. The more closely it is brought into communication with the object, the more full, also, and effectual will be the impression. And still further the more entirely the sensibility is surrendered to the impressing object, the more pure and perfect the impression. A consideration thus of the nature of objective beauty imposes this condition in experience that there be a sensibility, impressible, in close communication with its object, and exclusively occupied with it. The tenderer the sensibility, the more closely in connection with the object, that is, through the less medium of thought, of analysis, of criticism, of reflection, of association, of purpose, of aim, of mental activity of any kind, and the more exclusively the mind is surrendered to the object, the higher, the deeper, and wider, and purer will be the experience of the beauty.

Law of medium.

§ 332. Sensible beauty can reach the soul only through the bodily sense. So far all experience of such beauty is necessarily mediate. And we have found a properly mediate beauty—a beauty that comes to us only through some medium as the thought comes to us mediately through the written word. This first law of interpretation prescribes that all such medium be abstracted as far as possible from our regard in the contemplation of the object.

Of idea.

§ 333. Secondly, all idea revealed is from spirit which is essentially active in its nature. The dead forms of nature, as they are sometimes characterized, are but the ideas of the divine activity impressed in matter. We enter into the depths of natural beauty only as we discern these characters of activity. All objects, all events, says Jouffroy truly, are symbols of force, of spirit as the only force; and we catch the fullnesss of their forms only as we apprehend the force, the spiritual activity which they symbolize.

Of a revelation.

§ 334. Thirdly, we have found beauty to be essentially idea revealed; that is, a form of mind, of spirit is of the essence of objective beauty. But beauty is for mind, for spirit alone; only mind, only spirit can experience it. In all experience of beauty, accordingly, the essential thing in the phenomenon is that mind speaks to mind, spirit to spirit. The law hence arises that the more sympathetic the communion, the more deeply and tenderly the contemplating mind enters into the condition of the communicating mind, and moreover regards it as communicating, as revealing to itself, the higher and more perfect will be the experience of the beauty. It is a lower degree of conformity to this law when the contemplating mind looks no farther than the idea and not beyond to the revealing mind—sympathizes with the idea revealed, and with the revelation, but not with the mind revealing the idea.

We have familiar applications of the law which illustrate its nature and force. A poem written by one we have never known, may be to us beautiful; we may be in sympathy with the idea it reveals, from whatever source that idea may come. But if the poet be one whom we know, whose views, whose feelings, whose aims we understand, with which also we are in tender personal sympathy, a new brightness, significance, charm, and beauty at once invests it to our view. It is a more speaking form to us. We cannot thus enter into the idea of a stranger to us, or of one from whom our sympathies estrange us. So a man who has no heart can have "no music in himself;" he cannot sympathize with a speaking heart; "the motions of his spirit are dull as night, and his affections dark as Erebus." In the same way, the observer of nature that knows no spirit speaking in it, or has no sympathy with it in its views and feelings and designs, or none with the particular idea revealed in its divers scenes, is so far debarred from seeing beauty in it. Most justly as well as beautifully does the sweet poet of nature, Cowper, insist:—

> "Acquaint thyself with God, if thou wouldst taste
> His works. Admitted once to His embrace,
> Thou shalt perceive that thou wast blind before:
> Thine eye shall be instructed; and thine heart
> Made pure shall relish with divine delight,
> Till then unfelt, what hands divine have wrought."

Of intelligence. § 335. Fourthly, all idea revealed in beauty is from an intelligent source. The idea itself is characterized with intelligence. Even music which immediately reveals feeling, reveals the feeling of an intelligent spirit. How little of the power of music can he know who has no intelligence of the thought which moved the feeling of the composer. Mozart, before he can begin his composition, requires his *libretto*—the full, detailed narrative in character, scene, progress, issue. He first takes that into his intelligence; he ponders it, studies carefully out every personage, every incident, every development, and then yields his feelings to the varying thought, to be stirred more or less intensely, or in this or that direction, precisely as the details of his libretto impress him. Only till then does his proper artistic work begin. Then he begins to speak forth in musical sound those feelings thus awakened.

It is obvious that the full grasp of Mozart's soul put forth into his music cannot be without a knowledge of the objects, the same individually or the same in kind as it respects the feeling which they awaken. There must be intelligence of the ideas revealed, in order to the full enjoyment of the music of Mozart. But equally necessary is a knowledge of the material, the sounds in which the feelings are embodied, the principles of musical rhythm, melody, and harmony. How much higher and richer is the artist's enjoyment of music, who feels, because he understands, all the movements in modulation and counterpoint! Still farther, there is need of intelligence in regard to the whole matter of rendering—of embodying in sound. The power and skill of the composer reveal themselves everywhere in the music, and make up a part of its proper power over the spirit.

The "pleasure in poetic pains, which only poets know," is incorporated with the idea and the matter into the product, and contributes to its proper æsthetic value and effect. But such joys, belonging to him that sings, can be felt only by him that knows what power and skill and successful labor in art are. Accordingly, in familiar experience we find that a photographic portrait, accurate as it is, awakens but little interest as a product compared with a painting although not so perfect a likeness. In the photograph, there is little that is truly artistic; the production is mostly mechanical. In a picture, it is the accurate discernment of feature by the artist, his just reading of character in it, his skill in rendering in figure and color, the grace of his penciling and the delicacy of his touch, that give to it its charm as a work of art. The great beauty of a photograph lies in the revealed character of the subject in the sun-copied tracings of his features; the commanding artistic value of a painting lies this side of that in the rendering, fidelity and skill of the painter. The beauty of a painting is thus greatly heightened by a knowledge of the mental power and the skill which have been put into it. So there is beauty in mere musical execution, which successfully surmounts obstacles and achieves triumphs in vocal or instrumental endeavor, independently of the proper æsthetic character of the composition.

It is thus the intelligent taste that best appreciates beauty. The child's eye recognizes little beauty in a masterpiece of art; the expert artist catches the largest inspiration from all beauty. Not mere intelligence, knowledge of principles, critical learning, but practiced intelligence that is quick and sure to discern the divers constituents of beauty is a condition of æsthetic interpretation. Into every object of beauty there enter various elements, each of which contributes to its proper effect, and needs to be apprehended. The idea itself, in its manifold modifications and relations, the material in its absolute and relative fitness or unfitness, the rendering above all, comprehending the moral design of the producer, whether he be divine or human, the intelligence and the loving affection which he has breathed into it, in all their infinite degrees and modes, the skill and grace, too, in the countless forms in which they appear in every product of creative art, all these are for the æsthetic intelligence in its experience of beauty. And as intelligence here only appears as subordinate to the sensibility, to enlarge and exalt and intensify its movements, it must not be slow and groping in its action, and so make itself predominant or interpose itself between the object and the sense; but quick, self-moved, instinctive, as it were, and never lifting itself into distinct consciousness.

By this we understand in part, perhaps in chief, how it is that a product of art grows in beauty to the continued contemplation and prolonged study. The intelligence catches up one element after another, and brings it into the common storehouse; turns one ray after another into the common radiant, and so enhances its power. Thus it is that the lover of nature, of the beautiful work of the divine artist, becomes ever more and more enamored of its beauty, with fresh study and prolonged view being lifted to discern a fuller and richer beauty—

more of the divine idea of power and wisdom and goodness; more of the mysterious qualities of that strange substance—matter—into which this divine idea has shaped itself to make it discernible by his creatures; more of that marvelous skill and grace with which he has penciled all its outlines and tinged and blended all its hues.

Of moral element.

§ 336. Fifthly, all form, all beauty is from a moral source. Only a rational spirit can create beauty, and to be rational is to be moral. The artist cnanot wholly divest himself of his moral nature. Even the suppression of its higher and truer instincts is of a moral character. To be moral is to be good in respect to the end and aim and legitimate result of any act and to be right in moving towards this result. Even when genius is corrupt and art is depraved, it yet can never put itself entirely without the pale of the moral nature in which it participates. If the aim in art even be vicious and devilish, the work must yet to some degree disguise itself in a decent garb. All beauty thus is necessarily in the moral sphere. To apprehend it aright, therefore, and fully, it must be apprehended with a moral disposition and spirit.

From pure art, the pure soul imbibes most freely and most copiously. It enters into a warmer sympathy with both artist and product; it receives in larger supplies the blessing that comes from all true art. It appreciates better, interprets better than the impure and defiled spirit possibly can. But still this moral disposition and life must underlie the sensibility and only enliven and expand that. To be morally profited in the contemplation of beauty must be the indirect fruit and consequence, not the immediate effect. The moral nature is fostered, purified, and guided in art not by direct aim and effect on itself, but through the heightened and purified sensibility, only as that is made more quick and tender to the pure and good, more constant and more vivid in its pure suggestions, more engaging by its purer pleasure to whatever is pure and noble and good.

SPECIAL APPLICATIONS OF THE LAWS OF ÆSTHETIC INTERPRETATION TO THE SEVERAL ARTS.—

To architecture.

§ 337. I. *To Architecture.*—The question we are here to meet is this: How can we, in proceeding to the contemplation of a work of architectural art, interpret out to ourselves its proper beauty best and most perfectly? The general exposition that has been made of the laws of æsthetic interpretation will easily guide us in our procedure.

Surrender of sensibility to object.

We are first to bring our æsthetic sensibility as susceptively, closely, exclusively as possible into communication with the structure. It addresses us only through the sense of sight; and our æsthetic sense must apprehend it mediately through that. To what this sense of sight brings us we are to surrender our susceptible nature that it may fully engage us and purely and deeply impress itself upon us. We must bring not a dead, motionless passivity; but the sense of a living, active soul, that is awake and on the alert, that is free to move here and there, as the object may move us, and to feel from every part of it. We are to bring it as in sympathy with the benignant design that seeks a provision of shelter and of comfort and also of blessing to the æsthetic spirit, that our active sense may be warm and glowing as well as tender. We are to bring in also the full measure of all that intelligence which such a work addresses, in respect of idea, material, form; and our moral nature should be enlisted with our intelligence, to elevate, quicken, and expand our sense. This is our procedure regarded from the subjective side.

View of object as a whole.

Turning now to the object, we first apprehend it as a whole of such or such an outline and amplitude, just as it pictures itself on the retina. Never dropping wholly this its impression as a whole, as the eye rests upon it, parts come into our regard—site, and position, absolute and relative to surrounding objects; outline in all the particulars of vertical and horizontal figure, with those of color and hue, and then of the several parts passing from the more general to the subordinate, and viewing each in its individual figure and color, as well as relatively to the whole and the other parts.

Site.

Outline.

Color.

Idea.

The idea that has determined and shaped it, the ends of utility, of shelter, of comfort, of repose, and the like, and the more special ends of domestic, civil, religious, or memorial purpose, with the fitness to each of those ends; the material, its adaptation to its use, and all the elements that have determined the selection, and also entered into the treatment of it; the mechanical design in securing these economic and special ends; the æsthetic ends through those of utility and through outline, light and shade and color, as the support, vertical and lateral, the unity, contrasts, æsthetic number of parts, proportion, symmetry and harmony of parts; the moral aspects, too, coloring the design and work throughout, the power and skill, the love and patient care, the sound intelligence which mark the construction. The continued contemplation, keeping ever the sensibility in predominant exercise, making all intelligence and moral purpose subservient and in ministry to that, is thus to be kept upon the object as part after part presents itself to the study, as it passes now in this direction, now in that, causing every successive view to quicken and fill the sensibility. The historical knowledge of the art affording opportunity for comparing and contrasting and measuring may well form part of the intelligence which is to feed the sensibility. The true taste will characteristically dwell most on the excellencies, turning rather from the imperfections which enter and mar all human workmanship. The critic may bring both beauties and deformities into his view; the cynic revel in the spots and blemishes; the true æsthetic soul will

Material.

Mechanical design.

Æsthetic ends.

History.

rest upon whatever is truly beautiful there may be, and find a pure satisfaction in that.

Mathematical principles.

The more predominant and characteristic elements of architectural beauty are those which are founded in the intelligence, and are essentially mathematical. The principles of support and of proportion, thus, are the leading principles in architecture. The contemplation of this kind of beauty, therefore, will find its most proper and its most exalted and satisfying returns when directed upon these elements of the art. Accordingly, the mind most conversant with the laws of pressure and of cohesion in the materials used in architecture and most trained in the relations of quantities, will rise to be capable of the highest æsthetic enjoyment from architecture. But the rudest intelligence has some sense of these mathematical relations, and there remain outside of these elements manifold others to engage the eye and soul of every lover of art and beauty.

§ 338. 2. *To Landscape.*—In bringing the æsthetic sensibility to the reception of the proper beauty of landscape, it is obvious that while we must approach mainly through the sense of sight, as in architecture, this sense is not the only avenue. As we have seen, the hearing, the smell, the taste, are in a degree directly or indirectly instrumental to the enjoyment of landscape beauty. There is call here accordingly for a more widely diversified sensibility. There is call so far for a more active play of the sensibility, so that it may take in the

Call for a sensibility diversified.

varying object, as it offers itself at each of its several avenues. There is call, also, for a warmer, livelier sympathy; for here not dead forms of matter mathematically measured and shaped, but the forms of organic life offer themselves. Farther, a more intelligent as well as a higher moral sense is required.

Sympathetic.

Intelligent and moral.

For the right interpretation of beauty in landscape, there is the same procedure in the study of the object required as in architecture. The ideas proper to the art, both economic and æsthetic, are first to be present in the mind, prompting and shaping the sensibility. From the material in this art, however, will be derived the more peculiar and characteristic impressions. The medium of revelation in landscape is predominantly organic life. It is what is commonly called the beauty of nature, which properly engages the sense so far as material is concerned. At least, this is the kind of beauty which the highest and purest landscape aspires to reveal. Chiefly, although not exclusively, as we have seen, vegetable life gives character to landscape. It is the beauty of organic life and growth, the beauty of flower, of leaf, of branch, of tree, of garden, of lawn, of field, of forest, in the relations in which nature has placed them, which is here predominant. And the leading question which the demand for a right interpretation presents is: What shall bring in most of this beauty of organic life into our souls?

Study of idea.

Of material—organic life.

Or, what amounts to the same thing, what is the peculiar element in organic life which makes it beautiful, and which we are to apprehend in order to enjoy it most fully and perfectly? To make the answer more intelligible, we may put the question in the form of a still more specific inquiry: How do we apprehend the richest beauty in a single tree? The noble elm which stands before my window, with its roots that heave up in rounded ridges the turf and pavement above them, as they swell out to the dimensions needful to their functions of support and nutrition, its stately trunk cased in rugged bark, its sweeping boughs branching off at uniform angles and intervals, its intricate spray shooting off in every direction to hold forth the abundant foliage for freest ministries of air and light:—wherein does its beauty lie? on what precisely must the soul fix its sense in order most fully and exactly and perfectly to apprehend its proper beauty? We might rest satisfied with the general teaching of the poet, and recognizing it as the revelation of a great creative idea which expresses itself in its diversified forms in all nature, content ourselves with admiring

> "How exquisitely the individual mind,
> And the progressive powers perhaps no less,
> Of the whole species, to the external world
> Is fitted; and how exquisitely, too,
> The external world is fitted to the mind."

But we crave a more specific answer than this of the general correspondence of the human soul to the creative spirit speaking in nature. We ask why any form that exists is not beautiful; why an elm, evidently but half-rooted, with square trunk, with precisely horizontal boughs scattered at random from the center line, a spray and foliage different in position and shape and hue, a square smooth-lined black leaf, should not satisfy an æsthetic sense as well? Why an imperfect tree in any respect, imperfect because it was robbed of its needed soil and nutriment of light and warmth and vapor, or was scathed by excessive heat or benumbed by the untimely frost, or was mutilated by axe, or hurricane, or other instrument of rude violence, does not please our taste as well? The answer is, and the answer is the only answer that can be given while it is on the deepest æsthetic principles satisfactory, that somehow or other, more or less imperfectly, more or less unconsciously, we have come to know and to feel, that is to know deeply though imperfectly as to the grounds of our knowledge, so deeply as to move and shape our sensibility, that the creative idea of a perfect organic elm-life could be realized only with such roots, such trunk, such spray, and foliage. The constituent of the beauty lies in this or that particular form and shape because it is the necessary form and shape for the ideal of an elm in the creative mind. And just in proportion as our intelligence is enlightened and informed as to the relations of the branch and leaf to the perfection of the tree-life, the richer will be its beauty to us. If it be asked: Were things so constituted that a black leaf would be as fit for the life of the tree, would it be beautiful to us? the answer is that the

Why beautiful?

supposition itself is inadmissible, as much so as to suppose that twice two should make five; for we are authorized to believe that there is a like contradiction in it, although our minds cannot fathom the mysteries of creation quite so easily as those of mathematical quantities. The supposition is impertinent here on the theory that beauty, as perfect form, is revelation of idea in matter, since black leaf matter as it is, is incompatible with the idea of elm-life. The question is tantamount accordingly to this: If our minds and tastes were constituted otherwise than they are in reference to the realities of ideas and matter in which they act, would other forms be beautiful? The answer may wisely be reserved till our constitutions and the natures of things around us are thus changed.

Exclusion of deformities.

As even the natural world, like the moral, as if in sympathy with it and typical of it, has its imperfections, and beauty is perfect form, the æsthetic eye in scanning landscape as nature generally, should exclude so far as possible all the imperfection that unavoidably comes in. If trees are wrenched from their uprightness by storm or other rudeness, if decay has marred their native symmetry or turned rich-clothed limb into forbidding dryness and nakedness, or if other blot through alien force has in this or that spot defaced the proper beauty of the scene, it is the dictate of æsthetic wisdom to exclude it from the sense and let it enter as little as may be into the soul's vision and regard; just as the wise painter of landscape excludes from his ideal any feature in the real scene that has suggested his ideal which does not help out at least by contrast the perfect form he would design.

Study of sculpture as free beauty.

§ 339. 3. *To Sculpture.*—The beauty of sculpture is free beauty; and the æsthetic contemplation regards the pure form for its own sake. Not to be instructed, not to be benefited in any way except by being impressed, is the normal effect of all art, so far as free or purely æsthetic. The critical schools have long accepted the teaching that *free beauty is without all interest*—that the sentiment of the beautiful is not a want, but is wholly disinterested, without indicating the grounds or very sharply defining the meaning. If some philosophers have found the true effect of all free art in pleasure, it is only because their erroneous philosophy has failed to distinguish impression on the sensibility from the natural pleasure which is connected with such impression, and which consequently makes all feeling to be pleasure or pain. Or they have illogically inferred from the fact that perfect beauty, like perfect truth, must ever give pleasure to the apprehension, that therefore the beautiful is nothing else but the pleasing. The true view is, that free art proposes simply to impress its ideal most perfectly on the æsthetic sensibility. Other effects, as those of pleasure, instruction, culture, are consequential, and are not its immediate aim. That the work pleases is evidence of its success, the pleasure being but the satisfaction of the æsthetic sensibility.

From artist's point of view.

Sculpture addresses the æsthetic sensibility through outline and light and shadow. In order to its proper interpretation, therefore, the eye must regard it from the sculptor's standpoint, that it may receive the same effect of figure and of light and shadow which he purposed. The highest product of sculpture is the revelation of the human spirit and character. But the expression of the features varies with the direction from which they are studied. A photograph, although exact as the rays of light, may be almost expressionless, or express almost opposite characteristics, according as the rays fall directly on this or on that feature. To read a statue right, the eye must find its true position for observing.

With intelligence of character.

In apprehending the idea it is obvious the sensibility must be intelligent of the character represented. It can not be rightly impressed by an Apollo or a Venus without knowing what characters these are. The fuller and clearer this intelligence of the idea in the æsthetic sense, the fuller and richer will be the interpretation.

Of material.

To a certain extent, this intelligence of the material will help the interpretation; for marble and metal express very differently from each other as well as from native flesh. Certainly the skill of the artist, which enters largely in all æsthetic effect as a distinct element, cannot well be estimated or felt without such intelligence.

Why certain forms beautiful.

As no true art is mere copy, the question recurs here that emerged in the interpretation of landscape—why are certain forms necessary for art? Why do we recognize such a shape as beautiful and not another? The answer is as before—there is a relationship between rational life and the organic life such that the former may have its natural expression in the latter; such that any particular modification of the former demands for its full expression and realization a corresponding modification of the latter; such that an Apollo cannot be realized in the muscular shaping of a Venus-face; such that we are able, through a knowledge some way acquired, to identify this shape as a perfect expression of one character—of intellectual strength and symmetry; and that shape as a perfect expression of another character—of tender sensibility and affection. The organic conformation of a bird or of a beast is different from that of man. What is a beautiful shaping of force and majesty in a lion is not a beautiful shaping of human force and majesty. The beauty is not in the organization itself as organization; that which Schiller denominates architectonic beauty is not in any mere geometrical dimensions or relations; but the organization becomes beautiful as it is the perfect expression or realization of the idea—the animal or the human. The essence of beauty lies in this relation between the idea and the matter. The sensibility in receiving plastic form must intelligently apprehend the fitness of the matter to the ideal which it reveals.

The artist feels the necessity of long and close and careful study of the human anatomy, in its manifold modifications by age, sex, disposition, pursuit, culture, in order to express rightly his ideals; the observer, to catch the full power of his skill, needs something of the same intelligence which this patient study gives.

Summarily, then, for the æsthetic interpretation of sculpture, the sensibility, susceptible, quick, sympathetic, intelligent, and morally disposed, must reach its object through the vision directed from the proper standpoint, and receive successively element by element—ideal, matter, embodiment with all rendering grace and skill—into one whole of impression. The peculiar characteristic of art interpretation here, in the highest department of the art at least, is the apprehension of the rational spirit and character in its manifold modifications as they are realized in the human organization.

§ 340. 4. *To Painting.*—This art makes its appeal to the sensibility through the organ of sight like sculpture, but adds to outline and shadow not only a deeper, stronger tone, but the new medium of color. Its address is more direct to the heart accordingly. It demands the same accurate adjustment of the eye, that the light may come to it from the points which the artist designed to be more prominent; the same holding of the æsthetic sensibility to the constituent elements of idea, of shading and coloring, and of rendering in such way that all the artist has put upon his canvas may enter into the sense, and form one single image there, which shall be the full and exact reflection of what is studied. In the highest department of the art—historical painting—in which not human character in its fixed and unrelated features is the proper subject, but human achievement in related event and action, there is a higher call for a sympathetic sense, and also a sense more deeply and decidedly moved in the moral nature rightly disposed. The grouping of objects, which enters here, makes its corresponding demand on the intelligent sense. The proper artistic skill, moreover, in the artist invites a closer and more particular study. The grace not only in outlining, as in sculpture, but in blending as well as selecting colors, enters largely into the proper beauty of a painting.

Sympathy.

Intelligence.

Study of artistic skill.

§ 341. 5. *To Music.*—The art of music has for its characteristics that it expresses mainly feeling, and that its organ is the ear. In interpreting music there is, farther, the peculiarity that it is only for the moment—it passes and is gone—the contemplation must engage it at the instant and as it flits along. Further, feeling in itself having but the two modifications in quality of joyous and sorrowful, and the few of degree as of slow and quick, lax and intense, suffers manifold modifications from the objects which awaken it. These peculiarities guide us to the proper course for easy and right interpretation of music when it varies from that to be followed in the case of the arts before considered.

Demand of a sense practised.

As in the other arts the organ of sense, here the ear must be wholly enlisted, and to the exclusion of other occupations. There is a training for the ear as well as for the eye, which is only by practice. As the sharp, ready sight comes from long use, so the quick, accurate, discriminating ear is the result only of long and right exercise.

Wakeful.

In music, from its fleeting, transient character, the sensibility more needs to be awake and active than in the other arts. From the beginning to the end, each movement must be caught, or the whole effect is mutilated or destroyed. What escapes cannot be recovered, as in a new observation of a building, or a painting. To lose thus a passage or a part would be like having the eye blinded to a member of a group or a leading color in a painting, or a limb or a feature in a statue.

Sympathetic.

The sympathy is here more directly engaged than elsewhere; for feeling here comes immediately to feeling and heart speaks to heart. Whatever breaks or hinders this sympathy or play of soul mars the effect of music.

Intelligent.

The range of intelligence requisite in musical interpretation will depend mainly on the professional skill and on the foreign aid derived from operatic *libretti* or from the lyric songs to which the music is adapted. There are certain hints to be taken from the science of musical art, which will be helpful in obtaining the full æsthetic enjoyment from music. To pass over all that interest and pleasure which a professional musician realizes from his ready notice of the skill of the composer or the performer in surmounting difficulties or achieving masterstrokes of art, there is much help to be derived from a knowledge of the principles that lie at the foundation of all that is excellent in musical art. All music expresses a mood of feeling. To enjoy music properly, therefore, the hearer must needs allow his sensibility to be determined into that mood; and the general character of the mood which a given musical composition is to express, is or should be indicated in the few notes that express the theme. Then the theme extends itself into the melody, which should be fully apprehended. On the melody is built the harmony, the adaptation of musical consonances or chords to the melody. The introduction of the fugues, their character and relations, invite a separate notice. And then is to be apprehended the general succession of the movements characterized in respect to the joyous or plaintive, the quick or slow, the forceful or gentle, the allegro, the andante, the largo, the playful, the lively and quick. Even the unprofessional hearer of music will find his sense of its beauty greatly enhanced as he quickens and guides his sensibility by this underlying intelligence of the nature and import of music. One constituent after another he will be enabled to take up and weave into the one common woof of effect. Especially will he be able to recognize more readily the constituent to which the artist designed to give the chief effect, and to surrender himself more to it—to the air, or whichever of the other parts rises here or there above the rest, to the modulation or other change in the movement. His care should be not to allow himself to be drawn into an intellectual study. This is to defeat the very design of music, which is for the feeling alone — for the sensibility, between which and the sound that engages the ear nothing must be permitted to intervene. The intelligence must only minister to the sense, not dethrone or master it.

§ 342. 6. *To Poetry.*—In directing the æsthetic sensibility how best to receive the addresses of this art of arts, the best method will be to follow the order of the three constituent elements of all discourse — the subject or idea, the word as a sound, and the word as symbol.

Study of subject.

In regard to the subject of a poetical composition, the idea which runs through it and is revealed in it, very obviously the intelligence must be prominently enlisted for any proper sense of its beauty. Generally the highest order of poetry calls for the highest order of intellectual culture. So far from the doctrine being sound that the best poetry is that which best holds the popular mind in the sense of holding the uncultivated and the unintelligent mass, the contrary is just the truth. The best poetry is that which best holds the most cultured soul. This implies that good poetry, while it must be for all ages, all nations, all conditions, yet can be for them only as there is intelligence in them. The child, the ignorant, the undeveloped mind, is enraptured with Mother Goose's Melodies—with jingling nonsense. The illiterate mass delights in gross caricature, in uncouth tales of the wild and monstrous. Events of world-wide significance, truths of eternal moment, sentiments of the most etherial nature, it has no intelligent sense to apprehend. The call for intelligence in order to the æsthetic interpretation of poetry is heard everywhere. It helps this interpretation to know the poet himself, his age and times, his genius, his culture, his aim and object in writing. It helps it to know the relations of his subject, whatever its character, historical or intellectual, event or truth; as also the character and relations of each individual personage and each subordinate truth or sentiment. It helps to the full sense of a poem that the sensibility be informed by a full intelligence of all that pertains to the subject or idea in its character and specific development. A good poem grows in beauty as knowledge and culture grow.

Of word.

Again, the full æsthetic effect of poetry, as of all discourse, is conditioned upon the right apprehension of the word as the matter in which poetry and discourse reveal idea. The word, as we have seen, is sound filled with thought. It has a sound side, a thought side, and a proper symbol or imagery side, when it is correctly analyzed. We may dismiss here the consideration of the thought-aspect of a word, as the principles guiding to the right apprehension are the same as those which pertain to the apprehension of idea or subject generally. Never should it be forgotten, however, that the word, as symbol of thought, has a life and growth which reach the thought; that consequently the meaning or significance of a word has a history as well as the sound or the letters—the orthoepy or the orthography. He who has this notion of the nature of a word will ever enjoy most in discourse and poetry.

Its meaning.

The word is a sound; discourse and poetry are word-sounds in combination. As such they characteristically engage the æsthetic sense. Every word, as we have seen, has a true musical nature. Poetry, which in its normal form, is uttered, and must, to be enjoyed perfectly, when read silently, be rendered by the reader into imaginary sound, is thus true music. The poetic utterance goes out characterized by all the proper musical marks of sound. It walks along in simple tone-steps, with simple tone-slides or tone-skips up or down, as the feeling or the turn of the thought requires, or it breaks in tender feeling, into semitonic or minor gradations, or in intenser expression mounts through thirds, fifths, or octaves, or prolongs itself into combinations of tone-slides as the varying sentiment may prompt. The æsthetic effect of all poetry, as of all discourse, consists in a great part in the vocal word, so that its charm will depend not a little on the power of the voice to give in the utterance the proper musical movements to the several words.

Its musical nature.

Of Rhythm.

But we meet another oral element more peculiar to poetry, although not foreign to all human discourse, rhythm If there be poetry without what is commonly understood as poetical rhythm—a regular recurrence of poetic feet—such poetry for instance as the received English version of the Psalms, it is not poetry in its highest or richest form of diction. Poetry, generally and well nigh characteristically, has rhythm. Its verbal body is rhythmical. There can be no true æsthetic interpretation of a poem except as this rhythm is apprehended. And it is worthy to be borne in mind that the ear requires and is susceptible of training in its sensibility to rhythm. The true poet speaks in rhythm.

If he has the mastery of rhythm, as every true poet has, his thoughts and his feelings—his poetic mood determines the rhythm, and makes it an exact embodiment, conforming to itself in its successive variations the rhythmical body throughout. It is of course impossible to apprehend the mood of the poet, except as the rhythm is apprehended. To interpret poetry æsthetically, therefore, it is necessary that the nature of rhythm, the forms of rhythm, the expression peculiar to the different kinds of rhythm, be understood; that the sensibility be quickened and filled by a proper rhythmical intelligence.

Not only is this quick and susceptible sense of rhythm in itself requisite, but also its relation to thought must be apprehended so as to be æsthetically felt. Proper beauty implies an exact correspondence between the idea and the matter. In respect to poetical rhythm it implies an exact commensurability between the thought and the divisions of the rhythm. If the thought be direct, simple, sententious, like Pope's, the verse will end the thought; and the cæsural pause, the pause which the termination of the thought or of a part of it requires in a right reading, will frequently occur; the rhythm will be broken. If the thought be prolonged, more or less involved, expressing manifold modifications, like Cowper's, the rhythm will continue through the verse, or through successive verses unbroken. The beauty of the broken rhythm of Pope is one; that of Cowper is another; and the difference must be apprehended in order to a right æsthetic interpretation of the poetry of each.

Of Melody.

Moreover, there is, as we have seen, a poetic melody—a construction of the thought and of the sentence in harmony with the rhythm, which, in the right pronunciation so as to show the relations of the parts of the thought to one another, shall allow the variations in pitch to be in accordance with the principles of music. It is one of the æsthetic elements of all poetry. The sententiousness of Pope admits it but slightly; but the rich, varied thought of Cowper allowing and prompting it, his poetry owes a chief part of its charm to it. Its effect may be felt blindly, just as music has a certain pleasing effect on the dullest mind. But its full power can be experienced only by a sensibility enlightened by some intelligence of the nature and force of poetic melody.

Of Harmony.

A like observance of the harmony in poetry is as obviously necessary. To it the ear must be kept equally open.

Such are the conditions of a full æsthetic interpretation of poetry given by the sound-side of the word and of language. The sense must be prepared to receive the music of oral utterance in respect both to particular words and also to poetic rhythm and melody and harmony, which belongs to words in combination.

Of symbol.

Once more, for the full æsthetic enjoyment of poetry, the sense must be brought to take in the full beauty of the word as symbol—the full charm and power of rhetorical imagery. What demand is here made upon the intelligence in the æsthetic sensibility in order that the meaning and fitness of the symbol or imagery may be apprehended, it is unnecessary to indicate in prolonged detail. The object, the event, or the truth, which constitutes the symbol or image of the poet's revelation, must obviously be known, or this great element of poetic beauty is expressionless. How the Paradise Lost loses in its true charms on the mind ignorant of its rich classical allusions and imagery! So the poetry of the Hebrew scriptures is comparatively tame to one who has no idea of oriental scenery. The literature of a nation, that properly clothes itself in the national life, its history, its customs, its physical peculiarities, loses a great part of its beauty to a stranger's mind.

But above this intelligence of the object, which is taken to symbolize or image the thought, there is the proper poetic work of embodying it, which should engage the æsthetic sense. The beauty of poetry lies more characteristically in the skill and grace with which the idea is thus symbolized or imaged. It is enough here simply to indicate this as one of the particular elements to which the æsthetic sense is to be addressed; and its proper and full effect to be gathered up into the one total impression formed by the combination of all the elements of beauty. All art, it has justly been observed, is poetic; and, as justly may it be said, all poetry is allegorical. It is always putting thought or idea into other than its native form; always uttering in another speech-form; always allegorizing. Æsthetic interpretation in all art is essentially interpretation of the embodiment by the artist of his idea, gained in whatever way, in a new, original kind or form of matter. The interpretation of poetic symbolism and imagery is of the nature of the interpretation of all art. Only a more especial draft, perhaps, is made upon the intelligence in poetry than elsewhere in art. This one caution and reminder is consequently more fitting and needful here: that the æsthetic interpretation is by the sensibility as the immediate organ; that hence the intellect must be kept subordinate and subservient to the sense; lest the contemplation of poetry be not æsthetic, not such as gives the experience of beauty, but characteristically intellectual or critical; for the sake of knowledge or of trial, in order to approve or condemn.

BOOK IV.

RELATIONS OF BEAUTY.

CHAPTER I

INTRODUCTORY VIEW.

Method.

§ 343. We have now in the several steps of our progress ascertained the Properties of Beauty; we have distinguished the Kinds of Beauty; and have determined the Laws of Beauty, whether they respect its production or interpretation. The fourth step, as at the start was indicated, still remains—to consider the Relations of Beauty.

A two-fold distinction at once presents itself. We have on the one hand the beautiful in itself; and we have on the other hand the science of the beautiful. We have in other words the two departments of (1) the relations of Beauty; and (2) the relations of Æsthetics, or the science of beauty.

Moreover, we have a two-fold inquiry to consider in regard to each of these two divisions: (1) the relations to coördinates; and (2) the relations to ends—its uses; the where and the wherefore both of beauty and of the science of beauty.

We have, thus, the four particulars of study indicated to us, which we shall proceed to treat in separate chapters:—

I. The Relations of the Beautiful to the True and the Good.

II. The Relations of Æsthetics to Logic and Ethics.

III. The Uses of Beauty.

IV. The Uses of Æsthetics.

CHAPTER II.

THE RELATIONS OF THE BEAUTIFUL TO THE TRUE AND THE GOOD.

Place.

§ 344. We are first to seek the place of the beautiful — its geographical position relatively to other ideas in the same province of truth. From the earliest dawn of science to the present time there has been one universally accepted answer to this inquiry.

The three ideas.

The true, the beautiful, and the good have been accepted as occupying the same field of truth, as completely filling it — each the complementary and the coördinate of the others.

They have been denominated the three comprehensive ideas. They are the ideas of the true, the beautiful, and the good.

These three ideas have ever been viewed as standing in a very close not to say vital relationship to one another. Philosophers and poets have spoken of them as being but the same thing in essence. Cousin speaks of beauty as "blended with the true and the good in one, the same unity. If the true, the good, and the beautiful appear to be distinct and separate, it is not because they are so in fact, but because they are given forth [with different relative prominence] in different objects." In the same spirit Akenside speaks:—

> Truth and good are one,
> And beauty dwells in them, and they in her,
> With like participation.

The false, the ugly, the bad.

§ 345. Each of the three has its opposite or contrary; and each is recognized as of manifold gradations according as each is encroached upon by its opposite or mingled with it. The true has for its opposite the false: the beautiful, the ugly; the good, the bad. The false, the ugly, and the bad stand in the same relation to one another as the true, the beautiful, and the good. The interminglings of each with its opposite give us respectively the imperfectly true, the imperfectly beautiful, the imperfectly good. In some objects this intermingling is so equal that they become so to speak indifferent. We meet objects that we characterize as having no truth in them; or as having no beauty, or no goodness, although not positively false, or ugly, or bad.

We have recognized as an essential element in all beauty, idea—a form of mind or of spirit; some specific determination of spiritual activity, whether of intelligence, of feeling, or of purpose. So it is in all truth. There is in whatever is true, something which is received in this relation—an idea, here called a subject recognized as having some attribute belonging to it. It is the same with all that is good. There is a mind, a spirit in all that we regard as good or bad. In every thing good, there is a form of mind, a specific determination of spiritual activity — an idea. There is thus in the true, the beautiful, the good, in each alike, idea as an essential element.

Phases of the same.

§ 346. Moreover the same object is characterized as true, or beautiful, or good, according as we view it. Here before my eye, is a certain thing. It is oval in outline; it is thin like paper; it is green in hue; it is coursed with regular hollow veins running out at regular angles from a central stem; it is made up of a multitude of little vessels connected with all the veins and veinlets and filling out the whole outline. I say it is a true leaf. It is true because of it I can say it is oval, thin, green, veined, cellular:— I recognize these attributes as belonging to it This is my idea of a leaf — an object having the attributes named, others perhaps. My idea is true in so far as I regard it in this relation of something having certain attributes; in so far as I regard it in itself — in its relations as a whole to its several parts. Or if I take a part of this object, a vein, it is a true vein to me in so far as I regard it as a tube conveying sap between the central stem and the cells; in so far as I regard it and its relations not only to its own parts as tubular, but also in its relations to other parts of the same leaf-whole — the central stem and the cells. All my apprehension of this object in this way, all my experience of the leaf in its relations of subject and attributes, that is in its relations as a whole to its own parts, or as a part of a larger whole to the other parts of the same whole, is an apprehension, an experience of the true. It is a state or act of the intelligence, a knowledge or a cognition. If indeed I recognize the leaf in this interior relation of a certain thing with attributes erroneously, ascribing to it an attribute not belonging to it, I have a false idea of it. My experience is in the same realm of intelligence—of the true; but it is the opposite of perfect.

But I may take this object, this leaf into my experience in quite another way. I drop out of my regard these relations of subject and attribute. I contemplate the leaf only as a form in which an idea is revealed to me. The divine Former has expressed so far His idea of a plant-life; this idea has gone out into this oval-shaped, thin, green, veined, cellular thing. It is full of truth and full of goodness, but I regard these aspects only as they help out and minister to my sense of its form, of its beauty. I resign myself to the simple feeling of the object. I could not feel it, perhaps, my sensibility, being in its very essence, an intelligent moral sensibility—I could not receive it into my experience unless it were formed also in intelligence and in goodness; but it is its form, its simple revelation of the former idea which now engages me. I apprehend it now as beautiful; I have the experience of beauty.

Once more, I may regard this same object in its proper effect or end. I may regard the design of the Creator in giving it being and apprehend it as good—good as ministering to the life of the tree which itself is designed in beneficence to bring fruit or coolness to the hungry or the weary, and therefore good; good in its own parts, each ministering to the well being of the others. Or more exactly, I may apprehend it as good to me, as working joy, pleasure, by its engaging my intelligence and gratifying my love of the true, my desire of knowing; by its engaging my sensibility as a perfect form, as beautiful and gratifying my sense by its pleasing impressions, or still farther, by its working directly in blessing upon me by bringing food and coolness. I apprehend it now as good, the good comes into my experience.

Every object may be apprehended as true, beautiful, and good.

§ 347. We must go one step further still. Not only may the leaf, not only may this or that selected object be true, beautiful, or good, either and all according as it is regarded; but any object, every object that can come into our experience, whether thing, truth, or event, is either true, or beautiful, or good to us according as we apprehend it in its relations of a whole and parts, or as a form, or as producing effect. Every object has each of these characteristics. By our power of abstraction, of attending to this or that one of its aspects, it may become to us either. Some objects, it is true, are better fitted to engage the intelligence, and so to appear as true; others to engage the sensibility, and so to appear as beautiful; and others still to engage our souls as natures blessing or to be blessed, and so to appear as good. It is still true that all alike may appear to us in either aspect, and so shape our experience of it as to be either to us. An abstract proposition, for example, is in the form of a truth. It prominently addresses and more easily engages our intelligence. We do not so readily apprehend it as beautiful or as good. But yet it is possible to regard it in either of these aspects; and our experience of it will then be more prominently and characteristically an admiration of it as a form in which an idea is revealed in a perfect way, or as most important in its bearing on our welfare as interpreting to us more or less the world which is constructed in intelligence around us. We may pronounce the proposition bald which expresses the law of universal gravitation—that all bodies of matter tend towards each other in the inverse ratio of the squares of their distances from each other. But yet in another view how sublime is this revelation of the Creator's great idea in forming a material universe! and in another view still how beneficent, how good does this great law appear to us!

So, to take another example of a widely different character, the pebble that lies before our feet, while we regard it as a mere space-filling little body, with no orderly outline to indicate that a mind has been present to shape it, with no agreeable color to reveal a soul that has embraced and has left upon it the glow of its warm embrace, has no beauty for us. We either do not notice it; or we view it only as a thing of utility, if not as a cumbrance. But let us regard it, as it is in our power to regard it, as a product of power, of wisdom, of love; let us read these characters in the locality which it has chosen, in the quiet rest which it maintains, in its internal structure too, the harmony, order, loving union of its parts, and it becomes to us a thing of beauty, not by virtue of mere accidental associations which we throw around it, but by virtue of its own nature as revealed idea. There is more of truth even than of poetry in the familiar lines of the poet :—

> To me the meanest flower that blows can give
> Thoughts that do often lie too deep for tears.

The universe around us is thus full of truth, of beauty, and of goodness, in a fuller, richer sense than is sometimes supposed. It is literally true that there is not an object in it with which we can become conversant that is not alike true, beautiful, and good, in this interpretation of the proposition, that each object participates in this three-fold nature and belongs alike to the nature of truth, beauty and goodness. It may be false, it may be ugly, it may be bad ; it may be partially true, partially beautiful, partially good ; but it belongs alike to each of these three departments which respect our three-fold rational nature.

Whether true, beautiful, or good, how far determined by object itself.

§ 348. It follows from this view, in the first place, that an object may enter our experience more readily, either as the true, or as the beautiful, or as the good, according to its own determination or character. As already intimated, a proposition more readily engages the intelligence ; we approach it as a truth to be known. A fixed object in nature, a plant, a flower, a rainbow addresses more our sense ; we apprehend it more as a form as beautiful or otherwise. An action more readily arrests our moral nature ; we regard its rightness or its goodness.

Or by our own mind.

It follows in the second place that we may receive any given object more into our intelligence, and it will, whatever its more prominent and characteristic determination in itself, appear to us as true or otherwise; or we may receive it simply into our sensibility, and it becomes a thing of beauty to us; or we may receive it as a design and effect, and it becomes to us good or otherwise. We may so vary our apprehension of the same object by simple purpose, through transient inclination, or through settled habit. The philosopher thus politically looks upon the universe of objects and events, with the mere eye of his intelligence, and experiences it only as true or otherwise. Each object, each event, he studies in its relations to its own parts or attributes or in its relations as a part to other parts, and views it as that which in regard to its whole or any part, he can identify as itself, as true. The poet opens his heart to the impressions of things and actions, and dwells on them as forms fitted to impress or as impressing; and the universe is to him not a universe of truth, but of beauty. He cares little for the truth of things; he disdains analysis; he laughs perhaps at philosophy except as it ministers to beauty. He looks upon the rainbow and yields his sense to the free impressions that it makes upon his soul as a revelation of peace and goodwill, of wisdom and order, of power and skill and grace. The philanthropist scans the design and working and effect of all that appears, of all that transpires. It is to him right and good or otherwise. Only as nothing can be right and good which is not true and beautiful, does he care to recognize these characters in what he studies. The truth of things, the beauty of things, he sinks under the utility and the morality of things.

Confirmation from psychology.

§ 349. This general view of the relation between the true, the beautiful, and the good, receives a striking corroboration from the history of psychological science. The ancient philosophy recognized, as we have said, these three as the all comprehensive ideas. Whatever we can contemplate or experience, must, according to their teaching, be contemplated or experienced in one of these three aspects or characters. Modern psychologists have recognized also three departments of mind in its relation to outward objects — intelligence, sensibility, will. The former distribution of mental phenomena will be recognized as objective, the latter as subjective. Being both sound and true, they must be in exact correspondence with each other; the objective division must exactly correspond to the subjective; that is, the true must correspond to the intelligence, the beautiful to the sensibility, the good to the will. And the true, the beautiful, the good must exist together in the object in the same vital union, in which the intelligence, the sensibility, and the will exist together in the conscious subject.

CHAPTER III.

THE RELATIONS OF ÆSTHETICS TO LOGIC AND ETHICS.

Mutual interdependence.

§ 350. From the vital relationship of the three great ideas of the true, the beautiful, and the good, we are prepared to anticipate a like vital relationship between the formal scientific expositions of them—between the sciences of the true, the beautiful, and the good. This relationship we are prepared to anticipate will discover itself in an analogous unfolding of the elements that respectively enter into these ideas and characterize them; in a reciprocal determination of the limits and boundaries of the respective sciences; in a reciprocal modification of the particular departments in each; and generally in a reciprocal illumination and explicating light thrown by each upon the others. In truth it may be safely presumed that neither science can be fully and truly expounded except in the light of the others.

Proof from Æsthetic science.

§ 351. The name of Æsthetics, we have seen, has been given to the science of the beautiful, perhaps we may now be disposed to admit, with a greater propriety and fitness than Baumgarten himself recognized. Certainly we shall credit him with a keener sagacity and a nicer instinct in thus denominating the science than some critics have allowed. It is the science of the human sensibility — the capacity of form, an exact synonym of which we have indicated to be the passive imagination, as distinguishing it from its necessary correlate — the active imagination or the faculty of form. Beauty is perfect form ; and the whole realm of objective beauty has been denominated from the perfect in it.

We have found in all objective beauty, in all form, three elements — idea, matter, revelation of idea in matter — the last of these being the more vital and essential element, yet necessarily pre-supposing the others.

Moreover we have found, both in the production and in the interpretation or reception of form or of beauty, the modifying presence, indeed the actual governance of the intelligence and of the moral nature—of the true and the good ; a presence and governance so vital and indispensable, that we have found philosophers and critics on the one hand who have merged all beauty into the expression of some one principle of the intelligence, a form of the true, as of unity, or variety, or of harmony, and on the other hand, philosophers and critics who have merged all beauty into the expression of moral ideas, just as we have found other philosophers merging all beauty in the one element of idea, others in the one of matter, and others still in a union but only a subjective not an objective union—a union created by the intelligence, the judgment, or the faculty of thought. The grand underlying truth in all these partial and so far erroneous theories is that the same soul which experiences beauty, experiences also truth and goodness. Its nature is intelligent, feeling, moral, and in no specific act or state, however more fully shaped in either direction, can it wholly lay aside the other elements of its being. If it feels, it feels as an intelligent moral being feels, not as a blind irrational passivity; and if it thinks or purposes, it carries into its thought or its purpose equally its feeling nature.

But these departments of the soul's activity, although in our analytic thought distinguishable, are ever shading into each other. The sensibility grades itself into sentiment or intelligent sense. There are states of mind, in other words, in which feeling and intelligence both enter and in like or unlike proportions. It is the same with the moral. The true, the beautiful, the good intermingle in all relative degrees in the object—one object being as we have noticed, more characteristically for the understanding, another for the sensibility, another for the moral nature. Moreover in the same object, as we have seen, we may recognize either the true, or the beautiful, or the good, just as in harmonized music we may recognize either part and give attention to that, to the relative suppression of the others, or just, as in an act of thought, we may abstract one element as the subject of the proposition or the predicate from the others, and give attention predominantly to that. Now just as in music the knowledge of the principles of harmony will aid us in separating any one part from the others, so that we can exactly limit our attention to it unconfusedly with the others and with a closer, fuller, exacter apprehension of it; or just as in thought the knowledge of what the subject is in distinction from the attribute and from the copula element which unites them, will give us a clearer, exacter, fuller notion of the subject when we abstract it for closer investigation and apprehension; so the knowledge of the beautiful, of the true, of the good — of their peculiar distinctive characteristics and of their necessary relationships to one another, will naturally guide and help us to a fuller, richer, exacter apprehension of either. This knowledge gives us the key to unlock at will the door that opens to either treasure-house. It enables us to summon forth from any object offered to our experience just the element we desire; to recognize in any object at our will the true, the beautiful, or the good, all three of which we have seen alike participate in it; to assure ourselves in the experience of it that we have just the one we demand, and have it sharply and fully and exactly distinguished from the others, and so that all the light from the others is reflected upon it to enhance our experience of it. Thus these sciences enable us to drink in a purer, richer beauty from every object whose form we wish to engage our sensibility; to discern in clearer, distincter knowledge whatever is true in any such object; to apprehend in larger, purer measures its moral effect and bearing.

From logical science.

§ 352. The same view of the vital union and close relationship of reciprocally dependent and helpful sisterhood subsisting between these three fundamental and comprehensive sciences, is presented to us as we turn to the second of these sciences—the science of the true. To this science the name of logic has been given. For this representation of logic as the science of the true, we need present no higher or further authority than that of Sir William Hamilton, the most honored and able expounder of the science certainly since Aristotle. When undertaking to draw the lines of distinction between the three sciences in his seventh lecture on metaphysics, he says:—"Logic is the science of the laws of thought in relation to the end which our cognitive faculties propose, *i. e.* the *true*." This definition embraces both the knowing subject and the object known—the intelligence or the cognitive power, and the object of the intelligence—the true or the thing known.

For convenience in expounding, psychology analyzes the faculties of the intelligence, the cognitive powers, into the presentative and the representative. The first class, which includes the perceptive and the intuitive, are regarded as introductory, and preparatory. The mind does not rest in them; by a necessity of its very nature it passes to another stage which is attained for it by the other cognitive power, which consummates and makes complete the act of knowing. This is the so-called judgment—the proper product of the understanding, the intellect. For illustration, in perception we are said to be cognizant of *the sun* as object merely. But we cannot rest in this sense-perception; we of necessity recognize it as *bright.* That is, we recognize the object as having an attribute; we think *the sun is bright.* This is a judgment. We have attained no truth in the simple perception—*the sun;* we attain the true only when we think of the object in the relation of a subject to an attribute; when we think, in other words, *the sun is bright; the sun shines; the sun exists;* or the like.

It is obvious at once from this exposition of the experience of the true, which is technically called a judgment, that there are necessarily as in the experience of the beautiful, three elements, the subject, the attribute, and the relation of agreement or technically of identity between them—the copula. It is clear also that the more vital element of the judgment is found in the relation, just as we have found to be the case with the beautiful:—it is the copula element which identifies the predicate or attribute with the subject. The whole exposition of logical science accordingly proceeds essentially in a way exactly analogous to that of æsthetics. The right exposition of the one therefore must shed a bright, guiding light on the other.

But not only from the analogous unfolding of the elements of the beautiful and the true, but also in the second place, from the reciprocal determination of the limits of the two sciences, is this relationship seen to be most important and promising of help. The history of metaphysical science discovers no greater and no more common stumbling block and hindrance to truth, no more frequent or prolific source of error and dispute than the obscuration of the lines which bound æsthetics from logic, the province of the sensibility from that of the intelligence. It is enough here to refer to those voluminous discussions which have been carried on over the relations between sensation and perception and the obscure, vague, and unsatisfactory, not to say self-contradictory treatment of the imagination. An exile from the realm of the sensibility — it is admitted only as an alien in the domain of the intelligence with no native or acquired rights of residence.

The accurate and thorough scientific survey of the provinces of these sciences cannot but indicate the bounds of each; and as they are, on a portion of the boundary lines at least, continuous, these surveys must be of reciprocal service and help to each other.

Once more, the departments recognized in the one science may reasonably be presumed to modify and specifically determine the departments of the others. This reciprocal modification of the departments of the sciences will trace itself more or less definitely and clearly throughout the entire exposition. It will suffice here to indicate only its bearing on a fundamental distribution of the respective fields of the two sciences. We have found in æsthetics the two sides of form as addressing and received; — we have had given us accordingly, as leading departments, the production and the interpretation of beauty. We have in exact correspondence the two leading departments of the science of the intelligence — the intelligence as discerning and the intelligence as demonstrating. The laws of the production of beauty run a continuous line with the laws of the discernment of truth, so that with the line run for one science we have the data for running the line in the other. The laws of the intrepretation of beauty bear a similar relation to the demonstration of truth. We cannot well demonstrate truth, without imagining to ourselves the conditions by which the sense shall receive it. And so, on the other hand, we cannot interpret beauty well, but as we look over into the field of truth and discover what truth is demonstrated in the form that addresses us. We need to see the idea revealed to us in beauty, in its own interior relations, in the relations of its own parts to one another and to the whole, in order to apprehend the beauty of the revelation.

From Ethical Science.

§ 353. Turning now to the remaining one of the great sisterhood of sciences—the science of the good—the same interdependence and reciprocal relationship of helpfulness appears to us in like clear light. This is ethics in its broader sense as synonymous with what Sir William Hamilton denominates Practical Philosophy, which is defined by him in the same lecture on metaphysics to be "the science of the laws regulative of our will and desires in relation to the end which our conative powers propose—*i. e.* the *Good.*" Ethics, thus, is practical—it immediately respects an activity; more exactly it respects idea as activity; as having thus both a certain direction and also a certain end or result, and thus presenting its two correlative and equally primitive aspects of right, and of good in the narrower sense.

The very terms of Hamilton's definition mark the analogy in the subjective experience with the beautiful and the true. The introductory stage of experience in beauty, which we recognize by our analysis and abstraction for our convenience in study, but never separate in the concrete, is in what we call the mere passive sensibility, and reaches no farther than the impression. It is simply introductory and preparatory; the mind can never rest in it; but presses on by a necessity of its nature to the full experience of the form as revelation of idea. Just so have we found it in the science of the true—the preparatory perception or intuition leading necessarily to the consummating judgment or thought. And just so also in ethics. We have the preparatory desires leading on to the consummating purpose or volition in which alone all morality seats itself, just as beauty seats itself in the embodiment of idea in matter and truth in the union of subject and attribute.

Precisely analogous is the three-fold elemental constitution of the ethical or the moral. There is the subject acting, the object respected in the acting, the result itself which, regarded as action in respect to the direction of acting subject towards the object acted upon, we recognize as right or otherwise, or which, regarded as act in respect to the result, we recognize as good or otherwise. So we recognize love in the doer, good in the deed, rectitude in the doing, as each participating in the perfectly moral. Moralists may expound with equal correctness the great laws of ethics either comprehensively as the law of love, taking their outlook from the moral doer which all morality implies, or from the result — good — which all morality equally regards, or from the relation of the activity — its direction — the right. The analogy between this science and the sciences of the true and the beautiful is in this respect of the elements thus complete.

From their conterminous definition.

§ 354. Again, the reciprocal dependence and helpfulness of these sciences appears in the conterminous outlining of them. The very definition we have cited from Hamilton, in which he includes among the practical or ethical powers the desires, shows how ethics trenches immediately on æsthetics. The same is true of the bordering confines of logic and ethics — the conviction of duty is on one side purely intellectual, on the other purely ethical. The sharply drawn lines of scientific demarcation for one science bound also the others. We cannot bound one well without looking over into the others on which we bound ; we cannot bound on nothing. And so in bounding out all the departments of each, they must take their courses and bearings from metes and bounds which the other sciences may furnish or determine.

From history.

§ 355. The especial relationship of æsthetics to ethics cannot be more impressively evidenced perhaps historically, than in the remarkable fact that the nice sense of the Greek mind recognized the hue of beauty ever in the lineaments of moral perfection. The beautiful and the good were distinguishable in thought; but as if the separation were repulsive as suicidal to each, they in their utterance of their sense of the truly, perfectly good, would restore the union and call it the beautiful and good in one word — *καλοκάγαθον*. At all events nothing can be more certain than that only the perfectly beautiful can be perfectly true or good; as only the perfectly true or good can be perfectly beautiful. And so the provinces of the several sciences must be throughout in their outer boundaries conterminous and in exact correspondence.

CHAPTER IV.

THE USES OF BEAUTY.

Reasons for the inquiry.

§ 356. The beautiful we have found to enter into the very constitution of things. It is an essential in our idea of creation; for, as is well observed in the "Reign of Law" by the Duke of Argyll, "Creation is the outward embodiment of a Divine idea." It would be as inept consequently to inquire for the final cause of the beautiful as for the final cause of the true or the good. The perfect embodiment of a perfect idea, such as answers to our notion of creation, cannot but be beautiful—is nothing else, when regarded as to its form alone, than the beautiful.

But we have found that through the abstracting power of our minds, enabling us to attend to any one of various aspects of the same object, we are enabled to regard one of the three great ideas presented to us in every object to the relative exclusion of the others, and to establish thus a propensity or habit of regarding this rather than the other ideas. One thus, following what we loosely deem a native bent or yielding to the beck of circumstances, confines his views to the true in objects presented to him; he becomes by this predominant culture of his intelligence—a scholar or a philosopher—a man of learning or of science. This general fact prompts and justifies the inquiries; what are the peculiar benefits of gratifying this instinct of knowledge — what are the uses of the true? In the same way under the urgency of a similar instinctive love of the beautiful, we are prompted to inquire what are the special benefits from gratifying this instinct; from guiding and cultivating it; from wonting ourselves to seek out the beauty of things abstractly from their reality or the truth of things and the tendency or utility of things — what are the uses of beauty.

The love of the beautiful instinctive.

We start in prosecuting our inquiries on the broad ground that the love of the beautiful is as much a part of our natures as the love of the true — the sensibility to the forms of things as the faculty of apprehending the interior relations of things; that the true and the beautiful are exactly coördinate in the world around us; that hence the pursuit of the beautiful is as legitimate as that of the true, and culture of the love of the beautiful as essential to our highest perfection and well-being as that of the love of the true; that they stand in precisely the same relation to our moral perfection and can neither of them fully effect its end without the coöperative aid and ministry of the other. And the significance of our inquiry appears at once from the fact that through the abstracting and specializing tendency of our natures we are liable to give excessive attention to one part of the world around us, which is at once the incitement and the instrument of our culture, to the neglect of the other, and thus to deform and dwarf our spirits.

The pleasures of beauty.

§ 357. The first and most fundamental view which our search for the uses of beauty offers to us is in its relation to our enjoyment. So close is this relation that with a class of philosophers, as we have seen, the experience of beauty is synonymous with pleasure; that which is pleasing is ever the beautiful, as on the contrary that which displeases is ever ugly. But all this is error or, worse, confusion. There is a joy in the apprehension of the true—in knowing, as there is a higher joy in virtue. The pleasure that attends the experience of beauty comes from it and does not make it. Such is the divine ordering of our natures that the legitimate use of our endowments ever brings joy. This pleasure from the experience of beauty is a veritable sign and proof of its purity and its reality. The fact that the form of an object gives us pleasure is presumptive proof of its being beautiful; and the higher the pleasure, the higher its order of beauty. Precisely so the joy attending knowledge is a presumptive proof of its being real knowledge, not illusion, not deception. The exultant "*eureka*" of the philosopher was a token of his having reached truth. And just so too the joy that attends a virtuous deed, the complacency of the soul in a beneficent act, is presumptive proof of the rightness and the goodness of the act. But in neither case is the pleasure or the joy the æsthetic sense, the intelligent knowing, or the ethical willing;—it attends these states and attests their legitimacy and their purity. A natural satisfaction, pleasure, joy, is the proper boon of beauty.

Rank and worthiness.

§ 358. And this pleasure is altogether a worthy, wholesome, elevating pleasure. It can never degrade, never mislead, never discredit. Relatively to the joy proper to knowledge, or proper to virtue, it may be disproportionate ; but the pure effect of beauty is ever in harmony with our highest well-being. The pleasures of false beauty, of empty or distorted forms of things, may corrupt ; just as those of a false philosophy, of spurious or imperfect knowledge. But the pleasure that comes from a sympathetic sense of perfect embodiments of perfect ideas can never harm, except, as intimated, by being indulged disproportionally to the pleasures of intelligence and of right action. Art may minister to immorality and vice ; but only as it ceases to be true and perfect art. Just so, philosophy and science may be enlisted in the service of evil ; but it is ever an erroneous philosophy that subserves the vicious or the wrong. Even religion has been degraded to the vilest uses ; and the picture of good ends has been made a cover and a warrant for the worst morality in the use of means. The perversion of art or of the pursuit of the beauty in nature to excessive or vicious indulgences is but an abuse, not a true and right use of beauty.

Susceptible of indefinite increase.

§ 359. It is further to be remarked of the use of beauty in enhancing the legitimate joy of a good life, that the pleasing, joyous sense of beauty is susceptible of indefinite increase from culture. Unlike the animal sense which clogs and palls and becomes blunt and dim, the proper æsthetic sense, as we have seen, but enlarges its capacity and sharpens and quickens its apprehension with use and indulgence. The love of nature grows with the study cf nature. The delight in art deepens and strengthens with progress. The ecstatic, well nigh heavenly rapture of Mozart, as he fed on the musical forms, which the composition of his Requiem offered to his imagination, how immeasurably beyond and above all the pleasure possible to his immature genius in music. So in another department of art, how vast and how intense was the joy of William Blake, when in his riper years after long use had expanded and quickened his sense of beauty, in his garret he pitied the merely opulent in outward possessions as compared with his exalted condition in the high seats of art. And what an insight into the deep joys which the prolonged study of natural beauty brings, is given us in that immortal confession of Wordsworth, that the meanest thing that grows gave him thoughts too deep for tears.

Here, then, in its direct ministry to our most legitimate, highest, purest, safest joy and blessedness, do we find the first and most fundamental use of beauty. By virtue of the divine ordinance in creation, the proper experience of beauty brings a necessary and exalting pleasure — a pleasure which is pure and wholesome, and which rises ever in proper indulgence and culture. In its lower forms beauty fulfills this its ordained function of giving pleasure ; in its highest forms it allies the pleasure of the æsthetic experience with the joy of the perfected nature.

§ 360. But the use of beauty appears in a more indirect yet equally legitimate ministry to our highest well being. This indirect and more incidental use and ministry is of a threefold character as it relates to the æsthetic, the intellectual, or the moral nature.

Ministry of beauty to the taste and to art.

First, in its æsthetic bearings, the experience of beauty guides, animates, and nurtures the æsthetic spirit itself. We have already noticed the fact that the indulged sense of beauty quickens and enlarges by the indulgence. But we have here another view. The passive imagination quickens and feeds the active imagination ; the sensibility to beauty awakens and fosters the instinct to produce beauty ; the capacity of form stimulates the faculty of form. The artist catches his inspiration from contemplating art. The condition of high artistic skill is the study of art. This truth is of the most common and familar recognition, and in all the departments of the beautiful. To be conversant with the refined and graceful in manners is to become refined and graceful. The study of painting guides in the use of the pencil : the hearing of eloquence teaches how to be eloquent ; and the hearing of rhythm and melody in poetry makes and guides poets, even although there be unconsciousness of the nature of rhythmical feet and of melodious intonation. So all art, all production of beauty, remains meager, infantile, undeveloped, without the observation of beautiful form. Architecture sprang from the suggestion of beauty discerned in nature. Sculpture grew from the observation of the beauty of the human shape in the physique of the unclothed athlete. Thus does the experience of beauty in the contemplation of works of taste ever awaken, stimulate, guide, and nurture the faculty of form, and also further the production of beauty in manners and in morals, as well as in all departments of proper art.

In the same way the beauty of nature's forms is familiarly recognized as a quickening power to taste and to artistic skill. The aspiring student of art is by every judicious and experienced teacher earnestly directed and exhorted to the diligent study of nature as the well-furnished repository of all the divers forms of beauty, where all kinds of idea — divine intelligence, love, and goodness — are revealed in all the diversities of sensible matter and in the most perfect grace. The inspiring, elevating, refining power of this devoted study of nature as a cabinet of beauty is too well exhibited in all worthy literature to require here more than the simple mention of the truth. It is most forcibly as well as beautifully set forth by the great poet of nature — Wordsworth — who not only gave himself up to the influence of nature upon his own spirit, but also philosophically studied the degree and modes of this influence upon the human soul. Its power to impress and nurture he recognizes in these suggestive verses :—

Nor less I deem that there are powers
  Which of themselves our minds impress;
And we can feed this mind of ours
  In a wise passiveness.

So in his little poem "Three years she grew," he intimates the specific effects of conversance with nature. It is the promise of nature to her fondling, that she shall not fail to see

Even in the motion of the storm
Grace that shall mold the maiden's form
By silent sympathy.

And beauty born of murmuring sound
Shall pass into her face.

Indeed, as it has been well expressed, "life and beauty, it seems to the poet, utter far deeper things than do final causes or evidence of design. Were this goodly frame, the earth, but a silent temple, its beauty would speak to him of a divine occupant; but when the presence of the Lord,

In the glory of his cloud,
Has filled the house of the Lord,

when the voices of worshipers are heard in solemn adoring, or in choruses of triumphal jubilation, he has no need of a physico-theological argument, and is apt perhaps to think it an impertinence." Such is the power of nature as beautiful, as form, over the human spirit, as it is introduced by it into immediate communion with the all-perfect and is by its beholding there his glory transformed into the same image.

To the intelligence.

§ 361. Secondly, we discover another important indirect use of beauty in its relations to the intelligence. From the vital intimacy between the true and the beautiful on the one hand and between the æsthetic and the cognitive departments of our nature on the other, we are prepared to believe that the culture of the one must draw in and facilitate and extend the culture of the other to any supposable degree; that knowledge cannot grow surely and freely without the help of the æsthetic sense; and that its progress and perfection depend on its aid.

But more specifically, as the active intelligence is dependent on the passive intelligence, as the power to demonstrate truth pre-supposes the acquisition of truth, so this reception and acquisition of truth come only through the æsthetic sense; the truth and reality of things are given us through the form of things. The quick, nice, sure sense of the forms of objects is the necessary condition of the knowledge of objects. The captivating charm which beauty gives to the objects of knowledge and to the forms which knowledge attains, is the indispensable inspiration of true science. Altogether spiritless, lifeless, wanting in all enthusiasm, must science sink to be, if it lack the stimulus and tone and cheer which come from the beauty in those forms of the objects of knowledge and those forms which knowledge itself takes and embodies itself in that it may live. When science wins a form that truly pleases because beautiful, it rests content; its achievement is attested as a general result of truth. The highest attainments in the highest reaches of its enthusiastic complacency come forth in the most perfect forms of beauty. So essential, so constant, so helpful, is beauty to truth.

There is still another view of the ministry of beauty to truth. We have found the objective characters of true objective beauty to include certain proper intellectual elements, as of unity, contrast, number, proportion, symmetry, harmony; and that accordingly the æsthetic sense must be intelligent. The highest beauty cannot be reached except with the help of the intelligence. The more intelligent the æsthetic sense becomes, the more conversant with idea in itself, the more quick to discern it, the higher and richer will be the experience of beauty. The culture of the sense of beauty therefore leads directly to the culture of the intelligence. As we cannot interpret an object of beauty, whether it be a product of art or a thing in nature, without apprehending the idea it reveals, and as in proportion as the idea becomes richer in significancy to us the beauty shines out more fully, so our love of beauty puts us on improving our knowledge. So, we have seen, the beauty of a piece of art is enhanced to us by a knowledge of the nature of the material and of the principles of æsthetic production, which are concerned in it.

Thus every way does æsthetic culture draw in and constrain the culture of the intellect; the enlarged experience of the beautiful ensures the enlargement of knowledge. The more of the beautiful, ever the more of the true; the more perfect and exalted the beautiful in our experience, the higher and purer the true in it.

To the moral nature.

§ 362. Thirdly, still another important indirect use of beauty is in its relations to morals. As we have seen, all beauty participates in a moral nature; and the full interpretation of beauty demands an æsthetic sense that is characterized as moral. The endeavor to produce the beautiful—every aspiration in art and also the desire to experience the beautiful in the fullest and richest measure and degree, must lead to the enlistment of the moral nature. It must put on the study and practical experience of virtue. In all the general respects in short in which the beautiful ministers to truth does it also minister to goodness.

But we need to dwell on the more peculiar and characteristic ministry which beauty lends to virtue. All that is properly moral is of an active nature in a higher sense than is true of the æsthetic and intellectual. It pertains ever either to an individual act or a permanent disposition which is the determination of a man's own proper active faculty—his will. The very nature of mind or of spirit is indeed activity; but all that spontaneous activity which underlies the voluntary and in which the voluntary inheres, is rather to be accounted the ordering of the Creator, and the expression of his idea. But the moral in man which is never separable from his freedom, and is ever the expression of that, is the active in man in the highest, strictest sense. The intelligence itself is a form of the divine activity, except so far as the free will of man enters it, and controls and determines it. The expression of this active free will, if it be perfect in all respects, if it be the proper legitimate action of the spirit, if it be put forth in its proper matter, and be rightly embodied or directed, cannot but be a form of perfect beauty, if our general view of the nature of beauty be correct and sound. So Milton recognizes sublimity and beauty as the very constituents of the form of moral perfection when he says that Satan at the sight of an unfallen angel stood abashed—

> And felt how awful goodness is, and saw
> Virtue in her shape how lovely.

Right action and pure moral disposition awes as sublime and charms as beautiful. It is called forth by this loveliness of its native form. It is encouraged and sustained by the pleasing, satisfying shape it necessarily assumes as it comes to be. How, when from fierce struggle with evil the right comes out triumphant, does the eye of the soul flash, and the inmost sense of the heart warm and glow as the abiding form which the action has assumed shines before it and presses itself upon it. An approving conscience is but the æsthetic sense in its ethical modifications; and the pale specters that haunt the guilty soul are but the forms which wrong actions have shaped in the spirit's life.

In this general view we find the grounds of those current maxims that companionship with the refined and virtuous refines and purifies, while society with the bad corrupts and degrades. A coarse, vicious spirit is rebuked, repressed in virtuous surroundings. Boorishness wears off in polite society. Purity of soul thrives when all around is pure. The love of beauty in nature brings into sympathy with God and keeps the soul in society with

Him, whose whole nature is a fostering atmosphere to goodness. The pursuit of art keeps one conversant with the truest beauty, which, as we have found, is ethical in its nature. Such at least is the legitimate influence of art—of art as it should be, and in order to be truest and most perfect, it must be. It is true that the ministry of art and of beauty may be perverted. Immoral ideas and impure or vicious designs, debasing matter, or foul embodiment may enter art. Even pure art-products may be vilely construed. But the same is to be allowed of truth. Science is often perverting, debasing. The false enters philosophy, the fiendish enters doctrine and teaching, equally as the ugly enters art with base design. But the false is not more opposed to the true than the ugly to the beautiful; nor the vicious and immoral in their nature more hostile to science than to true art. The cultivated æsthetic sense rejects the immoral as instinctively as the ugly.

It is a notion somewhat prevalent, that beauty as mere form can be only emptiness, a mere show without substance. It is thought that as mere form it is devoid of reason and consequently that reason can have no concern with it; that to give oneself to the production of beauty or the contemplation of beauty is to amuse oneself with empty show—to give oneself to play, that children may be indulged in, but that the serious earnestness of mature life should lay aside and shun. But long ago did Schiller utter the paradox that "man only plays when he is a man, and he is only entirely a man when he plays." The ripest culture only apprehends the highest, richest beauty, and true ripeness in the human soul is only when there is outlined in it the image or form of a true spiritual ideal shaping all its activity. The essential idea of *play*, as the term is here used by Schiller is freedom; when idea utters itself freely, exempt from all constraint from within or from without, then and only then is there perfect beauty. Just so to apprehend beauty, the soul must give itself freely to the full impressions of the object. This is play. But it is the play of a rational spirit which can never renounce or lay aside its rational nature. While it plays or acts out its freedom in art or in contemplation, and the whole outer surface of the spirit puts on a multitudinous ripple of playful, laughing joy, there is yet the deep flow of reason beneath, not only bearing it, but bearing it in its own way to its own end.

Moreover it is undeniable that the form is often of higher import and interest than even either the idea revealed in the form or the matter in which it is revealed. It is the gracefulness of an act of courtesy or of kindness often which gives it its chief value. The human form, in the sense of the union of a mind or soul with matter, of the embodiment of the spiritual in the material, overshadows in its interest the nature both of spirit in itself and of the dust into which it has breathed itself. The God incarnate is more to us in its claims upon our highest and most serious regards than the divine in its own nature or the created nature in which it revealed itself. Our chief concern lies in forming the ideal of the perfect in our shaping characters. Call it by what name you will, this bringing the spirit into the freest and fullest play in the glorious liberty of a divine sonship, is our most serious pursuit; and that divine form of a perfect beauty of character may well and wisely be kept before us as the model and the charm of our life's whole endeavor.

CHAPTER V.

THE USES OF ÆSTHETICS.

§ 363. The uses of æsthetics — of an orderly systematic exposition of the nature of beauty, of its essential elements, its modification in all the diversified kinds of beauty throughout the universe so far as it comes into our experience, the conditions and laws of its production and its interpretation — become obvious from the nature of beauty and its relations to the two other coördinated principles of our rational being — the true and the good.

A true science.

To it belong all the uses which pertain to science generally. Æsthetics is a true science; it has its definite subject matter; it has its systematic, logical development, as truly and as perfectly as any science.

Of the highest rank.

It belongs to the highest class of sciences. As coördinate with the sciences of the true and the good, making up with them the three comprehensive sciences — the three highest and broadest sciences including all others under them — it claims to itself the power to impart the benefits of proper science of a kind and to a degree unsurpassed by any.

The gate of all knowledge.

§ 364. Æsthetic science has the especial merit and peculiarity of being the very portal of all knowledge as we receive truth only through form by the æsthetic sensibility. It is of moment therefore, that the principles by which we inform our minds in all knowledge, be understood by us.

If we conceive of it as but a science of form, of show, of play, as we may in a legitimate, perhaps, but rather unfamiliar sense of those terms, it is as such the very charm and inspiration of all study and knowledge, and we need especially to be so instructed that we may never be misled by false show and be deluded by mere dazzle and glitter. Æsthetics teaches us what is true beauty; where it may be found; how it may be discriminated from the false; how it may best be produced, and how best enjoyed. It claims these preëminent uses as a science.

Aid to the science of the true.

§ 365. But in the next place its utility is obvious from its relations, as already indicated, to its sister coördinate sciences of the true and the good—logic and ethics. It is impossible to attain a perfect science in either of these departments except in the light of æsthetics and by the aid and guidance which it alone can render. The truth of things cannot be scientifically expounded unless it be carefully and definitely distinguished from the form of things. We are warranted in presuming this from the relations of beauty to truth. The history of science up to its present stage confirms this presumption. If there be any great defect and want, if there be any vice and hindrance to science, it will be found preëminently to arise from the ignorance of beauty as the perfect form of things and of its clear discrimination from the truth of things. The age is an age of marvelous intellectual activity which moreover is characterized by a remarkable keenness and thoroughness of observation. It lacks certainly logical discernment and skill; but its chief defect lies in its confounding the form with the idea in the form, which it is the function of æsthetic science to discriminate. Hence it is that mind and matter are made one and identical, or rather are annihilated; the unity of all things is in a mysterious inexplicable organism which is neither mind nor matter, has no origin, has no aim as it has no sight, works blindly but yet selectingly, is the unconscious parent of all things conscious and unconscious, and dies ever in the death of its offspring. This scientism itself is but organism; it has no sense of form as distinct from substance or idea. Idea and form are indistinguishably one and the same to it. This confusion, which is the legitimate effect of the one-sided training of the age, of its neglect to study the form-side of things as distinguished from the idea-side, is at once the vice of recent science and the hindrance to its sure and rapid advance.

A more specific illustration of the especial need of æsthetic science and also of its promise of a high utility is found in some of the leading speculations of the age in the highest of the subordinate sciences—theology. Two questions more than any others are agitating the theological world:—the one is, can the Infinite be known at all; the other is, can God reveal His will infallibly in language. It is evident that these problems can be solved and assurance of the truth in solution be gained only as the nature of form, of what communication of spirit, idea—infinite as well as finite—to other spirits is; what are the imitations, and what the true interpretation of form, of revelation, of spirit or idea in matter.

To ethical science.

§ 366. In ethics, also, the necessities of æsthetic knowledge are equally apparent. The noble and the beautiful in art and in character are recognized as having truly an ethical nature, as the right and the beneficent. But except from the light which æsthetics sheds upon them many unanswerable questionings arise which obscure and shake to their foundation all our ethical conclusions. Is the noble and the beautiful, right and praiseworthy in itself, because noble and beautiful? If so, how does it relate itself to the moral nature? If so, why not make ethics the science of the noble and the excellent? When the fair and noble mingle with the wrong and vicious what is the moral estimate it should receive? How comes the old "honest," meaning properly the beautiful, to lose its meaning and come to denote mere commercial integrity? How comes the æsthetic to interchange in language and in the opinions of men with the right and the good? Why is unlovely love defective in morality? Why is the boorishly right censurable; and the uncouth deed of goodness morally entitled to no gratitude and rightly provocative of indignation and censure? Such are specimens of the questions which track the path of ethical science and which find no quieting satisfaction except in the light of æsthetic science. So do the threads of the true and the good interweave themselves with those of the beautiful, that only by the careful intelligent separation of each from the other and the distinct recognition of each by its own proper hue can any part of the great woof of our experience be clearly and perfectly discriminated and known.

§ 367. But the highest utility of æsthetic science is to be discovered in its relations to culture — to the development and shaping of character. In order to the fulfilment of this chief end of our earthly living, we need to know what are the ideals we are to select, where to find them, how to identify and prove them. To every individual and to every people there is one great ideal of character — one comprehensive end and aim of culture. But this comprehensive ideal breaks and changes itself into subordinate ideals in all the several stages of growth and progress. Æsthetic science has for its special object in part, as we have seen, to guide us in this relation. Further, character shapes itself in bodily movement, in word, in thought, in feeling, in specific purpose and endeavor, which again express themselves in all that outwardly belongs to us, our dress and habitation, and physical surroundings. It is æsthetic science which unfolds to us the principles and rules by which we are to select and use all this outward material in which our growing and shaping characters form themselves. This selection and handling can be wise and safe only as they are intelligent. We are not ordered or permitted with impunity to blunder into what is excellent and good. Then above all we need to understand how we are to incorporate all these ideals to be taken by us one by one with every advancing step of our progress as they change and vary in reference not only to the stage of our maturity but also to the material of specific word or act or thought into which they are to be shaped — how embody them freely, gracefully, well, in these outer forms. We need to understand this philosophy of form — its guiding principles and rules, all which lie in the realm of æsthetic science.

Use of models.

To take another view, æsthetic science teaches us the necessity and the utility of models in all culture. It instructs us where to find them, by what signs to discriminate the true from the false, the truly elevating, refining, from the meretricious and the misleading and debasing; what are fit and proper for our divers conditions and relations, for individuals and for communities; what forms of nature are to be sought out and studied, what products of art to be selected, that as models of the truly excellent, they may by our contemplation of them, be right molds for our fashioning spirits; and how to use these models and how apply them. This indispensable condition of all true culture in whatever department from the lowest to the highest, from mere manners and civil courtesies up through all social morality and personal refinement to the modes of our proper religious life — this indispensable condition and means of culture given in models, we go in vain to seek elsewhere than in the domain of æsthetic science.

Here in short, must we go to learn what it is to put principle into purpose and purpose into endeavor and endeavor into efficient act; to put thought into word and word into fit organ and instrument to penetrate and also to command the recesses of the human soul; to put fond affection into a golden chalice that shall be its own passport to the heart when craving sympathy, and shall make itself the sure recipient of grateful, confiding response; to put the forth-bringings of prolific genius into art-forms that shall live and endure for brightening, elevating, and blessing toilsome life; to put, in fine, the human spirit in its unshaped childhood and youth into the mold of the all-perfect that it may grow up into him in all things. In this scientific field of the beautiful alone do we find what all this is and how it is; the rule to guide, and the power to quicken and to enable in all true rational culture, in all worthy act, in all proper human life.

APPENDIX.

EMBLEMS AND SYMBOLS IN ART FROM HEBENSTREIT'S *Encyklopædie der Æsthetik.*

Anchor, hope; commerce.
Ant, frugality.
Ape, imitation, cunning.
Ashes, death.
Beaver, diligence, skill.
Bee, industry.
Blindfold and dagger in hand, fanaticism.
Blue, stupidity.
Bridle, moderation.
Butterfly, fickleness, frivolity.
Candle lighted, good example.
Candle paschal, light of the gospel.
Candlestick with seven branches, the seven sacraments.
Censer, prayer.
Chain about a globe, slavery.
Circle, completeness.
Crocodile, false.
Crown of thorns, expiation.
Cup with wafer, the supper.
Dove, innocence.
Dove hovering in flame, the Holy Spirit.
Eagle, genius, magnanimity.
Eel, misanthropy.
Eider duck, affection.
Elephant, moderation, intelligence; religion.
Ermine, predetermination.
Fire and water, purity.
Fly, impudence.
Fox, deceit; cunning.
Frog, inquisitiveness.
Globe with a cross, the Christian world.
Goat, foresight.
Gold, purity.
Goose with a stone in the bill, secrecy.
Hammer and nails, necessity.
Hands two, joined, good faith; fidelity.
Hare, fear; cowardice; forgetfulness.
Hawk, taste.
Heart burning, sympathy.
Hen, productiveness.
Horn from which flowers are falling, plenty.
Indian, pretension; pride.
Jacob's ladder, contemplation; meditation.
Keys crossed, sovereignty of the church.

Lamb, gentleness.
Lamb offered on the altar, the sacrifice of Christ.
Lamp, study.
Leopard, ferocity.
Lion, strength ; spirit ; magnanimity.
Lion with an arrow which he is drawing out, revenge.
Mask, hyprocrisy.
Mirror, truth ; wisdom.
Owl, acknowledgment.
Ox, moderation.
Oxhorns, industry.
Oyster, quiet ; weakness.
Palm, reward of the righteous.
Parrot, docility.
Partridge, appetite.
Pelican, sympathy ; motherly love.
Pillars hewn in the rock, firmness.
Quicksilver, unrest.
Rabbit, productiveness.
Rat, waste.
River horse, harm ; loss.
Rose white, innocence.
Scales and sword, justice.
Seal and key, fidelity ; secrecy.
Serpent, cunning.
Serpent holding its tail, eternity.
Serpent coiled around a rod, trade.
Sparrow, melancholy.
Sphinx, mystery.
Stork, gratitude ; filial pity.
Sun and open book, the truth of religion.
Swallow, floating success.
Swine, selfishness ; filth.
Tortoise, slowness ; dullness.
Triangle shining, trinity.
Trumpet, proclamation of the gospel.
Turtle dove, conjugal faith.
Veil, faith.
Viper, calumny.
Weather vane, unsteadiness.
Wheel, inconstancy ; fickleness.
Wild boar, violence.
Wreath of stars, glory ; reward of the righteous ; immortality.

INDEX.